Social Constructions of Migration in Nigeria and Zimbabwe

DIVERSE PERSPECTIVES ON CREATING A FAIRER SOCIETY

A fair society is one that is just, inclusive and embracing of all without any barriers to participation based on sex, sexual orientation, religion or belief, ethnicity, age, class, ability or any other social difference. One where there is access to healthcare and education, technology, justice, strong institutions, peace and security, social protection, decent work and housing. But how can research truly contribute to creating global equity and diversity without showcasing diverse voices that are underrepresented in academia or paying specific attention to the Global South?

Including books addressing key challenges and issues within the social sciences which are essential to creating a fairer society for all with specific reference to the Global South, *Diverse Perspectives on Creating a Fairer Society* amplifies underrepresented voices showcasing Black, Asian, and minority ethnic voices, authorship from the Global South and academics who work to amplify diverse voices.

With the primary aim of showcasing authorship and voices from beyond the Global North, the series welcomes submissions from established and junior authors on cutting-edge and high-level research on key topics that feature in global news and public debate, specifically from and about the Global South in national and international contexts. Harnessing research across a range of diversities of people and place to generate previously unheard insights, the series offers a truly global perspective on the current societal debates of the 21st century bringing contemporary debate in the social sciences from diverse voices to light.

Previous Titles

- *Disaster, Displacement and Resilient Livelihoods: Perspectives from South Asia* edited by M. Rezaul Islam
- *Pandemic, Politics, and a Fairer Society in Southeast Asia: A Malaysian Perspective* edited by Syaza Shukri
- *Empowering Female Climate Change Activists in the Global South: The Path Toward Environmental Social Justice* by Peggy Ann Spitzer
- *Gendered Perspectives of Restorative Justice, Violence and Resilience: An International Framework* edited by Bev Orton
- *Social Sector Development and Inclusive Growth in India* by Ishu Chadda
- *The Socially Constructed and Reproduced Youth Delinquency in Southeast Asia: Advancing Positive Youth Involvement in Sustainable Futures* by Jason Hung
- *Youth Development in South Africa: Harnessing the Demographic Dividend* edited by Botshabelo Maja and Busani Ngcaweni
- *Debt Crisis and Popular Social Protest in Sri Lanka: Citizenship, Development and Democracy Within Global North–South Dynamics* by S. Janaka Biyanwila
- *Building Strong Communities: Ethical Approaches to Inclusive Development* by Ifzal Ahmad and M. Rezaul Islam

- *Family Planning and Sustainable Development in Bangladesh: Empowering Marginalized Communities in Asian Contexts* by M. Rezaul Islam
- *Critical Reflections on the Internationalisation of Higher Education in the Global South* edited by Emnet Tadesse Woldegiorgis and Cheryl Qiumei Yu
- *Exploring Hope: Case Studies of Innovation, Change and Development in the Global South* edited by Marcelo Sili, Andrés Kozel, Samira Mizbar, Aviram Sharma, and Ana Casado
- *Rural Social Infrastructure Development in India: An Inclusive Approach* by M Mahadeva

Forthcoming Titles

- *Globalization and the Transitional Cultures: An Eastern Perspective* by Debanjana Nag
- *'Natural' Disasters and Everyday Lives: Floods, Climate Justice and Marginalisation in India* by Suddhabrata Deb Roy
- *Gender and Media Representation: Perspectives from Sub-Saharan Africa* edited by Margaret Jjuuko, Solveig Omland and Carol Azungi Dralega
- *Neoliberal Subjectivity at Work: Conduct, Contradictions, Commitments and Contestations* by Muneeb Ul Lateef Banday
- *The Emerald Handbook of Family and Social Change in the Global South: A Gendered Perspective* edited by Aylin Akpınar and Nawal H. Ammar
- *An Introduction to Platform Economy in India: Exploring Relationality and Embeddedness* by Shriram Venkatraman, Jillet Sarah Sam, and Rajorshi Ra
- *Unearthing the Institutionalised Social Exclusion of Black Youth in Contemporary South Africa: The Burden of Being Born Free* by Khosi Kubeka

Social Constructions of Migration in Nigeria and Zimbabwe: Discourse, Rhetoric, and Identity

BY

KUNLE MUSBAUDEEN OPARINDE
Durban University of Technology, South Africa

AND

RODWELL MAKOMBE
North-West University, South Africa

United Kingdom – North America – Japan – India – Malaysia – China

Emerald Publishing Limited
Emerald Publishing, Floor 5, Northspring, 21-23 Wellington Street, Leeds LS1 4DL.

First edition 2024

Copyright © 2024 Kunle Musbaudeen Oparinde and Rodwell Makombe.
Published under exclusive licence by Emerald Publishing Limited.

Reprints and permissions service
Contact: www.copyright.com

No part of this book may be reproduced, stored in a retrieval system, transmitted in any form or by any means electronic, mechanical, photocopying, recording or otherwise without either the prior written permission of the publisher or a licence permitting restricted copying issued in the UK by The Copyright Licensing Agency and in the USA by The Copyright Clearance Center. Any opinions expressed in the chapters are those of the authors. Whilst Emerald makes every effort to ensure the quality and accuracy of its content, Emerald makes no representation implied or otherwise, as to the chapters' suitability and application and disclaims any warranties, express or implied, to their use.

British Library Cataloguing in Publication Data
A catalogue record for this book is available from the British Library

ISBN: 978-1-83549-169-0 (Print)
ISBN: 978-1-83549-168-3 (Online)
ISBN: 978-1-83549-170-6 (Epub)

INVESTOR IN PEOPLE

Contents

About the Authors ix

Chapter 1	Introduction	1
Chapter 2	Contemporary Global Discourses of Migration and Migrants	11
Chapter 3	Frequency of Migration Discourse in Nigerian Everyday Contexts	29
Chapter 4	Social Media Narratives and Counternarratives of Migration in Zimbabwe: The Case of Hopewell Chin'ono's Facebook Page Post-August 2023 Elections	45
Chapter 5	Discourse of Politics and Security in Migration	65
Chapter 6	Co-existence of Power and Powerlessness in Nigerian Migration Discourse	83
Chapter 7	Discourse, Zimbabwean Migrants in South Africa and the Politics of Viscerality: The Case of the Zimbabwe Exemption Permit (ZEP)	101
Chapter 8	Post-Migration Discourse and Identity Crisis: The Case of Nigeria	123
Chapter 9	Further Thoughts: The Figure of the Migrant in Contemporary Discourse: Reflections and Lived Experiences	141

About the Authors

Kunle Musbaudeen Oparinde is a Research Associate in the Institute of Systems Science at the Durban University of Technology, South Africa. He is an interdisciplinary researcher with interests in areas such as communication, sociolinguistics, discourse analysis, decolonisation, and higher education. He has published several articles in reputable journals as well as book chapters. He is the pioneer editor of the *African Journal of Inter/Multidisciplinary Studies (AJIMS)*. He is a rated researcher with the National Research Foundation (NRF) in South Africa.

Rodwell Makombe is Professor in the Department of English at the North-West University, South Africa. He is a previous fellow of the African Humanities Program (AHP), the University of Michigan Presidential Scholars Fellowship (UMAPS) and the British Academy fellowship, completed at the University of Oxford, with Prof Elleke Boehmer as host. He has also been awarded the Humboldt Fellowship for Experienced Researchers (2024–2026) with the University of Bonn in Germany. His research focuses on postcolonial literary studies, social media, humour, satire, and poetics in literary and cultural texts. He has published several journal articles and two books titled *Cultural Texts of Resistance in Zimbabwe: Music, Memes, Media* (2021) and *Coloniality of Migrancy in African Diasporic Literatures* (2023, co-authored).

Chapter 1

Introduction

This book examines discourses of migration in Nigeria and Zimbabwe with a particular focus on how citizens in both countries imagine and narrate experiences of migration. For the purpose of this book, we perceive migration in the same view as Kok (1999, p. 20) who defines the concept in general terms as the crossing of a spatial boundary by one or more persons involved in a change of residence. In essence, migration involves the departure from one's place of residence to another. In this context, we discuss how conversations around migration are constructed vis-à-vis the realities of migrancy in contemporary Nigeria and Zimbabwe.

While Nigeria and Zimbabwe are two countries with diverse ethnicities and cultures, they share similar socio-political and economic realities. Both countries are former British colonies which gained independence 20 years apart – Nigeria in 1960 and Zimbabwe in 1980. Since independence, the two countries have witnessed and continue to witness heightened socio-political tensions and harsh economic realities that have led to continual migration. Nigeria, like Zimbabwe, has experienced many economic challenges associated with what has come to be known as 'the resource curse' in Africa. These challenges have been worsened by political instability which dates to the military coups of the 1970s and 1980s and the rise of terrorist Islamic groups that continue to wreak havoc in the northern parts of the country. A combination of these challenges, among others, has seen many Nigerians migrating to other countries inside and outside of Africa in search of better economic opportunities.

Zimbabwe, for its part, has a long history of migration which dates back to the precolonial era. Before the advent of colonialism, people migrated from one place to another in search of grazing pastures, fertile land and to break away from natural disasters such as droughts. The advent of colonialism saw new forms of migration, particularly from rural to urban areas in search of employment opportunities. For many years, Zimbabwe has been both a sending and receiving country. In the 1950s and 1960s, during the federation of Rhodesia and Nyasaland, Zimbabwe received migrants mainly from its neighbouring countries while it also exported migrant labours to South Africa. Patterns of migration in Zimbabwe have changed drastically in recent years, particularly after the land reform of 2000 which led to an unprecedented political and economic crisis. The post-2000 period has seen many Zimbabweans flocking out of the country to seek better economic opportunities around the world.

What unites Nigeria and Zimbabwe in this book is not only the historical trajectories of both countries but also their politics and economics which play a significant role in shaping migration trends and narratives. Like Nigeria, Zimbabwe has a highly educated population with over 98% literacy rates. However, the ongoing economic crisis has created a situation where young people graduating from various institutions of learning cannot find employment and end up seeking employment opportunities outside the country. Although Zimbabwe has enjoyed relative political stability since independence, it has, in recent years, taken a leaf from Nigeria's political playbook of the early years of independence characterised by cycles of contested elections, politically motivated violence and widespread state-sanctioned corruption. The coup of November 2017, which saw the end of Robert Mugabe's 37-year rule, has, arguably, taken Zimbabwe back to the era of military coups in Africa, which Nigeria has experienced with dire economic consequences.

Most citizens in both countries desire out-migration due to unfavourable conditions in politics, economics, governance, and security. Migration has thus become exceedingly prevalent in recent years contributing significantly to the migration of able-bodied and skilled citizens of both countries. Central to this book is the notion of discourse and how it is constructed in everyday communication. We explore *what* Nigerians and Zimbabweans say about migration as well as *how* they say it. According to Walsh (2023), migration has dominated media discourse because of its significance for society's character, future, and identity. Walsh further notes that the advent of digital platforms and technologies has broadened opportunities to produce, share, and access content online and ignited debates about migration and its discursive construction.

We discuss real-time migration discourses gleaned from social media interactions in the two countries under study. The novelty of this book lies in the fact that it explores uncharted territory in the study of migration and discourse in Nigeria and Zimbabwe. From an academic standpoint, the book has a broad focus that encompasses sociolinguistics (discourse analysis), narratology, and border/migration studies and partly involves the sociology of migration. We thus enrich these different fields with novel information that will serve as seminal work for future studies of a similar nature. Disciplines that use discourse analysis as an analytical framework such as sociolinguistics, migration studies, sociology and cultural studies, interact in this book as we discuss the practical discursive realities of migration in Nigeria and Zimbabwe. It should be noted that the major focus of the book is discourse (communication in use) in the context of migration. Priority is given to discourse while migration is only the milieu in which the discourse is studied.

Migration as a practice is as old as humankind. People have always migrated or changed environments for different reasons among which are material needs, national security, and climate changes. As Schewel and Debray (2024, p. 153) note, 'migration is a feature of every society. Most people migrate internally, or within countries, but a smaller share moves internationally, or across country borders'. There has been a recent surge in migration patterns from countries in the Global South to countries in the Global North. Other reasons include the search for greener pastures, human security, and career goals. Communication (discourse) is also as old as human existence. This book interrogates the intertwined current realities of communication and migration. Discourse plays a significant role in shaping and influencing the real world, and migration, being a popular occurrence especially in Nigeria and Zimbabwe, is bound to produce interesting discourses that shape/influence not only the people from these countries, but also the socio-economic conditions of the two nations. As reflected in the book, while intercontinental migration (outside of Africa) is highly popular, intracontinental migration (within Africa) is also a common practice amongst Nigerians and Zimbabweans although not as widely reflected on social media as the former. This is a point entrenched by Yaro and Setrana (2024) that intra-migration is prominent with many African migrants crossing from one country on the continent to another country, unlike the misconceived narratives that portray African migrants as persons moving irregularly through the Mediterranean to the Global North.

Migration-motivated discourses in the two countries can be viewed from intercontinental and intracontinental perspectives. The nature of the book and its contents demand concurrent analyses of migration and popular discourse. As these concepts are the major focus of the book, they are therefore intertwined in a way that renders it challenging to discuss one without the other. This is also perhaps why the book is likely to appeal to different readers from different disciplines: discourse and migration are multi-pronged. Besides its specific focus on discourse and migration, the book also reflects on aspects of culture, identity, history, professions/careers, politics, governance, and security in relation to how they interact with migrants, discourse, and migration. In this book, we argue that one way to understand migration is to explore stories, narratives, and conversations about migration. How do stories about migration and migrants shape perceptions in society and influence policies that govern migration and migrants? Hence, the book does not discuss the phenomenon of migration itself but what is said about it. Among the questions we hope to answer are: What is the common social media rhetoric surrounding migration in Nigeria and Zimbabwe? How does this rhetoric reflect on the socio-economic conditions of the two countries? What are the motivating factors for migration in the two countries? How are these factors reflected on social media?

Our understanding is that to fully comprehend migration from an African perspective (Nigeria and Zimbabwe), the different views and opinions of the people in and from these countries are valuable. In the age of digital technology, social media is probably the most appropriate site to access information about migration trends and discourses of migration from the migrants themselves and others who have migration stories to tell. A point conceded by Dekker et al. (2018) is that digital social networks are becoming common in a way that enables potential migrants to understand better migration options and destinations for settlement. The discourses of migration produced and shared on social media are important records of lived experiences which may not be captured in any other way. Van Leeuwen

(2009, p. 144) opines that the term discourse is an 'extended stretch of connected speech or writing – a text', while Foucault (2013) describes discourse as 'practices that systematically form the objects of which they speak'. Blommaert (2005) explains that discourse 'comprises all forms of meaningful semiotic human activity seen in connection with social, cultural and historical patterns and developments of use'. In the same vein, Cameron and Panovic (2014, p. 3) view discourse as language in use; a form of social practice in which language plays a central role.

The fundamental connection between all the views above is that discourses are socially constructed forms of social practice from which interpretations are drawn in relation to their inherent roles within the larger community. The discipline of discourse analysis can be divided into critical discourse analysis (CDA) and multimodal discourse analysis (MDA), otherwise known as multimodality. While CDA dwells heavily on the critical deconstruction of discourses, MDA emphasises the multiple modes used by discourse participants to produce meaning. Hence, this book is premised on the assumption that discourses of migration reveal important insights on both migration and discourse as the different chapters in this book will reveal, spotlighting the everyday realities of Nigerians and Zimbabweans, and by extension Africans, in their quest to relocate for different purposes.

Since discourse plays a central role in everyday communication, discourses of migration have also proliferated with rising migration across the entire world. In several parts of the world, different motivations prompt people to migrate from one area to another. The frequency with which migration occurs makes it part of daily conversations on and off social media in Nigeria and Zimbabwe. It is, however, surprising that very few scholars have done extensive work that focuses on discourses of migration in and about these countries. Although there are several studies on migration especially in the Global North, few addressed it from a discursive perspective let alone compare migration discourses in two African countries. This book contributes to new literature on the concept of migration and its accompanying human realities in Nigeria and Zimbabwe from a linguistic point of view.

Guccione (2022) notes that if the importance of immigration in human affairs cannot be ignored, neither can the countless sociolinguistic consequences of migration. Migration discourse is an umbrella term that covers all the communication practices related to migration as a social and political phenomenon. In the view of Guillem (2015, p. 1):

> Migration discourses are the specific and distinct communicative practices that accompany the phenomenon of migration. They include lay discourses generated among migrant and host communities as they interact with each other in everyday contexts, as well as elite discourses about migration, often situated in institutional contexts, that frame it in particular ways and for different kinds of purposes. The study of migration discourse in everyday contexts has offered in-depth descriptions of the experiences of western-based migrants that reveal their struggles and strategies as they try to successfully adapt to their new environments. The discourses also emphasise the difficulties faced by migrants as they

strive to construct meaningful identities away from home, as well as the ways in which members of host societies discursively negotiate what is often perceived as a threatening immigrant presence.

What is important for our purposes is how discourses 'frame' migration, influencing perceptions and shaping attitudes towards migrants and migration. It is through discourse that migrants and citizens of host nations narrate their experiences of living in foreign lands and living with others respectively. Van Dijk (2018, p. 228) has provided a more extensive definition of discourse and its permutations:

- Discourse is a form and unit of language use.
- Discourse is an ordered sequence of words, sentences or turns – each with its own structures.
- These sequences express coherent sequences of local and global meanings.
- Discourse is a form of communication.
- Discourse is a multimodal message (spoken, written, images, sounds, music, gestures).
- Discourse is a form of social interaction.
- Discourse may instantiate a social relation, such as power, domination, or resistance.
- Discourse may be a political action, such as a speech in parliament or party propaganda.
- Discourse is a cultural phenomenon, such as a conference paper or editorial.
- Discourse is an economic commodity or resource (it may be bought or sold, e.g. as newspaper or book or represent a form of power).

What we regard as a discourse in this study relates holistically to Van Dijk's descriptions of the term. The texts selected for the purposes of this study draw significantly on the scholar's propositions. Van Dijk's (2018) description of discourse lends credence to our argument that any textual data relating to migration can be perceived as migration discourse. To have a nuanced understanding of discourse, Van Dijk (2018) recommends that the communicative situation or context must be examined by focusing on *Who, When, Where, for Whom,* and *How* the discourse is used, as well as its style and meanings.

According to Van Dijk (2018, p. 230):

> [...] migration discourse not only may be about migration or its many aspects, but also be a constituent part of migration as a phenomenon, as would be the stories of migrants, as well as immigration policies. Thus, migration as a social phenomenon not only consists of (groups of) participants, institutions, many types of social and political (inter)action, but also, quite prominently, of many genres of migration discourse as social and political acts and interaction.

For us, current conversations about migration do not only reflect discourse as a form of language use but also a form of social and political (inter) action.

Van Dijk (2018) provides several case studies of migration discourse through what he refers to as 'genres' of migration discourse among which are:

- Media discourse: news reports (press, TV, radio, internet), editorials, interviews, reportages, cartoons
- Political discourse: parliamentary debates, bills, policy documents, party programmes, speeches of politicians
- Legal discourse: bills/laws, international agreements, treaties, police discourse, crime reports, interrogations, trials
- Educational discourse: textbooks/lessons, classroom interactions, teacher–student interactions
- Administrative discourse: interactions with officials, forms, applications
- Social movement discourse: official declarations, meetings, protests, slogans, conversations among members
- Internet discourse: websites, blogs
- Artistic discourse: novels, poetry, theatre, TV shows, and soaps
- Personal discourse: everyday face-to-face conversations, letters, e-mail messages, internet participation (Facebook, Twitter, Chats)

Van Dijk (2018) emphasises that the explicit understanding of the genres above derives from their communicative situations, because discourse genres are, first, a type of social activity. As such, the communicative situations may be characterised by the following:

- Time/Period
- Place/Space/Environment/Institution
- Participants
- Social identities, e.g. ethnic identities, origin, etc.
- Communicative roles: speaker, recipient, etc.
- Social roles, e.g. politician, teacher, police officer, judge, etc.
- Social relations, e.g. of domination (power abuse), cooperation, resistance
- On-going (Inter)Action
- On-going discourse
- Speech acts (e.g. assertion, question, promise, accusation)
- Other social acts (e.g. cooperation, protests, etc.)
- Personal and social cognition
- Goals of the current interaction
- Shared and mutual generic knowledge (common ground) of participants
- Shared social attitudes and ideologies about migration

According to Van Dijk (2018), the analysis of these genres can be approached from different perspectives. An analyst might identify themes and topics, schematic superstructures, local meanings, modalities, implications, presuppositions, as well as actor and action descriptions depending on their relevance to the investigations on migration discourse. For this study, we focus our analysis on themes and topics as well as on local meanings. The analysis of the themes and topics demystify the overall meaning of the discourse. Van Dijk (2018) maintains that topics are fundamental because they subsume the local meanings of discourse, i.e. through topics or themes one can develop an interest in the deeper meanings of issues. Although such summaries do not provide all the details, they at least provide a global idea of the meaning of a larger corpus of text or talk (Van Dijk, 2018). The common themes used in everyday discourse to refer to migration in Nigeria and Zimbabwe are reflected and analysed in this book. Besides the study of the overall meanings (topics, themes) of migration, the study of 'local' meanings, which are the meanings of words, sentences, or sequences of sentences is important in discourse analysis (Van Dijk, 2018). Local meanings are ensembles of semantic associations embedded in specific social groups (Basov et al., 2021); how meanings are negotiated and restricted in a particular society. This study focuses on how Zimbabweans and Nigerians debate migration discourse.

Van Dijk (2018) genre of *personal discourse*, particularly internet participation (Facebook, Twitter, Chats), is the nucleus of this study which reflects on data produced through social media. In the current reality of migration, social media plays an important role. As pointed out by De Fina and Baynham (2012), the construction and negotiation of meanings by immigrants are not confined to narratives in interviews but extend to many other kinds of communication. So, if we must carefully study migration, we cannot ignore discourses produced on social media which is one of the 'many other kinds' that De Fina and Baynham encouraged researchers to also consider. We consequently examine personal and social cognition, the goals of current interactions, the shared and mutual generic knowledge (common ground) of the participants, shared social attitudes and ideologies about migration plus social relations, roles, and identities in our analysis of discourses produced in Zimbabwe and Nigeria.

People of similar and diverse societies exchange views and information on social platforms and although discourse analysts have researched the human realities of social media, the authors of this book are unaware of studies which address migration discourse either distinctly or jointly in Nigeria and Zimbabwe. We juxtapose data from the two countries to assist in deepening comparisons across other countries in Africa. In this sense, our book could be used as source material for global readers, researchers, and scholars in similar fields. Discourse analysis offers a wide scope when it comes to the scrutinisation of texts. Several studies have shown that discourse is invested and ideological and it is through the analysis of discourses that the invested meanings are brought to the fore. Similarly, migration discourses in everyday context are heavily invested with substances that interpret and shape the current realities of migration, especially on the African continent. The intertextual nature of migration discourse in Nigeria and Zimbabwe, where the citizens of the two countries use many forms of written and visual texts to discuss migration issues, makes discourse analysis a significant part of this book.

This book adopts a qualitative approach using netnography method to identify and gather relevant data. Netnography is a method that involves listening-in to and/or following online conversations or discussions without actively participating. Some scholars have defined netnography as the application of ethnographic methods of collecting and analysing data such as observation and document analysis to virtual platforms. Bainbridge (2000, p. 57) defines netnography as 'a relatively passive examination of websites, without full interaction with the people who created them'. For Makombe (2022, p. 160), netnography is a research method that seeks to transfer ethnographic research methods such as observation and document analysis to the online platform. Dekker et al. (2018) note that there are barriers and hazards to the use of social media by migrants on a dangerous journey, suggesting that there is a state of data precariousness regarding access to and trustworthiness of social media content. As such, they argue that social media data involves untested and instrumentally relevant statements that can be identified as rumours (Dekker et al., 2018). Notwithstanding this limitation, we believe that netnography offers us a unique exploration of Nigerian and Zimbabwean migration discourses on social media platforms. Our view is that social media produces rich data since many social media platforms reflect the emotional and immediate feelings of users – very often as they occur (Benski & Fisher, 2013, p. 6).

We purposively selected online media data on migration discourse with the main criteria being that they must address migration and relate to Nigeria or Zimbabwe. Certain measures were employed to ensure the rigour and trustworthiness of the data collection so that it would be credible, transferable, dependable, and confirmable. Specific keywords were used in searching for relevant data which ensured that the social media posts addressed migration. The frequency of usage of these keywords in the context of migration already suggests that they are important discursive elements for the purpose of this study. The frequency of the posts, as well as the impressions and perceptions they reflect also determine the popularity of such views and opinions. The data collected was analysed and juxtaposed to make comparisons and identify patterns and similarities.

According to De Fina and Baynham (2012):

> Discourse perspectives on migration start from very different theoretical and methodological premises. On the one hand, they emphasize the need to analyse what migrants themselves say about their experience in order to understand the processes that change their lives. On the other hand, they argue for the constitutive nature of discourse in the construction of identities, stances, and worldviews. It should not come as a surprise then that many of the studies that take as their object the discourse of immigrants, that is, the way they construct and represent their experiences, have focused on narratives.

The data emanated from several sources including X (formerly Twitter), Facebook, YouTube as well as other online sources such as mainstream online newspapers and blogs in order to have nuanced and balanced perspectives. In each chapter, specific details regarding sourced data are discussed in order to enhance clarity. The collected data was examined through discourse analysis taking into account the context of the data as well as the social worldviews reflected in the data.

From a discursive perspective, efforts were made to unpack the lived-in realities of Nigerians and Zimbabweans. Their reasons for migration, as well as the dominant discourses post-migration are also presented in this book. The inherent feelings of the migrants, potential migrants, unwilling but forced migrants, as well as those who have chosen to remain in their countries despite the harsh socio-economic realities have all been retrieved from social media platforms and are discussed in relation to how they divulge important migration matters. The book addresses the prevailing motives of migrants in the two countries, the popular utterances used to discuss migration, migration destination interests of the Nigerian and Zimbabwean citizens, post-migration conversations and other significant matters.

In a nutshell, the book addresses the concept and realities of migration in Nigeria and Zimbabwe. However, the discourses and repertoires of migration discussed in this book are of course not exhaustive; further studies drawing from different contexts are required to enrich the knowledge in the field.

References

Bainbridge, W. S. (2000). Religious ethnography on the World Wide Web. In K. Hadden & D. E. Cowan (Eds.), *Religion on the internet: Research prospects and promises* (pp. 55–80). Elsevier.

Basov, N., de Nooy, W., & Nenko, A. (2021). Local meaning structures: Mixed-method sociosemantic network analysis. *American Journal of Cultural Sociology*, *9*, 376–417.

Benski, T., & Fisher, E. (2013). Introduction: Investigating emotions and the internet. In T. Benski & E. Fisher (Eds.), *Internet and emotions* (pp. 1–14). Routledge.

Blommaert, J. (2005). *Discourse*. Cambridge University Press.

Cameron, D., & Panovic, I. (2014). *Working with written discourse*. SAGE Publications Ltd.

De Fina, A., & Baynham, M. (2012). Immigrant discourse. In C. A. Chapelle (Ed.), *The encyclopedia of applied linguistics* (pp. 1–8).

Dekker, R., Engbersen, G., Klaver, J., & Vonk, H. (2018). Smart refugees: How Syrian Asylum migrants use social media information in migration decision-making. *Social Media + Society*, *4*(1), 1–11.

Foucault, M. (1972). *Archaeology of knowledge*. Routledge.

Guccione, C. (2022). Migration discourse and the new socially constructed meanings of the English Lingua Franca. *European Scientific Journal*, *18*(18), 33–49.

Guillem, S. M. (2015). Migration discourse. The international encyclopedia of language and social interaction. In K. Tracy & T. Sandel (Eds.), *The international encyclopedia of language and social interaction* (pp. 1–10). John Wiley & Sons.

Kok, P. (1999). The definition of migration and its application: Making sense of recent South African census and survey data. *Southern African Journal of Demography*, *7*(1), 19–30.

Makombe, R. (2022). Social media, COVID-19 and the 'Second Republic' in Zimbabwe Memes as instruments of subversion on President Mnangagwa's Facebook page. In T. Mangena, O. Nyambi & G. Ncube (Eds.), *The Zimbabwean crisis after Mugabe multidisciplinary perspectives* (pp. 154–171).

Schewel, K., & Debray, A. (2024). Global trends in south–south migration. In H. Crawley & J. K. Teye (Eds.), *The Palgrave handbook of south–south migration and inequality* (pp. 153–187). Palgrave Macmillan.

Van Dijk, T. A. (2018). Discourse and migration. In R. Zapata-Barrero & E. Yalaz (Eds.), *Qualitative research in European migration studies* (pp. 227–245). IMISCOE Research Series.
Van Leeuwen, T. (2009). Discourse as the recontextualization of social practice: A guide. In M. Meyer & R. Wodak (Eds.), *Methods of critical discourse analysis* (2nd ed, pp. 144–181). Sage.
Walsh, J. P. (2023). Digital nativism: Twitter, migration discourse and the 2019 election. *New Media & Society, 25*(10), 2618–2643.
Yaro, J. A., & Setrana, M. B. (2023). The dynamics of south–south migration in Africa. In H. Crawley & J. K. Teye (Eds.), *The Palgrave handbook of south–south migration and inequality* (pp. 183–199). Springer International Publishing.

Chapter 2

Contemporary Global Discourses of Migration and Migrants

Keywords: Migrants; borders; neoliberal; the other; crisis; Global South

In many ways, contemporary migration patterns resemble migration patterns of the 19th century, which were largely driven by colonial adventures. The difference, however, is that contemporary migrations are South to North as opposed to North to South and the migrants are largely desperate people escaping difficult economic conditions, wars, and various kinds of persecutions in Africa and South America. In fact, the general trend about contemporary migrations is that people move from economically weak countries to economically strong countries, either within the Global South or without. In recent years, the world has witnessed large numbers of people migrating from countries in South America such as Honduras, Guatemala, and Mexico to the United States and from Africa and the Middle East to Europe. The latter trend has been associated with the war in Syria, the collapse of Muammar Gaddafi's regime in Libya, and more recently, the Russia–Ukraine war. One common thread in all these migrations is economic strife and the breakdown of governance systems in the sending countries. Decolonial scholars have explained contemporary global migration patterns through the notion of coloniality which designates the persistence of quasi-colonial systems and structures of governance in former colonised territories of the Global South. According to decolonial theorists, the Global South constitute what they call 'the darker side of modernity', a zone of none being which must remain in the darkness of economic strife, poor governance, hunger, disease, etc. to maintain the bright shine of modernity in the Global North. It is from this perspective that we see a connection between contemporary migrations and colonialism and its legacies. The legacy of colonialism that we have in mind is not only that of economic plunder and dispossession but also that of negative stereotypes and misrepresentations of people of the Global South.

Social Constructions of Migration in Nigeria and Zimbabwe
Discourse, Rhetoric, and Identity, 11–28
Copyright © 2024 by Kunle Musbaudeen Oparinde and Rodwell Makombe
Published under exclusive licence by Emerald Publishing Limited
doi:10.1108/978-1-83549-168-320241002

The objective of this chapter (and by extension, this book) is to read contemporary discourses of migration as narratives that, in quasi-colonial style, resuscitate and in some instances, regurgitate, colonial discourses about the 'other'. Two questions guide our analysis. Firstly, we explore how migrants are represented in contemporary discourses of migration? Secondly, we examine how these discourses resonate with colonial discourses and contemporary narratives about borders and nations. We argue that contemporary narratives of migration draw largely from the colonial archive to construct migrants as problems and threats to the social fabric of countries in the Global North. We also argue that contemporary migration discourses tend to associate the Global South with dystopia (lacks and deficits) and the Global North with the utopia of endless economic opportunities.

Most available literature on contemporary migration show that migrants are generally represented in negative terms, sometimes using images of animals and natural disasters. We will explore this further in the review of relevant literature below, but first we must explain the linkage between contemporary discourses of migration and colonial discourses. Among the many definitions of discourse that Van Dijk (2017) proposes, we see discourse as a form of language use and a form of communication. Scholars such as Mudimbe (1988) have argued that Africa is an invention of Europe because most of what is 'known' about Africa and Africans in the global imaginary was recorded and disseminated by European travellers and anthropologists and reinforced by missionaries and colonial administrators through discourse. The stories that the colonialists recorded were usually based on their ignorance of African cultures and epistemologies, yet these stories were adopted as fact and regurgitated by many other Western scholars. Mudimbe cites authoritative Western historian, Herodotus, who in his work recorded stories of two-headed human-like creatures and cannibals that he claimed lived in some parts of Africa. Other artists such as painters and writers went on to construct images of Africa based on these false narratives. Mudimbe gives the example of the painting, *The Exotic Tribe* by Hans Burgkmair which depicted Africans as primitives based on scanty information from Bartolomaus Springer's travel diaries. The point of Mudimbe's work is that narratives (stories) were instrumental in the construction of a certain image of Africa and Africans in the Western imaginary. Similarly, Edward Said's *Orientalism* (1978) has also demonstrated how Western literature was responsible for producing and popularising the image of the East as feminine, exotic, and evil. These colonial narratives created a binary which has endured to the present day – the North as the citadel of reason and the South as the realm of emotions and instinct. Contemporary anti-Islamic discourses in the West can be traced to these narratives, which were largely produced by artists who either had never visited the Middle East or had limited knowledge about its cultures and traditions.

Postcolonial scholars such as Elleke Boehmer (2005) in *Colonial and Postcolonial Literature*, Benedict Anderson (1983) in *Imagined Communities* and Homi Bhabha in *Nation and Narration* have also emphasised the centrality of text/discourse in the constitution of nations. Boehmer's work shows that the British Empire was as much a cartographic entity as it was a textual exercise. This means that the colonisation of physical territories was often accompanied by narratives (stories) that portrayed British culture and civilisation as superior to the culture and civilisations of colonised territories. To colonise was thus, in Boehmer's formulation, not only to take over territories but also to write them into existence through texts. Colonial texts such as novels, legal documents, minutes, diaries, and travelogues participated, one way or the other, in the discursive constitution of empires. The point of Boehmer's theorisation is that nations, like empires before them, are constituted discursively.

The advent of the nation-state, which incidentally coincided with colonialism for most countries in the Global South, also came along with the idea of borders. These ideas (of nations and borders) are quite instructive not only because they highlight the centrality of narrative in the constitution of nations/people but also the ways in which narratives of nations and borders entangle with discourses of migrants and migration. To migrate, in the contemporary present, is to cross a border. Homi Bhabha (1990) postulates that nations are narrations, and in the context of our analysis, to narrate a nation is also to assert its borders and to determine by law or by any other means, who belongs and who does not belong to it. Contemporary nations, as Bhabha (1996) would argue, are obsessed with questions of identity, belonging, and citizenship. In every nation, there are those who belong and those who do not (or who are perceived as not belonging). To narrate the nation, in Bhabha's formulation, is to create boundaries between those who belong to it and those who do not belong to it. Benedict Anderson's (1983) seminal text *Imagined communities*, traces the origin of the nation to the advent of print capitalism and the novel, two inventions which enabled people to 'imagine' themselves as belonging to the same nation. Anderson's work shows that the ideas of nation, nation-ness, and nationalism are recent phenomena, having been invented in the aftermath of the fall of monarchs in the 18th century in Europe.

The point of Anderson's theorisation is that nations are not only physical entities but also discursive constructs. Ideas about empires as texts (Boehmer, 2005), narrations (Bhabha, 1996), inventions (Mudimbe, 1988) and imagined communities (Anderson, 1983) are important to our reading of contemporary discourses of migration, firstly because migration narratives are ceased with the notion of national borders which migrants transgress, and secondly, because migration is not only about the movement of people from one place to another but also about how that movement is imagined and narrated through text. Blinder's (2015) work on imagined migrants in Britain shows that migrants are not only real people who live in a foreign land (either temporarily or permanently) but also images in the minds of citizens. Blinder's study suggests that the migrants that enter the UK and appear in official statistics are different from the migrants that British citizens imagine when they think about migrants. The point of Blinder's work is that when we talk about migrants, we are not only talking about physical human bodies but also imagined entities.

We argue that migrants are imagined in Benedict Anderson's (1983) sense because one does not need to meet and know migrants to hold certain views about them. Blinder's (2015) study shows that 'attitudes towards migrants are shaped by "imagined migrants", rather than the reality of migrations'. If British citizens have different migrants in their imaginations, then the British government's focus on reducing net migration does not address the issue of the specific migrants that citizens consider as migrants. We make a connection between colonial discourses of the 19th century (and earlier), narratives of the nation, and contemporary imaginaries of migration because most contemporary discourses of migration target the same groups of people that were targeted by colonial discourses, and secondly, because one cannot talk about migration without talking about nations and borders and thirdly, because knowledge about migration is always mediated. To talk about migration and migrants is thus also to talk about images and narratives. Blinder's (2015) study submits that while the British government follows generic definitions of migrants, as prescribed by the United Nations, most Britons imagine migrants as people from 'racial and cultural backgrounds different from their own' (Blinder, 2015, p. 83). Perhaps, the question is who these 'different' migrants are, and why do British citizens perceive them as threats?

We focus firstly on Western discourses of migration to reflect, somewhat in reverse, on African (Nigerian and Zimbabwean) discourses of migration, which often depict Western countries in positive light as spaces of endless economic opportunities. Reflecting on what he calls 'the desire for borders and thus, for separation and provincialisation', Achille Mbembe (2021, p. 133) argues that European society (particularly France) has seen a resurgence in neo-revisionist and provincialist discourses that 'cultivate the phantasm of "man without Other"'. These two schools of thought (neo-revisionist and provincialist) are apologetic towards colonialism and its ravages on colonised societies, insisting that former colonised societies should in fact be grateful for the 'good' that colonialism did. This group, according to Mbembe (2021, p. 133), aims to 'reactivate the myth of Western superiority' by among other things, insisting on a narrow, nativist vision of the nation and national belonging. The nation is conceptualised as a closed space where a group of carefully selected people must belong while the rest are kept out, lest they slip into *our* way of life and poison it (Mbembe, 2021, p. 133). Moreover, this group sees the world as engaged in a 'global civil war' wherein the nation-state is facing an existential threat, and therefore, must prioritise border security and the policing of identities through all kind of legal and extra-legal measures. In all this, it is not only the security of the state that is at stake but also the very survival of Western civilisation. The foreigner, especially the Arab and the African immigrant, is redefined 'either as an illegal immigrant (the figure par excellence of the intruder and the undesirable) or as the enemy' (Mbembe, 2021, p. 133). If Western civilisation is perceived as under threat, then this civilisation must be protected by keeping others (read as threats) out of the national borders. In fact, it does not matter anymore whether this immigrant has legal documents or not. If she has documents, Mbembe argues, then she must undergo endless checks and verifications to prove her authenticity. The immigrant is thus an enemy, especially if he is Muslim, because his culture and religion (often seen as one) are a threat to the Christian values of the West.

In the aftermath of the rise of the Islamic state and terrorist attacks in Western cities, Islam as a religion has been lumped together with irrationality and terrorism. In most Western cities, Islam and Muslims are perceived as threats to secularism and democratic values of liberty, fraternity, and equality. The contemporary present, Mbembe (2021, p. 134) argues, has become a space where governments are preoccupied with ensuring the protection of the rights of some while others are 'deprived of all rights, abandoned to precariousness, and denied not only the possibility of having rights but also any legal existence'. The state (particularly the Western state) seeks to impose secular values on everyone because secularism is perceived as more rational than religious fanaticism, and those who are perceived as fanatics must be saved even against their will. Muslim women are seen as objects of religious and cultural oppression from 'their husbands and brothers [… and …] an inegalitarian religion' (Mbembe, 2021, p. 135). Mbembe (2021, p. 136) makes a connection between the objectives of the colonial civilising mission and the way the French state, for example, sees itself as on a mission to 'emancipate individuals "for their own good" and, if necessary, against their will'. The point that Mbembe is making is that we must understand contemporary discourses of migration within the context of a fundamentalist world, obsessed with the idea of borders and the nation as a closed space for others.

This negative perception towards migration and migrants is not only limited to France or to countries in the Global North. In 1983, Nigeria expelled over two million migrants, half of whom were Ghanaians on the pretext that they had no legal right to live in the country (Daly, 2022). In recent years, South Africa has witnessed violent outbursts of xenophobic violence aimed at migrants from African countries. We also know that during Idi Amin's reign in Uganda, the government expelled many migrants of Asian descent claiming that they had deprived Ugandans of economic opportunities. Similarly, in the contemporary South African imaginary, migrants from the continent figure as embodiments of all kinds of social ills ranging from criminality to witchcraft.

Migration Discourse

Martinez Guillem (2015, p. 1) defines migration discourse as 'the specific and distinct communicative practices that accompany the phenomenon of migration'. Research on migration discourse has thus focused on 'the role of narratives as sites where particular understandings of what it means to be a migrant may emerge, develop, and/or be challenged' (Guillem, 2015, p. 3). The starting point for most of these studies is that 'identities are not a priori, fixed categories, but they are intrinsically linked to discourse and interaction' (Guillem, 2015, p. 3). The way in which migrants are imagined (perceived and narrated) has a bearing not only on how they are treated but also on policies that governments implement to deal with them. In other words, migration discourses tend to reveal the ideological positions of interlocutors (political actors or ordinary citizens) – are they racist, nationalist, multiculturalist, etc. Migration discourses often categorise migrants as good or bad, bona fide, or bogus, thus creating two broad categories of deserving and undeserving migrants, those who are desirable and those who are undesirable. Guillem (2015) notes that reports on television tend to present issues related to migration in the category of bad news. News reports often make connections between migrants/migration and problems, crisis, risk (security, health, culture) and in this discourse, non-white migrants feature as posing a bigger threat, and more risk. In fact, the demonisation of black migrants in contemporary discourses of migration is not only limited to Europe. When the Russia–Ukraine war broke out, some Ukraine officials denied Africans transport to evacuate from dangerous areas to safe zones (Moopi & Makombe, 2023) preferring to prioritise the lives of their own citizens. Similarly, when COVID-19 broke out in China, African migrants in some Chinese provinces such as Guangdong were evicted from their homes and barred from restaurants because they were perceived as carriers of the disease. In addition to the 'bad news frame', Guillem (2015, p. 6) submits that other media such as newspapers usually use photographs that 'remove all agency from immigrants through the blurring of their faces, or the representation of scenes where they are consistently looking down or away from the readers'. Such representations promote narratives that associate immigrants with victimhood, cultural differences, criminality, and inability to integrate into the host culture.

Migration as a Crisis or a Problem

Longitudinal studies of migration and migration discourse suggest that perceptions about migration differ from context to context, and it is not always the case that migration is associated with negativity. Guccione's (2022) study of migration in Germany from the postwar era to the present suggests that the mass arrival of immigrants in Europe after the 1990s 'transformed the phenomenon of migration from a benefit into a problem and opened the debate to issues of first aid, security, expulsion, and rejection' (p. 33). After the Second World War, migration was generally perceived as positive because most countries needed skilled labour to rebuild their economies. Today, most countries especially in Europe no longer see migrants as socio-economic resources to be protected and regulated, but as apotential social problems affecting areas such as the economy, health, and national security (Guccione, 2022, p. 33). Similarly, Fröhlich's study of German migration discourse from 1949 to the present shows that Germany has witnessed shifting perceptions towards migrants over the years. However, the overarching perception is that of 'migration as crisis'. The only time that migrants were perceived as beneficial is when they came as skilled workers to alleviate shortages in critical sectors of the economy. Since the Syrian refugee crisis of 2015, the 'migration as crisis' narrative has become dominant in European migration discourse.

In 2015/2016, most European countries saw the influx of migrants from the Middle East as 'an extraordinary event' that would lead to 'instability and danger and affecting a preexisting reality which [was] perceived as "normal"' (Fröhlich, 2023, p. 2). Fröhlich (2023, p. 2) explains the general hostility towards migrants in Europe in terms of the Westphalian state model, which is based on 'the differentiation of an in-group from an out-group, of citizens from noncitizens'. The Westphalian state is built on a logic of inclusion and exclusion. The state, according to this model, has a responsibility only to the in-group, hence those who come from outside become intruders who are likely to jeopardise the rights of the in-group and destabilise the perceived tranquillity of the inside. For most countries, migrants tend to be seen as threats because they are not easy to control given that they are moving targets and 'and marginal figures with unclear potential, making them hard to read and control' (Fröhlich, 2023, p. 2). This model of the state has also been responsible for negative attitudes towards foreigners in African countries such as South Africa, Uganda (during Idi Amin's reign), Nigeria (in the 1980s) and Botswana. Zimbabwean migrants who flock into Botswana to escape the spiralling economic crisis are often met with arrest, detention, and deportation.

In recent years, countries such as the United States and Australia have witnessed an insurgence of far-right politics that aim to protect the state through erecting borders and keeping 'others' out. Similarly, South Africa has experienced violent xenophobic attacks against foreign nationals who have been accused of causing all kinds of socio-economic problems. Dodson's (2010) study of migration discourse in South Africa shows that South Africans see migrants in negative terms. Migrants are associated with social ills such as crime, drugs, unemployment, and poor service delivery. Senior government officials have promoted this narrative by blaming 'illegal immigrants for placing strain on state resources or engaging in criminal activity' (Dodson, 2010, p. 5). Dodson (2010, p. 5) argues that xenophobia in South Africa is not 'isolated, aberrant, or the work of a few rogue elements' but 'entrenched and systemic' thus, it requires 'similarly systemic responses if it is to be meaningfully addressed'. South African politicians tend to deny that South Africans are xenophobic, preferring to characterise attacks against foreigners as acts of criminality. There is also a tendency, Dodson (2010) argues, for politicians to associate migrants 'not only with illegality but also actual criminality, despite evidence that African immigrants are far likelier to be victims than perpetrators of criminal activity' (p. 7).

Although South Africa has a significant population of migrants from other continents such as Asia, xenophobic violence only targets migrants from the continent. Dodson argues that xenophobia in South Africa has its roots in apartheid's policy of racial segregation and isolationism, a claim that resonates with our argument that contemporary discourses of migration intricately intertwine with colonial discourses of othering. Black South Africans had no serious interaction with Africans from the continent until the end of apartheid in 1994. In Dodson's (2010, p. 4) view, 'the end of apartheid did not bring a clean break with the past' because most South Africans continued to see Africans as outsiders who had no right to be in South Africa. As it is in many European countries, the unwanted immigrant' in South Africa is not an anonymous, generic figure but a particular one, with a race and a nationality.

Dodson (2010) identifies at least six axes of explanation for negative attitudes towards migrants in South Africa. The first is the economic or material explanation which posits that migrants compete with South Africans for

> jobs, housing, and other services and resources to which they themselves [South Africans] feel entitled, while wealthier South Africans, black and white, resent paying taxes to provide shelter and services to people seen to be pouring into South Africa to

escape political incompetence and economic mismanagement further north. (Dodson, 2010, p. 5)

The perception that migrants are a burden to the national welfare system is also prevalent in many European countries. There are many parallels between the way in which African migrants are perceived in South Africa and the way they are perceived in Europe. In Europe, African migrants are usually perceived as bogus asylum seekers escaping chaos in Africa, ranging from war to endless economic crises. Similarly, South Africa has, in recent years, become the destination of choice for migrants escaping economic hardships from all over the continent. While in Europe, migrants are often seen as a threat to the socio-cultural fabric of society, in South Africa, migrants are often blamed for 'flashing money around and stealing women from local men' (Dodson, 2010, p. 5).

Achille Mbembe (2021, p. 234) has argued that in France,

> the foreigner is not only the citizen of another state: he or she is above all someone different from us, whose dangerousness is real, from whom a proven cultural distance separates us, and who in every form, constitutes a mortal threat to our mode of existence.

The othering of the foreigner in contemporary European society has overtones of the colonial discourse of stereotyping as Bhabha (1994) has theorised it. Like the colonised of yesteryear, the immigrant is an embodiment of negativity, an abject. In the South African context, the way in which the South African citizen treats the foreigner is not far from the way the apartheid government treats its black citizens. In fact, the end of apartheid, which was a system of othering, meant the creation of a new oppositional other in the form of the foreigner/migrant. Like the Muslim immigrant in contemporary Europe (especially France), who according to Mbembe (2021), embodies a difference that threatens the core values of the Republic, the foreigner in South Africa is also perceived as a threat to the cultural fabric of society. The foreigner, like the Muslim, is accused of unwillingness to integrate into the community, even when the latter is not willing to embrace the foreigner's difference.

The obsession with borders, separation and provincialisation that Mbembe discusses in relation to France is also relevant to the South African context. The nation, in South Africa, is seen as a closed space where only citizens have rights and privileges. Foreigners are seen not only as intruders but enemies who must be physically removed by any means, including violence. After having acquired the rights of citizenship, to which they were denied until 1994, South Africans feel that they have a responsibility to protect their rights and space from foreign intruders. The migrant is a usurper whose presence creates numerous problems and inconveniences for those with citizenship rights. Dodson (2010) argues that ordinary South Africans do not make a distinction between legal and illegal migrants. In fact, the distinction does not matter because in any case citizenship is understood as indigeneity. For ordinary citizens, migrants are not people with or without papers but those who look different from us, regardless of their status, those whose skin pigmentation speaks difference and foreignness. Generally, migrants tend to be perceived as 'dangerous and undesirable, including by the media' (Dodson, 2010, p. 6). In the case of France, Mbembe (2021) argues, the authorities often deny racism against non-whites prefer to treat it as 'mere cultural difference'. Similarly, in South Africa, politicians from Nelson Mandela to Cyril Ramaphosa have insisted that South Africans are not xenophobic and that the violence that often happens in poor communities is criminal and not xenophobic. Considering these denials, Dodson (2010, p. 9) describes xenophobia in South Africa as 'the hatred that denies its name'. In Europe, xenophobic attitudes are easier to justify because those who are 'unwanted' are visibly different, but in South Africa and other parts of Africa, the hatred against the 'other' is complicated because the other is not quite different.

Neocosmos (2006, p. 587) identifies three core elements of xenophobia in South Africa namely, 'a state discourse of xenophobia', 'a discourse of South African exceptionalism', and a 'conception of citizenship founded exclusively on indigeneity'. These core elements are also applicable to migration discourses in Europe and the United States. During the migration crisis of 2015/2016, there was a consensus across Europe that migrants were a threat that needed urgent attention. This was also the case in the United States during Donald Trump's tenure, when official discourses characterised migrants from South America in negative terms. In fact, Donald Trump went on to commission to construction of a border wall on the Mexican border to keep the 'unwanted others' out. According to this formulation, both Europe and America were exclusive territories of Americans and Europeans, and others were not welcome.

Heidenreich et al. (2020) study of migration sentiment in six European countries shows that right-wing political actors tend to portray migrants negatively, and migration as a threat to the social-cultural fabric and security of receiving countries. The study notes that 'overall perceptions of migration are negative […] and in Europe, […] immigrants are frequently portrayed […] as dangerous or a threat to the society in general' (1264). These findings resonate with Dodson's (2010) study of xenophobia in South Africa where most political parties, including the ruling African National Congress (ANC), blame migrants for worsening the country's socio-economic challenges such as crime, drug abuse, and unemployment. In Europe, Heidenreich et al. (2020, p. 1265) cite the example of the right-wing Belgian party 'Vlaams Blok' which has pursued a strategy of excluding, stigmatising, and blaming immigrants for a wide range of problems in the country.

Castles (2010) submits that most available research on migration is framed by a sedentary approach which firstly views migration as a problem and secondly believes that people should rather stay at home than migrate. The people who are often told to stay where they are despite the problems that they face, are those that Mbembe (2017) calls 'the new wretched of the earth':

> […] those to whom the right to have rights is refused, those who are told not to move, those who are condemned to live within structures of confinement – camps, transit centers, the thousands of

sites of detention that dot our spaces of law and policing. They are those who are turned away, deported, expelled; the clandestine, the 'undocumented' – the intruders and castoffs from humanity that we want to get rid of because we think that, between them and us, there is nothing worth saving, and that they fundamentally pose a threat to our lives, our health, our well-being. The new 'wretched of the earth' are the products of a brutal process of control and selection whose racial foundation we well know. (2017, p. 177)

It is interesting to note that Frantz Fanon (1963) used the term 'the wretched of the earth' to refer to the colonised, those who, in the colonial system, were condemned to live under a regime of violence. The contemporary present that Mbembe writes about is just as compartmentalised as the colonial world, and like the latter, it still upholds the colonial logic of bodies that matter and bodies that do not matter. In fact, 'a dominant political discourse [especially in Europe and America] sees migration as a problem that needs to be "fixed" by appropriate policies' which might include introducing tighter border controls and deportation of illegal/unwanted migrations. Castles (2010) argues that this approach is misplaced in that it does not recognise that migration is inevitable, and that it cannot be prevented, because it is part of broader changes taking place in the global economy. In fact, the sedentary approach assumes that people move from poor communities/countries to richer countries to improve their economic status, which implies that if economic problems in their countries improve, migration will cease. Castles (2010) submits that this is not the case because people migrate for different reasons as dictated by transformations taking place in society. Migration is, in Castles (2010, p. 1568) words, 'a normal part of social relations'. The sedentary bias in migration research is partly responsible for the 'migration as a problem' discourse in contemporary iterations about migration.

The Media and Discourses of Migration

Today, it is almost impossible to talk about discourse, especially migration discourse, without talking about the media. The media is responsible for framing news and setting the agenda in terms of what is, and what is not, newsworthy. Most of what the world knows about migrants and migration is disseminated through various media channels such as television, newspapers, and social media networks. Helene Schmolz's (2019) study of migration discourse in three English-speaking countries, the USA, the UK and Australia, notes that newspapers play a significant role, more than government, in creating certain discourses about migration. Newspapers tend to focus on 'action stories' which they consider newsworthy, such as instances of migrants drowning in the Mediterranean or migrants scaling fences on the US-Mexican border. These representations tend to create negative images about migration and these stories are often accompanied by photographs that conjure certain mental images. Viola and Verheul's study of migration discourse from 1900 to 2000 shows that the media plays a critical role in shaping public opinion and attitudes towards migration and migrants.

Other studies have shown that 'American and European media have framed migrants in a negative way, either by emphasizing the dichotomy of "us" vs. "them" or by creating an urgency of crisis' (Viola & Verheul, 2020, p. 5). Some scholars have also noted that 'public discussion – rather than the actual facts – plays a crucial role in creating political positions and in informing policy priorities and government choices' (Viola & Verheul, 2020, p. 5). Dhëmbo et al.'s (2021) study of migration discourse in Albania, a sending country in Europe, shows that the media often portrays Albania as facing a demographic crisis of 'population ageing, falling birth rates and changing social structures' due to migration. In fact, these scholars note that Albanian newspapers often carry alarmist headlines that create the impression that the country would disappear if current migration trends continued. The issues that the media report on, and the way they report on those issues, tend to create a hype that may influence authorities to act in certain ways, sometimes without any substantive evidence. A case in point is that of the UK which decided to exit the European Union in the context of the 'migration crisis' of 2015/2016. The fact that many scholars now put the migration crisis in scare quotes suggests that the crisis was more of a media hype than a substantive crisis.

Similarly, media discourse on migration, as Giorgi and Vitale (2017) observe, does not make a distinction between generations of migrants. In many European countries, second-generation migrants should not be categorised as migrants because most of them are now citizens of the host nations. However, in most cases, those that are easily identifiable, either because of their race, religion or general appearance are likely to be branded as migrants. The media often represent migrants in terms of their legal status, for example, documented and undocumented, legal, or illegal, and again these categories reinforce the binaries of good and bad migrant. This narrative is usually accompanied by a moralising discourse whose aim is to ascertain who is more deserving and who is not, who is more vulnerable and who is not, who is legitimate and who is bogus. The attempt to categorise migrants is usually problematic because it is often inconsistent and arbitrary. For example, Giorgi and Vitale (2017) argue that in most European countries, domestic workers are usually tolerated while asylum seekers are generally perceived as bogus. The war in Ukraine has exposed what Mbembe (2021) sees as Europe's obsession with keeping the racialised migrants out of its borders. Fröhlich (2023, p. 16) argues that in contemporary European migration discourse, Ukrainian refugees are considered 'fellow Europeans, with the president of the European Commission, Ursula von der Leyen, stating that 'Ukraine belongs to the European family' and unlike the Syrians who came in 2015, Ukrainians are seen as "real refugees"'. Deserving migrants are usually those escaping war situations; however, the Ukraine war has shown that some real refugees are more real than others. The way in which migrants are folklorised, exoticised on one hand and stereotyped based on their religion or country of origin (Giorgi & Vitale 2017) on the other in Western media reminds us of what Said calls, in a different context, orientalism. Orientalism is the stereotyping of people from the East, which according to Mbembe (2021) manifests in countries such as France where Muslims are expected to assimilate into the Republic for their own good. Dhëmbo et al.'s (2021) confirm that in some countries, the media portrays migrants as 'linked with crime, terrorism, and a threat to state security' and 'Muslim migrants in particular have suffered in a media that repeatedly portrays them as extremist, stereotyping and presenting Muslim women as victims of oppression' (Dhëmbo et al., 2021, p. 3).

Dhëmbo et al. (2021) identify several media frames about migration which shape migration narratives especially in receiving countries. The first relates to the issue of security, particularly the perception that migrants constitute a threat to the national security of receiving and host nations. The perceived threat posed by migrants is not only limited to issues of terrorism and criminality but also extends to issues of the cultural composition of receiving countries. The second is the economic and labour migration frame, wherein migrants are perceived as a threat to the economy and welfare systems of receiving countries. This frame suggests that migrants cause problems such as unemployment as they compete for job opportunities with citizens. Thirdly, migrants are also perceived as likely to cause strain on social services provided by the state. Dhëmbo et al.'s (2021, p. 3) note that negative frames about migrants in the media are often promoted through 'terminology that describe refugees and migrants in terms of natural disasters including waves and floods', creating the impression that if more migrants continued to enter the receiving country, they would cause a national catastrophe equivalent to the said natural disasters. The fourth is the victimisation frame, which portrays migrants as helpless and in need of a saviour. During the migration crisis of 2015/2016, 'Syrian refugees were often described as desperate and helpless victims' (Dhëmbo et al., 2021, p. 3).

In fact, in media discourse, the use of names of individual migrants is almost absent as migrants are described as influx and groups (Dhëmbo et al., 2021, p. 6). In the Albanian context in which Dhëmbo et al.'s (2021, p. 6) study is situated, the security frame tends to implicate migrants in social ills such as 'murder, rape, fighting, terrorism, drug trafficking, human trafficking, and robbery'. Since Albania is both a transit and a sending country, its media discourses of migration are two-pronged. On one hand, migration is represented as 'an opportunity for economic development' for those Albanians who migrate to other countries in the EU, while on the other, it is 'a threat to a country's economy' (Dhëmbo et al., 2021, p. 7) in relation to the 'other' migrants.

Scholars such as Eberl et al. (2018) have also highlighted the two-sidedness of economic frames about migration, with migrants seen as economic burden on one hand and economic benefit on the other. Dhëmbo et al.'s (2021) study shows that migration discourses differ from country to country. Countries that have serious labour shortages in some sectors of their economy tend to perceive migrants as economically beneficial (as was the case in Germany in the post-war period), but those with poorly performing economies such as South Africa view them as a threat. In 2015/2016 countries such as Italy and Greece reneged on the Dublin agreement which required migrants to register as asylum seekers in their first country of entry because they felt overwhelmed and let down by other European states.

Images and Imagining of Migrants in Contemporary Discourses

The notion of images and imaginings which we invoke in this section seeks to capture the ways in which migrants are represented visually either through images and language or visualised mentally, imagined. Giorgi and Vitale (2017) identify four main discourses of migration in academic literature. The first is that migrants tend to be identified as groups rather than individuals, for example Arabs or immigrants. Secondly, migrants are represented as victims who have gone through horrible experiences and need support or as threats to the economic and social fabric of host societies. Thirdly, migrants tend to be represented as bodies without voices. Usually, the migrants are spoken for, either by officials, media, or citizens of host nations. Lastly, host nations tend to talk about migrants within a specific local context, outside broader global developments. This is true for South Africa, for example, where Dodson (2010) argues, migration is discussed in relation to socio-economic problems within the country, as if it is a unique South African problem. The failure to situate migration in broader contexts promotes a decontextualised narrative that whips emotions without providing sufficient information on why things are the way they are. In the case of South Africa, this normally culminates in the formation of vigilante groups and right-wing political formations that seek to address migration by physically removing migrants and introducing stricter immigration laws. The case of South Africa is quite instructive because most migrants in South Africa are Zimbabweans escaping the economic crisis in their country, yet the South African government has done very little (if anything) to address the Zimbabwean crisis, which is the source of the migration crisis in South Africa.

The use of words is critical in the development of narratives. Guccione (2022) argues that words such as migrant, immigrant, alien, asylum seeker bear certain connotations about migrants. In official discourse, the way someone is defined determines whether they have rights or not, whether they can work or not, whether they have access to social welfare or not. More importantly, each category conjures certain images in the minds of citizens. Scholars such as Eberl et al. (2018) have shown that refugees (especially those escaping war situations) are perceived as more legitimate than asylum seekers, who are often seen as opportunity-seekers. A study called *Migration in the news* conducted by the University of Oxford (2013) 'found that the adjective *illegal* is the most common modifier of *immigrant*, while *failed* is the most common modifier of *asylum seeker*'. In the context of the migration crisis of 2015/2016, asylum seekers were seen as bogus because some applied for asylum in more than one European country. The term 'asylum shopping' was used to describe the process of applying for asylum in more than one EU country. Guccione (2022, p. 41) notes that the term 'ascribes a relaxed freedom of choice to the migrant applicant and places the EU in a slightly inferior position, as victim of this freedom of the migrant'. It also takes away the victimhood often associated with migrants, creating an image of the asylum seeker as someone with the liberty to choose which country to live in.

The media is responsible for shaping discourse on migration by 'choosing certain words or emphasizing others that can easily change perceptions of reality, since language creates realities' (Guccione, 2022). While words such as 'clandestine' are used to refer to migrants (often racialised) who enter the borders of a country illegally, fancy words such as expatriate have been applied exclusively to Western white people who go abroad to work, placing them above other ethnic groups for whom only the adjective *migrant* is reserved (Guccione, 2022, p. 41). Since the 1990s, Guccione (2022) argues, the increasing use of negative or alarmist terms in public migration discourse has affected the way migrants are perceived around the world, mostly in the states that have come under pressure from the large number of migrants who have crossed the Mediterranean. Guccione (2022, p. 43) also reports that 'migrants or asylum seekers are often labelled through the vocabulary of numbers (e.g. thousands, millions, tens), terms from legal or security discourses (e.g. *terrorist, suspected*) and the language of vulnerability (e.g. *destitute, vulnerable*)'. The use of numbers to refer to migrants not only reduces them to objects but also promotes negative sentiment against the thousands that will engulf *our* city/nation and completely change *our* way of life.

The discourse of migrants as terrorists often justifies 'the proliferation of lawless zones at the very heart of the rule of law' and the categorisation of people into those 'whose protection and safety the state tries to secure' on one hand, and those, on the other hand, who are 'literally harassed and, on occasion, deprived of all rights, abandoned to precariousness, and denied not only the possibility of having rights but also any legal existence' (Mbembe, 2021, p. 134). The language of migrants as vulnerable not only puts migrants into a position where they can get assistance but also justifies government intervention into the lives of vulnerable migrants, sometimes without seeking their consent. In fact, a study by news channel, *Aljazeera*, in 2016 revealed that the word 'migrant' had lost its dictionary meaning and was being used as 'a tool that dehumanizes and distances, a blunt pejorative' (in Guccione, 2022, p. 44). In the context of the migration crisis of 2015/2016, the word 'migrant' became synonymous with all kinds of problems (real and imagined) – from terrorism to economic and socio-cultural problems. Considering the *Aljazeera* study, scholars have emphasised the need to use neutral terms that do not dehumanise migrants such as 'migrants in an irregular situation' as opposed to 'illegal migrant'. Guccione (2022, p. 46) notes that 'it is better to use *irregular* or *undocumented* because the use of *illegal* associates the migrant with a criminal behaviour which threaten national security and not with his/her action of crossing borders without a regular permission'.

Fröhlich (2023, p. 8) notes that the period after the Second World War in Germany was generally associated with negative migration discourse. Terms such as 'unwanted', 'masses of refugees', 'illegal inflow', and 'onslaught' were prevalent in public discourse, constructing migrants as threats to national security. In the post-1945 period, even German nationals who were migrating from the Soviet controlled areas were seen as threats because of differences in dialect, religion, and possible economic difficulties. Fröhlich (2023) reports that in the 1950s, Germany recruited many guest workers and discourse around these workers remained positive as long as the economy was doing well, or the migrants were perceived as directly contributing to the economy. In the 1990s, when most asylum seekers were perceived as 'competing with German nationals on the labour market and with regard to housing and social services' (Fröhlich, 2023, p. 11), the discourse changed, and migrants became threats again. The negativity associated with migration is sometimes evident in the metaphoric language used to describe migrants. Arcimaviciene and Baglama (2018) study of metaphors and myths in media representations of the 2015/2016 migration crisis in Europe and the US shows that the media used negative metaphors, for example, migrants as objects, migrants as animals and terrorists. These images often drew on mythical representations with no factual basis.

The Nation, Its Laws, Borders, and Migration

We have argued that discourses of migration intricately intertwine with the ways in which nations are imagined and narrated in the contemporary present. Castles (2010, p. 1567) argues that 'the postmodern utopia of a borderless world of mobility has not yet dawned, so that it still seems appropriate to focus on migration as a process based on inequality and discrimination and controlled and limited by states'. Mbembe (2017) in *Critique of Black Reason* argues along the same lines, that the contemporary present is obsessed with excluding others from the boundaries of the state. Mbembe (2021, p. 134) has also written about how the state (especially in Europe) has adopted 'a specific form of governmentality that could be called the *regime of confinement*' that is preoccupied with managing 'undesirable populations' through 'countless legal, regulatory and surveillance measures ...] to facilitate practices of detention, custody, incarceration, confinement to camps, or deportation'. Scholars such as Fröhlich (2023) have argued that attitudes towards migrants are shaped by the ways in which existing legislation constructs them. Migrants who are categorised as refugees (for example those escaping the war in Ukraine) 'are commonly considered deserving of protection, while labour migrants are seen as not needing protection' and often they are seen as the responsibility of their consulates and embassies (Fröhlich, 2023, p. 2). What Mbembe calls the 'regime of confinement' is enabled by narratives that put migrants into different categories, sometimes in ways that are arbitrary. For example, migrants fleeing from the war in Libya are often perceived as threats while those from Ukraine are seen as victims of Russian aggression.

Studies on migration discourse such as Giorgi and Vitale (2017) have also shown that institutional definitions of categories such as migrant, asylum seeker and refugee have had far reaching consequences on the lives of migrants. Definitions tend to affect the way a problem is perceived in public discourse and represented in official discourse. Giorgi and Vitale (2017) submit that statistics about migrants depend on official definitions on who is (and who is not) what kind of migrant. It is also important to note that 'institutional definitions come with rights and entitlements' (Giorgi & Vitale 2017, p. 7). The categories legal and illegal immigrants do not only have an impact on the way the said migrants are perceived and treated but also on what they do for everyday life. For example, someone who has been categorised as 'illegal' is not likely to get a decent job or have access to official services. Giorgi and Vitale (2017, p. 7) also argue that institutional definitions have 'symbolic power' even when they cannot be implemented because they send a certain message 'from government to citizens'. This is in fact the problem in South Africa where government officials often single out 'illegal' migrants as social vermin that have infested the state, creating all kinds of ills. The symbolic power of this narrative is that it emboldens vigilante groups and opportunistic political actors to target and victimise migrants without following due process. Recently, an opposition political party in South Africa, the Pan African Congress (PAC) attempted to enforce border control at the Beitbridge Border post by chasing and threatening to shoot alleged illegal migrants.[1]

Discourses of national identity that develop in times of crisis, such as the massive influx of migrants into Europe between 2015 and 2016, tend to be exclusionary. The nation, constructed as one homogenous entity, must be protected by preventing others from entering its territorial boundaries. In a study of national discourses of migration in Germany, Fröhlich's (2023) observed that the idea of 'Germanness' as a national identity is sustained through rejecting other identities, otherwise it is an empty signifier' (4). The same can also be extended to the idea of South Africanness as an identity marker. Oftentimes, the identity of the citizen is affirmed and authenticated through the exclusion of the non-citizen. The non-citizen, the migrant, is the quintessence of difference, and this difference, Mbembe (2017, p. 24) argues, 'is seen as inscribed in the very body of the migrant subject, visible on somatic, physiognomic, and even genetic levels'. The double standards of the 'migration as crisis' discourse is that as some migrants are prevented from entering the European Union borders, others are accepted, especially those from 'selected nationalities and with […] specific skillsets' (Fröhlich, 2023, p. 7). Unlike undesirable migrants from Libya and Syria, Fröhlich (2023) notes, 'refugees from Ukraine were granted temporary blanket protection, including a residence permit and access to employment and social welfare'. In Europe, migrants from EU countries are generally seen as 'fellow EU citizens' while those from the Middle East and other non-European countries are seen as fundamentally different and likely to destabilise 'a supposedly homogenous group of dominantly White and Christian [European] citizens' (Fröhlich, 2023, p. 13). These double standards not only speak to the resurgence of nativist ideas about the nation but also the resurgence of colonial discourses of othering.

This chapter has argued, through a review of a wide range of literature on discourses of migration, that contemporary discourses of migration, not only regurgitate colonial stereotypes and misrepresentations about people of the Global South but also promote nativist narratives that construct the nation as a closed political space. Since the migration crisis of 2015/2016, most European countries have adopted harsh immigration policies that seek to exclude migrants from countries in the Global South. Often, these migrants are represented in negative terms, as threats to the socio-economic and cultural fabric of Western society. Discourses of migration do not make a distinction between legal and illegal

---

[1] https://bulawayo24.com/index-id-news-sc-local-byo-238960.html

migrants. While official systems may recognise someone as legal, ordinary citizens tend to regard everyone who looks different as an immigrant, and potentially illegal. This is the case in countries such as South Africa where migrants are identified and policed based on their complexion. Similarly, in European countries, narratives about who is and who is not a refugee are contradictory and selective. While refugees from countries in the Middle East are often treated with suspicion (as potential terrorists), refugees from Ukraine are accepted and regarded as fellow Europeans. In countries such as France, as Mbembe's work has shown, the government has adopted policies and technologies of exclusion, designed to identify, apprehend, imprison, and expel those who are perceived as not belonging or posing a threat to the Republic.

References

Anderson, B. (1983). *Imagined communities. Reflections on the origin and spread of nationalism*. Verso.
Arcimaviciene, L., & Baglama, S. H. (2018). Migration, metaphor and myth in media representations: The ideological dichotomy of 'Them' and 'Us'. *SAGE Open* (April–June), 1–13.
Bhabha, H. (1990). *Nation and narration*. Routledge.
Bhabha, H. K. (1994). *The location of culture*. Routledge.
Blinder, S. (2015). Imagined immigration: The impact of different meanings of 'Immigrants' in public opinion and policy debates in Britain. *Political Studies*, *63*, 80–100.
Boehmer, E. (2005). *Colonial and postcolonial literature*. Oxford University Press.
Castles, S. (2010). Understanding global migration: A social transformation perspective. *Journal of Ethnic and Migration Studies*, *36*(10), 1565–1586.
Daly, S. F. C. (2022, July 30). Ghana must go: Nativism and the politics of expulsion in West Africa, 1969–1985. *Past & Present*. https://doi.org/10.1093/pastj/gtac006. ISSN 0031-2746.
Dhëmbo, E., Çaro, E., & Julia H. (2021). "Our migrant" and "the other migrant": Migration discourse in the Albanian media, 2015–2018. *Palgrave Communications*, *8*(1), 1–10.
Dodson, B. (2010). Locating Xenophobia: Debate, discourse, and everyday experience in Cape Town, South Africa. *Africa Today*, *56*(3), 2–22.
Eberl, J., Meltzer, C. E., Heidenreich, T., Herrero, B., Theorin, N., Lind, F., Berganza, R., Boomgaarden, H. G., Schemer, C., & Strömbäck, J. (2018). The European media discourse on immigration and its effects: A literature review. *Annals of the International Communication Association*, *42*(3), 207–223. https://doi.org/10.1080/23808985.2018.1497452
Fanon. (1963). *The Wretched of the Earth*. Presence Africaine.
Fröhlich, C. (2023). Migration as crisis? German migration discourse at critical points of nation-building. *American Behavioral Scientist*, 1–22.
Giorgi, A., & Vitale, T. (2017). Migrants in the public discourse, between media, policies and public opinion. In S. Marino, R. Penninx, & J. Roosblad (Eds.), *Trade unions, immigration and immigrants in Europe in the 21th century: New approaches under changed conditions*. ILO-Edward Edgar.
Guccione, C. (2022). Migration discourse and the new socially constructed meanings of the English Lingua Franca. In Leotta P.C., Language Change and the New Millennium. *European Scientific Journal*, *18*(18), 33. https://doi.org/10.19044/esj.2022.v18n18p33

Guillem, S. M. (2015). Migration discourse. In K. Tracy (Ed.), *The international encyclopedia of language and social interaction* (pp. 1–10). John Wiley & Sons.
Heidenreich, T., Eberl, J.-M., Lind, F., & Boomgaarden, H. (2020). Political migration discourses on social media: A comparative perspective on visibility and sentiment across political Facebook accounts in Europe. *Journal of Ethnic and Migration Studies*, 46(7), 1261–1280. https://doi.org/10.1080/1369183X.2019.1665990
Mbembe, A. (2017). *Critique of black reason* [Translated by Laurent Dubois]. Duke University Press.
Mbembe, A. (2021). *Out of the dark night: Essays on decolonisation*. Columbia University Press.
Moopi, P., & Makombe, R. (2023). *Coloniality and migrancy in African diasporic literatures*. Routledge.
Mudimbe, V. Y. (1988). *The invention of Africa: Gnosis, philosophy, and the order of knowledge*. Indiana University Press.
Neocosmos, M. (2006). *From 'Foreign Natives' to 'Native Foreigners': Explaining Xenophobia in Post-Apartheid South Africa*. CODESRIA.
Schmolz, H. (2019). The discourse of migration in English language online newspapers: An analysis of images. *Open Linguistics*, 5, 421–433.
Van Dijk, T. A. (2017). Discourse and migration. In E. Yalaz & R. Zapata-Barrero (Eds.), *Handbook of qualitative research in European migration studies* (pp. 227–245). Springer.
Viola, L., & Verheul, J. (2020). One hundred years of migration discourse in the times: A discourse-historical word vector space approach to the construction of meaning. *Frontiers in Artificial Intelligence*, 3(64), 1–17.

Chapter 3

Frequency of Migration Discourse in Nigerian Everyday Contexts

Keywords: Nigerians; japa; motives; social media; migration

Migration within and outside Africa, by Africans, is not a new development. In fact, it is an age-old practice that has existed for centuries of human existence. Since communication is also as old as human existence, one would be right to argue that migration-motivated conversations are as old as the practice of migration itself. With migration now becoming a daily occurrence, the topic also appears in daily conversations. Supporting this notion, Olawale and Ridwan (2021) argue that the relationship between social media and migration, especially in the light of information and communication technology and globalisation, cannot be contested.

In Nigeria for instance, the discourse of migration occurs in everyday contexts. While some people discuss migration in the context of work, others discuss it in the context of study, survival, and greener pastures. Evidence of this is visible in social media engagements. Drawing from online media data, this chapter analyses migration discourse in the everyday contexts of Nigerians and Zimbabweans. Since X (formerly Twitter) and Facebook form major social media platforms in Nigeria, discourses stemming from these platforms regarding migration were used to establish the fundamentals of migration in Nigeria. The chapter interrogates the intersection of everyday life, i.e. the realities of life (socio-economic issues) and migration discourse in Nigeria. In other words, the chapter explores how the social realities of life in Nigeria shape discourses of migration. It further delves into how the discourses of migration represent the social context of the communities in which they are produced. Migration in Nigeria has become an unprecedented phenomenon in the last decade; both the young and the old are relocating from the country in droves due to socio-economic realities.

To create a clearer picture, everyday migration in Nigeria has seen established and mature people with families of many children grab opportunities to relocate abroad for study purposes in the hope of leveraging on post-study immigration opportunities, many of which are accessible in the global north countries (e.g. Canada, UK, Australia, and the United States). Middle-class families in Nigeria also focus on sending their children and wards abroad for postgraduate studies. For many, the education route to migration is less complicated thus becoming the most popular since Nigerians look for colleges, universities, and other educational institutions that can metamorphose them into expatriates in the long term. The foundational goal is to depart Nigeria. Many would argue that the goal to depart Nigeria is not to attain instant riches and wealth, but to raise children in better societies devoid of the harsh socio-economic realities which they have had to grapple with in Nigeria all their lives. For many Nigerians, the decision to relocate abroad stems from the realisation that the country is nose-diving and on the verge of self-destructing. In fact, migration has become so popular in the country that many Nigerians have lost family and friends to other countries without prior warning since many Nigerians plan migration silently and only make it public once the process is complete.

In recent years, Nigerians have produced several interesting discourses in everyday conversations, one of which is a popular local parlance that has become entrenched in the country's relocation conversations. There is now a shift in the country's migration discourse to address the urgent need to emigrate compared to when the discourse merely concerned potential personal benefits of migration. For Okunade and Awosusi (2023), *japa* is a novel term used by Nigerians to describe the outmigration trend into Europe and other parts of the world. *Japa* refers to the mass exit of people from Nigeria which represents the aspirations of Nigerians to leave the country for good (Afunugo, 2023). This colloquial term embraces a rich rhetoric that captures the overt and covert realities of Nigerian migration. Translated, *japa* is a Yoruba word which means to 'escape', 'flee', or 'run away completely'. Etymologically, the word is composed of *ja* + *pa*. *Ja* implies 'run' while *pa* connotes 'entirely'. The combination of the two words refers to running away from a situation or circumstance, completely. In the Nigerian context especially, it implies running away from a dangerous location. The social ills in Nigeria which comprise economic conditions, security issues, and bad governance are considered dangerous to the personal growth of many Nigerians thus leading to discourses which suggest that people should abscond from an alarming situation in the country. Therefore, to *japa* is to do everything possible to leave Nigeria for 'any' country with better socio-economic prospects.

Scholars such as Afunugo (2023) and Okunade and Awosusi (2023) refer to the mass exit from Nigeria as the *japa* syndrome. In this book, we extend their scholarly observations by referring to it as *japalisation*. As a concept, *japa* syndrome is a migration activity that ends whereas, for us, *japalisation* represents migration as a process that continues even when people have migrated. As such, migration discourse does not end pre-migration; it addresses current migration as well as post-migration realities. In short, *japalisation* involves the conscious process of departing one's country for intentions of personal growth and development often propelled by the lack of the same in one own's country. *Japalisation* in current Nigerian society means it is impossible for anyone who has migrated to complete the activity since the process continues after relocation. Recurring migration renders *japalisation* an unfinishable process which involves among other things: (i) helping people in Nigeria in the migration process, (ii) providing advice to people back home based on personal experience, and (iii) providing financial assistance to people in Nigeria. All these factors influence the migration process, and the surrounding discourse is of academic significance.

While the concept of 'fleeing' or 'running away' might indicate desperation, Adegoke (2023) cautions that *japa* is not illegal or irregular migration; it suggests that persons with legal means leave their country with material possessions they can pawn to satisfy a desperate wish for a better life outside of their own country. Unlike several previous studies on the concept of migration that have mostly relied on sociological perspectives, this chapter takes a linguistic perspective to interrogate *japalisation* in everyday migration-motivated conversations. What is migration about in Nigeria? What are the common views on migration in Nigeria? What is the rhetoric of migration in Nigeria? How does the rhetoric relate to the socio-economic conditions of Nigerians? These questions and related nuances are of interest to our intellectual enquiry.

Method

As discussed in the introduction, netnography was employed to gather relevant data for this chapter. Bainbridge (2000, p. 57) defines netnography as 'a relatively passive examination of websites, without full interaction with the people who created them'. For this chapter, data were collected from both X (formerly Twitter) and Facebook. We purposively selected information that align with the objectives of this chapter with the main criteria being that the selected discursive texts appear frequently in Nigerian migration conversations. To keep the authors of the posts selected anonymous, we refer to the authors using initials. The terms/phrases *japa, then vs now, welcome to a new dispensation, #EndSARS, Goodbye Nigeria, the evil you have done is enough, excited to love you from afar, Delete VPN*, were found to be frequently used in the context of migration discourse in Nigeria. A quick classification of these terms/phrases revealed that Nigerians often deploy them to (i) announce/celebrate their departure from Nigeria, (ii) communicate their motivation for migrating from Nigeria, and (iii) display their enthusiasm about their destination country.

Motivating Reasons in Nigerian Migration Discourse

This section briefly unpacks the many motivating reasons and circumstances leading to migration in Nigeria. Understanding the context makes it possible to crystallise the discourse. Moopi and Makombe (2023) state that global patterns of migration in Africa have seen large numbers of migrants continue to flow from poor countries in the global south to rich countries in the global north in search of better economic opportunities. In so doing, Baynham and De Fina (2005) notion becomes relevant that analysing the narratives of migration are seen as particularly useful to study and understand how people deal with social processes of 'uprooting' and 'unsettlement', or more in general, with great personal and social changes.

For Nigerians, motivating reasons may be economic, security, welfare, social status, political, career growth/progression, family reunification, and/or family goals. All these reasons are reflected in social media migration-motivated discourses.

Most evident in Nigerian migration discourse is the desire for 'greener pastures'. To relocate for greener pastures would be to move to a country with more promising economic opportunities in several ways that exceed the opportunities one can find in Nigeria in several years to come. Greener pastures represent multidimensional opportunities from multidirectional angles. Semiotically, the colour green can be said to connote freshness, newness, growth, and abundance. Thus, for migration purposes, it is the perception of many Nigerians that the colour green represents abundance of growth not only financially but in all other spheres of life. Etymologically, greener pasture is a borrowed concept from agriculture where it signifies an area of land rich enough for the purpose of grazing or planting. Since cattle herders locate favourable pieces of land to feed their livestock, it is essential to lead animals away from a non-nutritive environment to enriched and beneficial ones. This concept has been transferred to human lives where relocation from one area to the other for the purpose of nourishing opportunities is ably perceived as looking for 'greener pastures'.

Based on the foregoing, our understanding of 'greener pastures' in this book resonates with Pineda et al. (2023) in their findings that when the grass is greener for migrants, it signifies numerous opportunities for professional growth, personal security, and privileges. In their study based on Filipino immigrants, the participants reflected on how the pastures were indeed greener in their destination country compared to the Philippines. Firstly, it was discovered that financial gains were evident in higher earnings within a short period. At the same time, the quality of lives improved significantly with migrants having more freedom and owning properties and assets. For others, greener pastures derive from access to healthcare as well as living in an environment that is safe and clean compared to the environment in their country of birth. It is the view of Khun Eng (2006) that 'greener pastures' denote not only economic but also socio-psychological and political landscapes in which lifestyles are of paramount significance. 'Greener pastures' for migrants according to Pineda et al. (2023) promise improved living conditions and opportunities that are absent in one's own country. However, it is important to note that for Nigerian migrants, the search for greener pastures is not restricted to financial gains only. Other concerns such as healthcare, education, family, and career opportunities are equally important.

In this book, greener pastures are expressed through discourses that concern socio-economic transformation of the lives of African migrants often premised on the notion that opportunities and privileges in destination countries significantly outweigh those in the home country. While greener pastures can be subcategorised into other nuances, the overarching concept is the significant motivating reason for Nigerian outmigration. This search is reflected in social media discourses that foregrounds the possible transformation of Nigerian lives once they migrate to more economically advanced countries. The presence of greener pastures in destination countries reflects predominantly in Nigerian migration discourses which as a result, make motivating reasons diverse.

In a post made on X (formerly Twitter), Fisayo Fosudo – a popular Nigerian YouTuber seeks to understand the reasons for Nigerian outmigration. The post reads 'people who left Nigeria, what was the thing that made you finally decide to leave?' The post generated thousands of social media responses stating reasons for leaving Nigeria. Some of these include:

1. *I spent almost two years in one level in school, that summer, I just told my parents I was done! (TM, X).*
2. *With every promotion/salary increase, I was getting poorer (FO, X).*
3. *Came back from work one evening, no light. Went to 'on' gen, rope cut. Heat and sweating everywhere. Kids couldn't sleep that night. Woke up the next morning and told myself enough is enough (FA, X).*
4. *It wasn't one thing, it was a culmination of things the country carry my eyes see since birth. Just knew it wasn't an environment ideal for sane humans to inhabit (AD, X).*
5. *I realised very much early that it wasn't an actual country, just a gangsters' paradise. Too many experiences with cultists, police, and principalities (SA, X).*
6. *It was just the craving for a new place for a while. Was meant to come back but I saw that life is better here, though few struggles. But I love it (FA, X).*
7. *I got robbed in traffic the 2nd time, and that was it for me. Very traumatic experience till date, I would have died, the guys kept punching me in the face, thankfully I wasn't stabbed, I saw people get robbed in traffic several times, someone was shot right beside me in a public transport. It was the insecurity for me (YO, X).*
8. *Second passport, the liberty and freedom to travel without stereotype or discrimination (LA, X).*
9. *Nigeria police oh, those people in black uniforms are frustrated devils. No two ways about it, had to move. Safety first (TA, X).*
10. *Bad governance and the Nigerian police made me leave (RF, X).*

Although the viral post received thousands of comments, the above are hydra-headed enough to reflect the extent of Nigerians' desire to leave their country for better destinations. TM's response illustrates the country's poor education system which the author attempts to make a mockery of. In essence, the author bemoans the amount of time spent studying especially in Nigerian public higher institutions. In Nigeria, the term 'school' can be used informally to refer to higher institutions as is the case with the above example. To establish a clearer picture, the Nigerian higher education system is plagued with an interruptible academic calendar mainly stemming from industrial actions (strikes) by staff unions in the country's higher institutions. The higher education system in Nigeria is made up of universities, polytechnics, and colleges of education. Employees in these institutions are generally divided into academic staff (involved in teaching) and non-academic staff (responsible for administration). Universities have an Academic Staff Union of Universities (ASUU) and a Non-Academic Staff Union (NASU) while the polytechnics have an Academic Staff Union of Polytechnics (ASUP) and a Non-Academic Staff Union of Polytechnics (NASUP). The popular unions at colleges of education are the Colleges of Education Academic Staff Union (COEASU) and the NASU.

In discharging their duties, these unions launch strike actions (refusal to work) in order to achieve an objective or a set of objectives which the government is unwilling to grant. This practice often disrupts academic calendars in higher institutions making it challenging for students to complete their qualifications within the set timeframes. In some cases, academic and non-academic staff unions embark on strike actions at divergent periods thus making institutional activities less efficient further delaying academic calendars. The strike actions can last for a period of several months resulting in students remaining in the same academic year for 2 years or spending 6 years for a 4-year qualification. Thus, for TM, this is the ultimate reason for leaving Nigeria. This situation has long permeated the Nigerian higher education system and is so deeply rooted that no lasting solution has been in sight. Ogunode et al. (2022) argue that the unstable academic calendar remains a strong reason why most young Nigerians are seeking foreign higher education. Continuous strike actions are often the result of disagreements or lack of understanding between government and unions arising from non-implementation of previous agreements. This seriously impacts on students' abilities to learn and grow academically.

The second example by FO reflects on the economic situation of the country. With rising global inflation, low- and middle-income countries are more adversely affected by continued increases in the prices of goods and services. This economic reality informs the decisions of many Nigerians to migrate with the hope of living in an environment where they can better cushion themselves from the effects of inflation. According to Aderounmu et al. (2021), Nigeria as of 2018 ranked 158 out of 189 countries on the human development index and 39.1% of the population lives below the income poverty line of US$1.90 per day despite the country's enormous natural resources. With a large percentage of Nigerians living in poverty, without any interventions from the government, the only option for citizens is to flee the country before they are consumed by poverty. FO's post suggests that working and earning money in Nigeria, where salaries are received in a weak currency (in this case, Nigerian Naira), cannot lead to economic prosperity. FO points out that being promoted and receiving a higher salary in Nigeria does not translate to more wealth. Instead, the reverse is often the case. This post captures the motivation for many Nigerians to migrate. The desire to earn hard currency in an economically viable country continues to motivate several Nigerians to find the means to leave the country and settle down in better countries.

In the third example, FA ridicules the epileptic power supply in Nigeria which has forced many Nigerians to explore alternative means. For a long time, Nigerians have relied on equipment such as generators and solar inverters to generate power for everyday use. Although these alternative sources provide power, they are not without challenges. For instance, generators cause noise pollution and are operated with fuel which is currently expensive in Nigeria. Solar inverters on the other hand are extremely expensive to install and maintain, which means that many Nigerians cannot afford this option. Thus, for this social media user, it is the power crisis that motivated him/her to leave the country. The author's frustration was fuelled by the electricity situation in the country. Each time he/she returned from work, there would be no power. The attempt to use an alternative power supply also proved abortive since the generator recoil starter rope, often referred to as the 'generator rope', became faulty. As a result, the family spent the night in an extremely unpleasant situation which prompted the author to relocate his entire family from Nigeria to a country with better electricity. It is worth noting that the sub-standard electricity situation in the country has long been problematic with no signs of improvement. Since many businesses rely on sustainable electricity, many Nigerians experience challenges in this regard as well. Poor service delivery by the government is one of the main reasons many Nigerians opt to relocate. This point is also made in the 10th example where the author cites bad governance as the reason he left the country.

Lack of security also weighs heavily in the migration discourse and the fifth chapter fleshes this matter out. In fact, this is one of the most common reasons many Nigerians decide to migrate. The 5th, 7th, 9th, and 10th examples above all allude to issues of insecurity. Of great concern is the fact that the state actors who are meant to prevent insecurity are at the forefront of making the country insecure. The 5th, 9th, and 10th examples all highlight the incompetence of the Nigerian Police Force (NPF) contribute to migration. The ninth example especially emphasises this factor with the use of 'oh'. The author refers to the Nigerian police as 'frustrated devils' and 'people in black uniforms'. Black is the colour of police uniforms in Nigeria. Cases of police brutality, violence, profiling, extortion, exploitation, and extrajudicial killings have long permeated Nigerian society with no end in sight. While 'gangsters' and 'cultists' also terrorise citizens, the latter's fears are multiplied by the fact that police, who are meant to protect them, are equally culpable and often complicit. Obarisiagbon and Akintoye (2019) state that the Nigerian police is viewed with suspicion and are perceived to be 'unfriendly', 'brutal', 'trigger-happy', 'extortionist', 'crime collaborators', and 'gross violators of fundamental human rights'. Lack of trust in Nigerian law enforcement therefore contributes significantly to outmigration. The seventh example cites the unpleasant experience of a Nigerian who was robbed while in traffic for a second time, increasing this person's degree of insecurity. Recent harsh economic realities have also increased levels of insecurity for many Nigerians struggling to survive and resorting to robberies, thefts, and other types of violent activities to make ends meet.

Social media discourses show how many Nigerians face discriminatory and stereotypical reactions especially at international airports while travelling with Nigerian passports. The eighth example is a social media post expressing the desire to embrace different citizenship and by extension, a different nation's passport. The additional degree of scrutinisation that Nigerians are subjected to by airport and travel personnel is a further motivating factor. Adebayo's (2022) study shows that Nigerian travellers are differently treated, profiled, and stereotyped at international borders. An X post by WW advises that: *'When you decide to have kids, please try to give them another passport if you can. Your unborn children don't deserve Nigeria. This green passport is not it.'*[1] For many Nigerians, having access

---

[1] https://x.com/WunmiWonka/status/11559249817310822240

to a different passport is a 'dream come true'. They also face integration problems, limited access to employment opportunities and experience discrimination in the labour market. These challenges stemming from the image of the country heavily impact citizens internationally. Nigerian citizens with dual citizenship can strive to avoid this stereotyping.

However, migration discourses in Nigeria also reveal that motivating reasons for relocation from Nigeria are not always negative. The sixth example presents a Nigerian whose initial intention to migrate emanated from the need to explore a fresh and unfamiliar environment. The author also expressed the intention to return to Nigeria, but this did not happen since life was seemingly better in the new environment. Even though there are some challenges in the new country, the author prefers living outside of Nigeria, nonetheless. It can thus be argued that this social media user never perceived the ills in the country as reasons to leave the country. Equally, it did not initially appear to the author that the destination country would present better economic opportunities and living conditions. The current example, although not common in Nigerian migration discourse, is an indication that migration-motivated discourses are propelled by different reasons. Based on the current case, it can be assumed that the desire to remain in Nigeria by some Nigerians, and the thought of temporary migration, are merely because such Nigerians are yet to experience better living conditions in other developed countries.

Common Rhetoric in Nigerian Migration Discourse

The discourse of migration in Nigeria is filled with rhetoric terms that inspire the desire to relocate to another country. In this section, we explore popular terms or slang that Nigerians use when discussing migration-related matters. We analyse how selected linguistic terms drive migration narratives in Nigeria. Phrases, slangs, as well as memes have all been utilised in migration discourse in Nigeria. Perhaps one of the most popular is the meme 'welcome to a new dispensation'. As discussed earlier, *japa* became an extremely popular term in Nigerian discourse with the word appearing almost daily on social media in relation to migration. For many Nigerians, the solution to the ills in Nigeria is *japa*. Some instances of the usage include: 'The way tribalism dey go for Nigeria, make God help man make I don japa before una begin shoot on sight'.[2] The above, although written in what is popularly known as Nigerian Pidgin (a creolised English-based language spoken as a lingua franca across Nigeria), can be translated as 'with tribalism tendencies heating up in Nigeria, I pray God perfects my travel plans so I can escape from this country before violence erupts.' In recent times, following the 2023 general elections in Nigeria, tribal tensions have heightened. Thus, *japa* has become the go-to option for many Nigerians to deal with the socio-economic struggles in the country.

A Nigerian social media user, RW, posted on Facebook: 'If you have the means, try every possible means to *japa* from Nigeria. The economy is bad, the security is

---

[2]https://x.com/idandizzy/status/1720892029247373673?s=46&t=slBsAwqcpXInCgut3FU1hA

bad, everything is bad. The only option for the common man is to *japa*'. Another user also advised: 'If you are young and get the opportunity to leave, leave. Go get an education outside this nation. This government does not care about you'. These posts reflect the concerns of many Nigerians who perceive *japa* as the only option to live a fulfilling life. However, it is worth noting that the current *japa* discourse in Nigeria does not cater only for the youths but also involve middle-aged adults, including those who already have senior and successful careers in the country. According to Adegoke (2023), the *japa* migration cohort is not limited to aspirational youths; it also consists of middle-aged adults who want to avoid the uncertainty of life after retirement and sudden redundancy.

The popular meme named 'welcome to a new dispensation' has also become a strong *japa* rhetoric in Nigeria. The meme has been exploited for several migration reasons. Taken from a popular Nigerian movie titled *King of Boys: The Return of the King*, the scene showed Sola Sobowale, a popular Nigerian actress, grinning and raising a wine glass suggesting she wanted to have a toast. In the movie, the actress toasted after she achieved her goal of returning to her seat as 'king' after a long journey of planning and plotting. The character, who was initially overthrown in the movie, managed to scheme her way back to the throne. She then welcomed her followers to a new dispensation where she was the leader. Although the movie is not connected to migration, the message resonates with Nigerians' migration desires. Some Nigerians have appropriated Sola Sobowale's reaction to celebrate their migration goals. The 'new dispensation' in the meme is reimagined as a new destination country in Nigerian migration discourse. Nigerians utilise the meme to welcome themselves to the new country (dispensation). The scene represented the imagined reality for many Nigerians who aspire to relocate for their own reasons. Toasting is usually a symbol of celebration and joy. It defines the mood and atmosphere of celebration. Like Sola Sobowale who is happy after regaining her seat, Nigerians adapt the meme to display their happiness about migrating to another country.

The frequency of the meme on social media has become a source of constant motivation for Nigerians who wish to japa/leave the country. The continuous use of the meme has also attracted comic reactions such as: *(a) please allow mummy Sola Sobowale to drop the glass of wine for a bit, (b) I hope Sola Sobowale's arm is doing okay from raising that cup, (c) Sola Sobowale has been raising glass for the new dispensation for the past few days now, her hand must be paining her*, and *(d) This Sola Sobowale's picture has faced a lot this week and it's just Tuesday*. The meme became so popular that social media users on platforms such as X (formerly Twitter), Facebook and Instagram used it to announce their relocation from Nigeria. In many instances, the users posted it online alongside a picture of themselves at the airport, walking into a plane, or sitting in a plane. Some users labelled Sola Sobowale the Nigerian *japa* ambassador despite the original movie having no connection with migration. Regardless of which country one migrated to, and the experiences one would encounter in the new country, many migrating Nigerians celebrate their migration using the meme while those who desire to migrate make remarks such as: *(a) I will be using this meme soon in Jesus name, (b) I have saved this meme, (c) You are not the only one who will use this meme*, and *(d) I want post this Sola Sobowale picture so bad, my tired is tired in this country*.

Hendriks and Bartram (2019) intimate that migrants naturally expect moving abroad to improve their quality of life and/or that of their families. As such, the celebratory mood of Nigerians migrating for different reasons can be traced back to the long-held assumption that living in an economically advanced country translates to individual economic prosperity. However, Hendriks and Bartram (2019) note that migration decisions are commonly based on incomplete information about the consequences of migration because most migrants have never previously lived in or travelled to the destination countries. They sometimes receive overly positive information via the media or from immigrants in the destination country who are reluctant to reveal disappointing outcomes to people in the home country. Nigerians who leave the country often believe that the situation in destination countries cannot be worse than in Nigeria. It is the view of many Nigerians, especially the young ones, that the country inhibits their careers and individual development. Those can afford migration therefore waste no time in leaving the country. In fact, it has become the topmost priority for many Nigerians to leave the country because the challenges are becoming too difficult to overcome.

Another popular social media utterance on migration is: *Goodbye Nigeria, the evil you have done is enough, excited to love you from afar*. Like 'welcome to a new dispensation', 'the evil you have done is enough' is used to refer to the declining ecosystem in Nigeria. Not only does the country lack economic prosperity, but also a good education system, infrastructure, and healthcare. These are the perceived evils in the Nigerian nation which migrants refer to and attempt to escape by relocating to countries with better infrastructure, education, healthcare, and economic growth. The pressing motivations to migrate from Nigeria vary from individual to individual. However, the overarching factor remains the harsh realities which many Nigerians have had to endure from a young age. This, coupled with the fact that Nigerians living abroad seem to be financially better off, has made many Nigerians believe that their prosperity lies elsewhere. The meme became more conspicuous following the nationwide #EndSARS protests in October 2020 when many Nigerians became vocal against police brutality towards the youths. *'Goodbye Nigeria'* shows that although Nigerians are migrating because of the ills in the country, they still remain emotionally connected to the country.

The experiences surrounding the #EndSARS protests intensified the need for many Nigerians to relocate. The protests were followed by a series of killings, harassments, extortions, exploitations, and brutality by a certain unit of the NPF referred to as the Special Anti-Robbery Squad (SARS). For many Nigerians, it was time for this SARS unit to be disbanded hence the hashtag #EndSARS on different social media platforms. The protests which lasted for days did however not achieve this end as the government merely announced a reform to SARS. The killings after the protest were the turning point for many Nigerians who felt it was necessary to migrate from a country where gross human violations are condoned. The following year, specifically June 2021, saw the government of Nigeria officially banning X (formerly Twitter) and restricting its usage in Nigeria.[3] This followed Twitter's decision to delete a tweet by President Muhammadu Buhari which it claimed was controversial and violated its 'abusive behaviour' policy. In an attempt to take a stern stance against secessionist agitators, the President tweeted:

> *'Many of those misbehaving today are too young to be aware of the destruction and loss of lives that occurred during the Biafra war. Those of us in the fields for 30 months, who went through the war, will treat them in the language they understand. I think we have given them enough latitude. They have made their case, they just wanted to destroy the country. Whoever wanted diversion or destruction of the system at this point, I think will soon have the shock of their lives'.*

These remarks by the President generated serious reactions with many Nigerians accusing the President of making reckless war-inciting comments that could degenerate into ethnic violence in Nigeria. As a result, several Nigerian Twitter users reported President Muhammadu Buhari's tweets calling for his Twitter account to be suspended.

For many Nigerians, the Twitter ban not only represented the absence of human rights in Nigeria, but also represented negative economic implications for millions who used the platform for business purposes and had barely recovered from the economic blows of the COVID-19 lockdown. These issues became prevalent in Nigerian migration discourse because citizens often feel neglected and disregarded by the government. At the same time, many feared that the Twitter ban would be the precursor to what appeared to be a pattern of attacks aimed at muzzling free speech in Nigeria – although the country claimed to be a democracy (Obiaje, 2021). This lack of confidence in the ability of country's leaders to make the right decisions permeated the Nigerian migration discourse at the time. Anyim (2021) admits that the Twitter ban in Nigeria was an act of insensitivity considering the fact many Nigerians made a living through the site. Anyim (2021) further argues that the Twitter ban caused serious damage to the economy as many Nigerians relied on Twitter to support their work. This is a point also conceded by Obiaje (2021) who

---

[3] 'Nigeria suspends Twitter after the social media platform freezes president's account'. *Washington Post*. ISSN 0190-8286. Retrieved 15 May 2024.

opines that social media platforms have become an escapist strategy, a tool for start-ups and an economic advancement pedestal for businesses run by the youth. Obiaje (2021) also raised concerns that the Twitter ban sent a wrong message to foreign investors whose interests in the Nigerian economy would be hampered.

The above scenario, coupled with the role Twitter played during the 2020 #EndSARS protests where young people used it to mobilise support for the protests as well as disseminate the message of the protest beyond the shores of Nigeria, arguably ignited the reaction of the federal government to ban the Twitter platform. On the one hand, there was the perception that Twitter had disrespected Nigeria and her President. On the other hand, there was also the belief that Twitter had emboldened Nigerians to challenge the government. For these reasons, the Nigerian government resorted to banning Twitter. This exacerbated the perception that the Nigerian government did not respect human rights. The ban forced many Nigerians to devise other means to use the platform.

Several Nigerians bypassed the Twitter ban and used a virtual private network (VPN) to access the platform. Many users of the VPNs lamented the negative effects among which were strained batteries, over-consumption of internet data, overheating problems, and the cost of subscribing to efficient VPNs. It is for this reason that many Nigerians who migrated during the ban celebrated their departure from Nigeria since they relocated to countries where they did not need VPN to access Twitter. Many Nigerian migrants announced their departure from Nigeria on Twitter with a screenshot displaying the deletion of their VPNs from their smartphones. Highly common during the periods were screenshots displays such as: 'Delete protonVPN', 'Delete Windscribe' and 'Delete TurboVPN'. For many active Twitter users, the period was highly challenging since the platform was not accessible without a functioning VPN. The deletion of VPNs was followed by messages such as: 'If I can't use Twitter in Nigeria, I will use in New York', 'It is time to uninstall this VPN', and 'VPN can go forever, bye Nigeria' among others.

The phrase 'Then vs now' is also popular on Nigerian social media. This phrase captures pre- and post-migration experiences. Olawale and Ridwan (2021) perceive the 'then vs now' trend as a social media event that presents a picture of a Nigerian youth at 'home' and in the 'diaspora'. It involves a combination of pictures of African migrants, especially the youth, showing off their former status in Africa and their upward social mobility in the West (developed countries are often considered greener pastures). Olawale and Ridwan (2021) perceive the role of social media in migration discourse as twofold: (a) it facilitates people's decisions to migrate, and (b) changes people's attitudes towards migration by exposing the hazards that are associated with irregular migration. For Olawale and Ridwan (2021), the 'then vs now' message represents a comparative cross-section of lives in Nigeria and in the global north. The phrase generated everyday reactions from Nigerians, such as:

i. *Why is everything about Nigeria hard and harsh? Even your skin is dealt with in Nigeria. Then vs now cheiii. See when they left Nigeria and now in the abroad. I can't wait for my original skin when I travel (SJ, Facebook)*
ii. *Nigerians in diaspora are sharing amazing transformation after relocating abroad with these then vs now posts (IB, X).*

iii. *Then vs now challenge has increased my desire to leave Nigeria. See you people's skin (WS, X).*
iv. *Leaving Nigeria is the goal. Then vs now challenge be hitting me differently (FM, X).*
v. *I have already taken my then pics. When I leave Nigeria, I will take my now pics (OO, X).*
vi. *Some of us cannot join this then vs now challenge all because we have been stuck in Nigeria all our lives (SM, Facebook).*
vii. *The then and now trend got me thinking a lot…How can one be like roasted fish in Nigeria (then) and be like fresh fish (abroad) (DJ, X).*
viii. *So happy about these then and now pictures I'm seeing bruh…Nigeria has a way of letting its hardship show on your face (DB, X).*
ix. *It shows that the state of wellbeing in Nigeria is unpleasant, undermined and unproductive compared to life here abroad. An average Nigeria becomes exposed through social media and eventually realise they have been living a complicated life all through. Hence, their decision to migrate begins (DD, X).*

The 'then vs now' social media challenge made a mockery of the entire Nigerian society. For many Nigerians who have not been outside Nigeria, the before and after images instantly revealed the inherent differences between Nigeria and countries in the global north. The above social media text show how Nigerians lament the situation of the country, and the obstacles that they encounter every day. To emphasise the point, skin texture is also considered significant in establishing the difference between Nigeria and other countries. It is a popular belief in Nigeria that the weather abroad is more pleasant, thus making the skin naturally moisturised. One can argue that this particular social media phrase became popular because aroused the interests of many Nigerians who wished to *japa*. Adegoke (2023) stresses that pictures and memes on social media posts made by new emigres depict their newfound status in their destination countries while some even post pictures aboard aircraft with their passports conspicuously displayed to show that they have escaped awful situations for a hopeful future.

Since *japa* conversations have become a central component of everyday social media discourse in Nigeria, one can argue that there is a connection between the social media discourse of migration and the number of people who migrate or aspire to migrate from Nigeria. This is further validated by the concerns of many Nigerians whose families and childhood friends have all relocated from the country. The *japa* phenomenon has birthed a new migration discourse encapsulated in the statement – '*E be like say na only 3 people remain for Nigeria like this. Me and two other people*'. This statement has several variations but one meaning – Nigerians are migrating in droves. The statement is hyperbolic and can be directly translated as 'there are only three people left in Nigeria. That is, only me, and two other persons'. A discourse analysis of the statement suggests that the degree to which Nigerians are leaving the country has never been witnessed before. The everyday reality of people departing Nigeria, which is evident on social media, coupled with the observable realities where known friends, families, and associates, among others suddenly migrate without detailed long-term warning, has led to exaggerated views that only few people would remain resident in Nigeria.

The implication transcends quantitative departures to reflect the extent of brain drain in the country. Anetoh and Onwudinjo (2020) share the view that brain drain currently bedevils Nigeria since the country has continued to witness a mass exodus of her citizens to more developed countries. The social implications of outmigration, namely brain drain, is a matter of concern for Nigeria as a nation.

Although *japa* is perceived by many Nigerians as an escape route, the reality remains that migration has its own challenges. In fact, the major resource required for migration is finance and judging by the economic status of many Nigerians, *japa* is not feasible because of the associated costs. The realisation that everyone in the country cannot migrate, even if they genuinely want to, due to the required expenses also produces some of the common migration-discourses in Nigeria. For instance, there is the popular saying that *no be everybody fit japa* which can be interpreted as 'everyone in the country cannot migrate'. Worth noting is that the decision not to migrate is not solely impeded by funds. For some people, other factors such as family, thriving businesses, and different priorities hold sway. However, the associated cost is perhaps the major and first factor to consider as available resources will determine the migration destination. The financial capability of many Nigerians is one of the dominant concerns when matters of migration or *japa* emerge. In a Facebook post by BO, she posted: 'I really want to japa, but no money. Definitely, one day, I go leave this country'. This can be interpreted as 'I am highly interested in migrating, but I do not have the financial means. However, I am confident that whether now or later, I will also relocate from this country like others'. While this example speaks directly to the owner of the post, the next example generalises what many Nigerians feel and captures what seems to be an almost universal truth, namely 'Every average Nigerians wish to japa but there is no money on ground'. This suggests that almost every Nigerian is interested in migrating, however lack of available resources is a barrier.

This chapter has analysed discourses of migration in Nigeria majorly from two perspectives. As reflected in the chapters, migration motivations differ for many Nigerians. While many dwell on the economic reasons, others cite sociopolitical as their primary reasons. The findings of the chapter also reveal that certain rhetoric, which are often commonly understood by Nigerians, are used in migration conversations on Nigerian social media spaces. Based on mutual acceptance, the usages of these rhetoric contextually refer to migration. The motivating reasons and rhetoric discussed in this chapter explicitly connect to the discussion provided in Chapter 6 where Nigerians are made powerful, or in fact powerless, depending on the circumstances in the context of migration. The examples discussed in this chapter present Nigeria as a powerless country that citizens must flee in order to attain a sense of power in foreign countries.

References

Adebayo, K. O. (2022). 'They did not allow me to enter the place I was heading to': Being 'stuck-in-place' and transit emplacement in Nigerian migrations to China. *Mobilities*, *17*(6), 885–898.

Adegoke, D. (2023). 'Japa': An exploratory study of the roles of social media in an outmigration trend in Nigeria. *Social Media+ Society*, 9(4), 20563051231203691.
Aderounmu, B., Azuh, D., Onanuga, O., Oluwatomisin, O., Ebenezer, B., & Azuh, A. (2021). Poverty drivers and Nigeria's development: Implications for policy intervention. *Cogent Arts & Humanities*, 8(1), 1927495.
Afunugo, K. N. (2023). Japa syndrome and its challenges to the Nigeria's Labour Force: A search for religious solutions. *Ohazurume-Unizik Journal of Culture and Civilization*, 2(2), 70–93.
Anetoh, B. C., & Onwudinjo, V. G. (2020). Emigration and the problem of brain drain in Nigeria: A philosophical evaluation. *Journal of African Studies and Sustainable Development*, 3(1), 86–98.
Anyim, W. O. (2021). *Twitter ban in Nigeria: Implications on economy, freedom of Speech and information sharing*. Library Philosophy and Practice, 0_1-13.
Bainbridge, W. S. (2000). Religious ethnography on the World Wide Web. In K. Hadden & D. E. Cowan (Eds.), *Religion on the internet: Research prospects and promises* (pp. 55–80). Elsevier.
Baynham, M., & De Fina, A. (Eds.). (2005). *Dislocations/relocations: Narratives of migration*. St. Jerome.
Hendriks, M., & Bartram, D. (2019). Bringing happiness into the study of migration and its consequences: What, why, and how? *Journal of Immigrant & Refugee Studies*, 17(3), 279–298.
Khun Eng, K. P. (2006). Transnational self in the Chinese diaspora: A conceptual framework. *Asian Studies Review*, 30(3), 223–239.
Moopi, P., & Makombe, R. (2023). *Coloniality and Migrancy in African Diasporic Literatures*. Taylor & Francis.
Obarisiagbon, E. I., & Akintoye, E. O. (2019). Insecurity crisis in Nigeria: The law enforcement agents a panacea. *Journal of Sociology and Social Work*, 7(1), 44–51.
Obiaje, K. (2021). Nigeria Twitter Ban: An erosion of freedom of information? *International Journal of Management, Social Sciences, Peace and Conflict Studies (IJMSSPCS)*, 4(4), 37–51.
Ogunode, N. J., Akinjobi, F. N., & Musa, A. (2022). Analysis of factors responsible for Nigerians' patronizing of foreign higher education. *European Multidisciplinary Journal of Modern Science*, 6, 19–29.
Okunade, S. K., & Awosusi, O. E. (2023). The Japa syndrome and the migration of Nigerians to the United Kingdom: An empirical analysis. *Comparative Migration Studies*, 11(1), 27.
Olawale, Y., & Ridwan, I. (2021). Nigerian youth, migration narratives and social media: A perspective. *Electronic Journal of Social and Strategic Studies*, 2(2), 162–177.
Pineda, R. C., Abad-Pinlac, B., Yao, D. P. G., Toribio, F. N. R. B., Josephsson, S., & Sy, M. P. (2023). Unraveling the 'Greener Pastures' concept: The phenomenology of internationally educated occupational therapists. *OTJR: Occupational Therapy Journal of Research*, 15394492231205885.

Chapter 4

Social Media Narratives and Counternarratives of Migration in Zimbabwe: The Case of Hopewell Chin'ono's Facebook Page Post-August 2023 Elections

Keywords: Economic opportunities; economic crisis; narrative; Kwachustan; social media users

In this chapter, we explore how Zimbabwean journalist Hopewell Chin'ono used his Facebook Page as a platform to narrate the economic possibilities that migration offered to Zimbabweans in the aftermath of the contested elections of August 2023. We focus specifically on migration-related messages that Chin'ono posted and counter-narratives of migration by Zimbabwean social media users in response to Chin'ono's posts. Two questions guide this chapter. Firstly, we explore how Chin'ono narrated the liberatory potential of migration in the context of the post-election political impasse in Zimbabwe and the ongoing economic crisis which continues to negatively impact livelihoods of ordinary citizens. Secondly, we analyse how social media users responded to Hopewell Chin'ono's 'migration option' in relation to their lived experiences and the broader question of the future of Zimbabwe post the August 2023 election. Is migration the solution to Zimbabwe's endless political and economic crisis? How do Zimbabwean netizens perceive migration and its potential to offer alternative economic possibilities? We draw on theories of narrative and narratology (Eastmond, 2007), the notion of digital diasporas (Nedelcu, 2018) and transnational public spheres (Fraser, 2007) to explore how Zimbabwean journalist Hopewell Chin'ono and social media users narrated the pros and cons of migration after the election of August 2023 and in the broader context of the political and economic crisis in Zimbabwe.

The chapter argues that social media has become an important platform that citizens use to share views and give each other advice on important issues such as migration in the context of crisis.

The advent of social media has democratised the public sphere by creating alternative spaces where anyone with an internet connection can share lived experiences and contribute to public discourse. The proliferation of digital public spheres has in many ways bridged the communication gap between populations across space and time, enabling people from different spatial zones to share life experiences in real time. Before the advent of social media, stories of minorities, marginalised groups, and citizens in general rarely made the headlines (Makombe, 2021). Official news channels such as newspapers, television stations and radios, especially in repressive regimes, tended to prioritise the stories of public figures and/or the political elite. Eastmond (2007, p. 248) argues that stories reveal the 'meanings people, individually or collectively, ascribe to lived experience'. In fact, it is through storytelling that lived experiences assume material existence. This view resonates with the notion of 'nation as narration' propagated by scholars of the nation such as Benedict Anderson (1983), Elleke Boehmer (2005a), and Homi Bhabha (1990). Just as narrative enables people to imagine themselves as a national community as Anderson (1983) would argue, narratives also give form to lived experiences. In her book titled *Stories of Women*, Elleke Boehmer (2005b) argues that narrative is both 'form-giving and in-forming' to suggest that it is through narrative that experience takes form, but it is also through narrative that information is conveyed. Narrative analysis as methodology and critical reading approach is premised on the view that 'meaning is ascribed to phenomena through being experienced' and that 'we can only know something about other people's experiences from the expressions they give them' (Eastmond, 2007, p. 249). In thinking about narratives, we need to make a distinction between life as lived (the events that shape one's life), life as experienced (how one perceives and ascribes meaning to what happens) and life as told (how we frame experience for certain purposes). These levels of the textuality of life/experience show that 'experience is never directly represented but edited at different stages of the process from life to text' (Eastmond, 2007, p. 249).

Eastmond (2007, p. 251) further argues that 'stories are important sites not only for negotiating what has happened and what it means, but also for seeking ways of going forward' (Eastmond, 2007, p. 251) and while 'narratives [...] are not transparent renditions of reality, they call for our interpretation' (Eastmond, 2007, p. 252). Migration narratives are stories developed through communicative practices including framing, codifying, selecting, omitting, and silencing to offer a specific view on migration or migrants or a country's migration history (Sahin-Mencutek, 2020, p. 4). Narratives have a role in delineating what are considered publicly-acceptable opinions and behaviours, and who does – or does not – have a voice (Sahin-Mencutek, 2020, p. 12).

In an article titled 'Transnationalising the public sphere' Nancy Fraser (2007) argues that transnationalism and globalisation have ushered in new social configurations that have made Jurgen Habermas' notion of a public sphere untenable. Jurgen Habermas' concept of the public sphere theorised democratic deliberations within the confines of the nation state. However, the contemporary postnational constellation has seen the emergence of transnational public spheres where public opinion is shared outside the confines of the nation state. Following the economic crisis in Zimbabwe, many Zimbabweans migrated to different countries around the world, but they remained connected and continued to participate in national discussions back home through transnational digital spaces. We draw on the notions of 'transnational digital spheres' and the 'digital diaspora' to explore how citizens use virtual platforms to participate in national discourse. Candidatu and Ponzanesi (2022, p. 264) define the digital diaspora as an imagined community 'characterized by progressive efforts to maintain and reproduce shared cultural norms outside the homeland, [and] a simultaneous attempt to build new hybrid spaces of belonging'. It is also, in Bernal's (2020, p. 4) words, central to the formation of 'new public spheres, forms of protest, social groupings, and spaces of imagination'.

We explore how Zimbabwean netizens both at home and in the diaspora constitute a digital diaspora that reconfigures 'experiences of loss in agential forms of representation and use digital platforms to build social bonds of solidarity' (Witteborn, 2019, p. 180). We focus specifically on the Facebook posts of Hopewell Chin'ono, a Zimbabwean journalist who has played a significant role in setting the agenda of public discourse in Zimbabwe. We read these posts as the focal point around which citizens both at home and away share their views on the 'migration option' in the aftermath of the election of August 2023.

Hopewell Chin'ono: A Brief Background

Hopewell Chino'ono is a prominent award-winning Zimbabwean journalist who has been arrested and imprisoned by the Zimbabwean government for his anti-corruption activism. In fact, in 2020, he was arrested and remanded in prison for several months for exposing corruption related to COVID-19 funding by ministers in the governing regime. He has also been harassed and intimidated by government officials and security agents for internationalising the Zimbabwean crisis. For example, in April 2022, state security officials threatened to confiscate his goat farm, claiming falsefully that the farm belonged to the government.[1] In the context of Zimbabwe's economic collapse, Chin'ono has also been instrumental in highlighting the collapse of the country's healthcare system. In some instances, he has been involved in raising funds to support noble causes such as covering medical bills of the underprivileged.

He has received several awards for his work including the Henry Kaiser Foundation Award and the Desmond Tutu leadership award (2008). In December 2022, he received the International Anti-corruption Excellence Award from the Emir of Qatar, Sheikh Tamim bin Hamad Al Thani for his global contribution

---

[1] https://www.timeslive.co.za/news/africa/2022-05-02-goat-grab-by-zanu-pf-youth-foiled-by-zimbabwean-journalist-and-allies/#google_vignette

to the fight against corruption.[2] His work as a journalist has contributed not only towards exposing government-sanctioned corruption in Zimbabwe but also internationalising the Zimbabwean political and economic crisis, and the governing regime's aversion to democratic governance and the rule of law. Following the election of August 2023, which election observers, including the regional body, the South African Development Community (SADC), roundly condemned as shambolic and short of meeting the basic principles of democratic elections, Chin'ono became a voice of conscience in Zimbabwe, speaking on behalf of millions of Zimbabweans suffering under the brutal and corrupt regime of President Emmerson Mnangagwa (Mumba, N. & SADC Electoral Observation Mission, 2023).

Method

This is a qualitative study that uses netnography as method to identify and gather relevant data from Hopewell Chin'ono's official Facebook Page.[3] Netnography is a method that involves listening-in to and/or following online conversations or discussions without actively participating. Some scholars have defined netnography as the application of ethnographic methods of collecting and analysing data such as observation and document analysis to virtual platforms. Bainbridge (2000, p. 57) defines netnography as 'a relatively passive examination of web sites, without full interaction with the people who created them'. We purposively selected migration-related messages that Hopewell Chin'ono posted between November 2023 and January 2024 and responses by social media users to Chin'ono's call for the youths to leave the country and explore opportunities elsewhere. In this period, Chi'nono posted nine (9) messages related to migration. In some of the posts, he actively encouraged young Zimbabweans to migrate and explore economic prospects in other countries because there was no hope in Zimbabwe after the elections of August 2023. In other posts, he shared success stories of Zimbabweans who had migrated to other countries and his own experiences of travelling to, and living in, other countries. We have, therefore, categorised the data into three broad themes namely (1) narratives of Zimbabwe as a hopeless state, (2) success stories of Zimbabwean migrants, and (3) narratives of opportunities and possibilities offered by migration. We identified social media users with their initials to ensure anonymity and confidentiality.

Migration and New Life in the Diaspora: Leave the Republic of Kwachustan

Following the election of August 2023, which most people believed was rigged in favour of the incumbent regime, many Zimbabweans considered leaving the country because they had lost faith in ZANU-PF rule. This was evident in the long

---

[2]https://alinstitute.org/news/hopewell-chinono-wins-anti-corruption-award
[3]https://www.facebook.com/hopewelljournalist/

queues that were seen at the passport offices as citizens jostled to apply for passports. The results of the elections had dashed the hopes of many, including those living in the diaspora, who had travelled back home to vote for change. Hopewell Chin'ono's Facebook post just before the election results were announced was telling. It showed a picture of a desperate looking man holding a Zimbabwean passport. Many of his followers read the post to mean that the ruling party had 'won' the elections and that citizens were once again on the road seeking economic opportunities elsewhere. The long queues at various passport offices throughout the country was evidence that many Zimbabweans saw migration as one way of improving their livelihoods. Hopewell Chin'ono responded to the disappointing election results by urging young people to leave the country and explore opportunities elsewhere. For several months after the election, his Facebook page became a digital transnational public sphere where followers from different parts of the world deliberated the possible consequences of the election outcome. Those in the diaspora used the Facebook Page to not only 'build communities of belonging and reaffirm connections with their homelands, but also to establish new relations and networks of solidarity' (Candidatu & Ponzanesi, 2022, p. 266)

On 5 November 2023, Chin'ono posted a message about his visit to the Netherlands where he was received by Zimbabwean migrants who had made 'the right decision' by migrating in search of better economic opportunities. The message read as follows:

> I have received a warm welcome in the Netherlands from Zimbabweans who made the right decision and left Zimbabwe.
>
> My advice to young people in Zimbabwe remains the same, leave and focus on your lives.
>
> Someone who was 20 years old in 2000 and thought that they could hang around is now 43 years old with a wife, kids, no home, no job, no medical aid and no pension.
>
> Work on yourself and build yourself up, if I had stayed in Zimbabwe when I finished college, I would have been reporting to Reuben Barwe as my boss.
>
> I wouldn't have had the independence that I have today to speak my mind because I would have been beholden to my lived realities.
>
> Liberate yourself from the Republic of Kwachustan!

The message above conjured an image of Zimbabwe as a hopeless country that had no economic opportunities for its citizens. It constructed migration as a potentially liberating experience especially for young people who, in Chin'ono's words, should 'leave and focus on [their] lives'. In this post, Chin'ono described those that had migrated from Zimbabwe to other countries such as Netherlands as having made 'the right decision' because it is through migration that they were able to transform their lives for better. The 'warm welcome' that he received from Zimbabwean migrants in the Netherlands suggested, not only that the migrants were doing well economically, but also that the Netherlands was an enabling economic environment. Chin'ono's Page became a rallying point where citizens not only expressed their frustration but also established networks that they needed to leave the 'Republic of Kwachustan'.

Given his profile as an award-winning journalist, Chin'ono leveraged his social capital to develop an alternative narrative about Zimbabwe's political and economic situation. While the post-Mugabe regime of Emmerson Mnangagwa often claimed that Zimbabwe had turned a corner in its economic fortunes, in his social media posts, Chin'ono insisted that the Zimbabwean state continued to breed dystopia for those who chose to stay. He thus encouraged young people to leave the country by providing information about other Zimbabweans who had improved their lives through migrating to countries with better economic opportunities, especially in the Global North. His advice to young people 'remain[ed] the same' probably because the situation in Zimbabwe had not changed and it was not likely to change any time soon.

Since the beginning of the economic crisis, Zimbabweans were caught in endless cycles of disappointment, with each election cycle promising change, which often ended in yet another cycle of crises and frustrated dreams. The collective struggle for change had turned into a futile exercise especially after the coup of November 2017 and the contested elections of 2018 and 2023 respectively. Many Zimbabwean scholars such as Ndlovu-Gatsheni and Ruhanya (2020) and Nyambi (2019) concur that Zimbabwe under the presidency of Emmerson Mnangagwa is worse than that of his predecessor, Robert Mugabe. Under the Mnangagwa presidency, the democratic space continues to shrink as the economy slides downhill, with skyrocketing inflation that surpasses that of countries at war. By advising young people to 'leave and focus on [their] lives', Chin'ono was probably advocating an approach that prioritised the individual at the expense of the collective, given that the regime was determined to undermine the will of the collective. In tentatively theorising what she calls the transnational public sphere, Fraser (2007), distinguishes the transnational public sphere from Habermas' public sphere by arguing that it is not confined to the boundaries of the nation-state and citizenship, defined as membership of a bounded nation-state. Chin'ono's Facebook Page resembled a transnational public sphere not only because it brought together participants who did not necessarily reside in Zimbabwe but also internationalised the Zimbabwean political crisis.

The post above did not only encourage migration by painting a negative picture of Zimbabwe but also created a sense of panic. Chin'ono's hypothetical example of someone who was 20 years old in 2000, who is now (in 2023) 43 years old, painted a picture of a country that specialised in wasting lives. In recent Zimbabwean history, the year 2000 was a landmark year which marked the intensification of the economic crisis especially following the chaotic land reform of the same year. It also marked the entrenchment of anti-democratic tendencies by the governing ZANU-PF regime on the back of the popularity of the opposition movement and a deepening economic crisis. Chin'ono's hypothetical gave a sense of immediacy to the ongoing crisis by showing that the latter had real human victims – people who were ageing with nothing to their names, 'no home, no job, no medical aid and no pension'. The typical Zimbabwean character that Chin'ono portrayed was a negated personality. The things that he owned (a wife and kids) were in fact liabilities and everything about his life was in the negative as implied by the word 'no'. To live in Zimbabwe was thus to live a negated life, with a wife and kids but with no means to secure their lives by providing shelter, medication, and economic security.

In the last paragraph, Chin'ono rehashed the importance of focusing on the individual as opposed to the collective. The repetition of the word 'yourself' in 'work on yourself and build yourself' moved the struggle for emancipation from the public sphere to the private arena, from the corporate to the personal. The logic of Chin'ono argument was that people had individual dreams and aspirations that could only be achieved by taking certain decisions at individual level such as migration. Moreover, the success of a nation depended on the success of its citizens. To encourage Zimbabweans to migrate was therefore an act of patriotism on Chin'ono's part aimed at improving not only the welfare of individuals but also that of the nation. Chin'ono's digital public sphere became a counselling platform where he advised young people to forget the empty patriotic rhetoric of the state and focus on personal development.

It is also important to note that Chin'ono call for Zimbabweans to 'leave' happened in a context where the incumbent regime had made it impossible for the opposition to govern even after winning elections. Opposition political formations in Zimbabwe such as the Movement for Democratic Change (MDC) and more recently the Citizens for Coalition Change (CCC), have attracted a huge following because of their seductive message of change and newness (AfricaNews, 2022, March 28). For example, in the run up to the elections of August 2023, CCC ran under the slogan 'a new Great Zimbabwe for everyone' which implied that the change it envisaged was meant to transform Zimbabwe as a national collective. However, the party's failure to assume political power, despite allegedly winning the elections, suggested that the collective struggle had failed, and individuals needed to focus, not on building the nation, but on building themselves.

It is also interesting to note that Chin'ono cited himself as an example of someone who had made the right decision by leaving Zimbabwe at a young age instead of waiting for things to change. This example gave a human face to the migration option, as if to say, 'look, I am a living example of someone who left and changed his life for the better'. One would also notice that Chin'ono message speculated about what could have happened to him had he failed to leave Zimbabwe at the time that he did. The conditional word 'would', opens a range of imaginary possibilities, from 'reporting to Reuben Barwe' (a regime journalist) to losing the freedom to speak his mind to being 'beholden to [his] lived realities'. In Zimbabwean public discourse, Reuben Barwe is the archetypal regime journalist who has worked for government-controlled media since the days of Robert Mugabe. To report to Reuben Barwe, a figurehead of the regime, was to become a puppet of the regime and thus lose the freedom to express one's personal views, something which contradicted the basic ideals of the journalistic profession. To leave Zimbabwe (i.e. to migrate) was equivalent to gaining one's freedom, not only economically but also discursively. What is also important to note about Chin'ono's speculative discourse is that it depicted those who chose to remain in Zimbabwe as having no choice but to prioritise their 'lived realities' ahead of (and against) their conscience.

The last line, 'Liberate yourself from the Republic of Kwachustan' which reads almost like a political slogan is not only a summative punchline whose message is 'leave Zimbabwe for a better life' but also an apt representation of Zimbabwe as a socio-economic and political space where everything has fallen apart. The term 'the Republic of Kwachustan' conjures images of failed and crisis-ridden states such as Afghanistan and Pakistan. In Zimbabwe, the prefix 'kwachu' in *Kwachu*stan is associated with a song by popular Zimbabwean musician, Hosiah Chipanga, called Kwachu Kwachu. In this song, Chipanga lamented the culture of vandalism which citizens in Zimbabwe embraced in response to failure by the state to create economic opportunities for its citizens. The kwachu-kwachu phenomenon of Hosiah Chipanga's song referred to vandalism of public amenities, such as communal water tapes and bus stop shelters. This phenomenon was associated with individualistic and self-centred behaviour by citizens which mirrored the selfishness of the political elite. For Chin'ono, Zimbabwe was 'the Republic of Kwachustan' not only because of selfish tendencies exhibited by ordinary citizens, but also and more importantly, because of the political elite who were interested in wealth accumulation at the expense of rebuilding the nation for the benefit of everyone.

In another message which he posted on 6 November 2023, Chin'ono accused some Zimbabweans of being selfish by discouraging the youths from migrating in search of greener pastures. He characterised the nameless Zimbabweans as 'silly and selfish' because they were tweeting from the comfort of 'America, Europe and South Africa' and yet discouraging others from accessing the same comfort that they were already enjoying. America, Europe, and South Africa symbolised functional economies that provided economic opportunities for citizens, and thus were different from the Republic of Kwachustan (Zimbabwe) where people grew old with no home, medical care, or pension. In this post, Chin'ono discursively constructed migration from Zimbabwe as a positive move that would transform lives for the better. He dismissed those who 'own[ed] houses in Zimbabwe because they left' and yet discouraged others from leaving as selfish. Leaving Zimbabwe was thus construed as directly linked to the ability to buy/build houses and own properties. The implication was not only that those who lived in Zimbabwe could not afford to buy houses but also that those who left stood a chance to buy and own houses. To migrate was not only to escape the economic ruin in Kwachustan/Zimbabwe but also to leap into a world of better economic prospects and new possibilities of material wellbeing. Chin'ono used the digital platform to deconstruct official narratives and construct a new narrative that favoured migration from Zimbabwe.

Chin'ono's Facebook thus resembled a digital diaspora which 'allow[ed] for the identification of both shared vulnerabilities and oppressions, as well as common visions and possibilities of solidarity' (Candidatu & Ponzanesi, 2022, p. 265). Some Zimbabwean social media users responded to Chin'ono's post by arguing that migration was not a viable option because every successful struggle required the youths to participate in it. If Zimbabwean youths ran away to other countries, who would lead the struggle against tyranny in Zimbabwe? In response to this argument, Chin'ono ridiculed his opponents with three laughing emojis, accusing them of being 'uneducated'. The response subverted popular discourse which claimed that Zimbabweans were the most educated in Southern Africa. Chin'ono argued that 'any struggle needs people to fund it' and 'you can't fund a struggle when you have people sitting at home with no food to eat'. In Chin'ono formulation, migration had the capacity not only to empower citizens economically but also to promote the collective struggle because those who migrated had a chance to improve their economic status and consequently support the struggle financially. Migration was thus not an act of cowardice but a strategic move that had the potential to benefit both the individual and the collective.

Chin'ono used derogatory language to dismiss those who discouraged migration, arguing that it was 'foolish to tell a man who can leave the country and get a job in Britain not to leave when he has no job, no medical aid, no pension scheme and no home in Zimbabwe'. He gave the example of Zimbabweans who left the country during colonial rule to find jobs elsewhere and helped fund the struggle for independence. He further characterised as 'utter madness' attempts by some social media users to discourage youths from migrating because of an imagined revolution 'which hadn't happened in 23 years since the current crisis started'. The use of words and phrases such as 'silly' and 'utter madness' showed, not only Chin'ono's conviction that migration could transform lives but also the polarised nature of Zimbabwe's social media discourse.

In Zimbabwe, the governing regime often dismissed those who opposed its policies as puppets of the West and counter-revolutionary elements. Similarly, Chin'ono used derogatory language to dismiss those who did not see migration as a viable option. He concluded his message with a condescending statement, 'the fact that we have adults who discourage others from getting a better life shows why Zimbabwe is a failed state'. The statement not only ridiculed 'adults' who were not supportive but also associated migration with 'getting a better life'. Chin'ono also categorised the 'adults' who did not see migration as a solution to Zimbabwe's problems as part of the reason Zimbabwe was 'a failed state'. The 'adults' in Chin'ono statement could also refer to the governing elite (most of whom are elderly men) who were involved in the liberation struggle.

Most of Chin'ono's posts constructed migration as a liberating experience that could open economic opportunities. On 8 November 2023, he posted another message in which he congratulated a Zimbabwean national named Kumbirai[4] who had started a successful business venture in Germany. The message read as follows:

---

[4] https://miningbusinessafrica.co.za/zimbabwe-to-berlin-kumbirai-champions-human-centric-mining-technology/

> This is what leaving Kwachustan will do to your life, it opens up opportunities that were never there in Kwachustan, Kumbirai can now come back at any time of his choosing stronger and independent.
>
> Well done Kumbirai, unotsvirei tea yacho isina shuga.
>
> Almost ALL successful Zimbabweans globally are outside Kwachustan, Strive Masiyiwa, James Manyika you name them.

In this message, Chin'ono used Kumbirai's 'migration' experience in Germany to demonstrate that migration could transform lives. The line 'this is what leaving Kwachustan will do to your life' did not only point at Kumbirai's experience as an example of what might happen to those who leave Kwachustan/Zimbabwe but also created a narrative that equated the act of leaving Kwachustan with economic success. In this case, Kumbirai's experience becomes the standard for anyone who dared to leave Zimbabwe and explore opportunities elsewhere. It is the act of migrating, of moving to an elsewhere, that 'opens up opportunities that were never there in Kwachustan'. The difference between Zimbabwe and Germany is thus not only that Zimbabwe has limited opportunities but also that some opportunities that exist in Germany do not exist in Zimbabwe. Therefore, those who dare leave Zimbabwe are likely to be exposed to new opportunities. Transnational digital spaces, as evident through Chin'ono posts, create opportunities for the local and the global to interact and for individuals in local communities to access opportunities in other locations around the world.

In this post, Chin'ono constructed Zimbabwe as a limiting socio-economic landscape that muzzled individual freedom. Having established himself economically in Germany, Kumbirai 'could now come back home at any time of his choosing', suggesting that migration opened economic opportunities and enabled free mobility from one country to another. Unlike those that remained in Kwachustan, who often found themselves jobless, with no access to medical aid and other basics of life, Kumbirai would, after having established himself financially in Germany, come back to Zimbabwe 'stronger and independent'. The word 'stronger' suggests influence and power that comes with economic freedom. Kumbirai would come back to Zimbabwe 'independent' both economically and discursively like Chin'ono himself who could speak fearlessly against the regime because he did not depend on it for survival.

The Shona phrase '*unotsvirei tea isina sugar*' that Chin'ono used to describe the predicament of Zimbabwean citizens is associated with a song by Zimdancehall musician Enzo Ishal in which he discouraged people from pursuing things that had no benefit. The statement '*unotsivirei tea isina shuga*' means 'why burn your lips when the tea has no sugar?' to imply that it is futile to keep doing something that has no benefit. Zimbabwe is like tea with no sugar. It is tasteless, and therefore not worthy sacrificing one's life for. Just as sugar gives taste to tea, a country that has economic opportunities bestows a sense of patriotism on its citizens.

In a previous post (6 November 2023), Chin'ono had described Zimbabweans who discouraged young people from migrating to countries that offered economic opportunities as 'silly' because patriotism was a two-way street. It was only logical for citizens to move to countries that had economic opportunities (sugar) and abandon a life of drinking tea without sugar. Chin'ono demonstrated Zimbabwe's sugarless state by arguing that 'almost ALL successful Zimbabweans globally [we]re outside Kwachustan'. The word 'all' in capital letters suggests not only Zimbabwe's lack of opportunities but also its volatile economic environment which cannot guarantee success. Chin'ono gave only two examples of Zimbabweans who had established themselves economically outside Zimbabwe (Strive Masiyiwa and James Makamba), however, the phrase 'you name them' suggested that the list of successful Zimbabweans abroad was endless.

On 7 December 2023, Chin'ono posted another message in response to a purported agreement between Zimbabwe and Botswana in which the presidents of both countries had allegedly agreed to waive visa requirements and allow citizens to travel between the two countries using identity documents instead of passports. In fact, following a meeting between President Mnangagwa of Zimbabwe and President Masisi of Botswana, the former announced that the two countries had agreed to remove visa requirements and allow citizens to travel using identity cards. Although the deal was only going to take effect after it was endorsed by parliament in both countries, President Mnangagwa announced it as if it was a done deal. In his post, Chin'ono described the deal as 'a shrewd business and commercial decision on the part of Botswana to lure Zimbabwean traders away from Musina to Francis Town'. Musina is a small town on the border between South African and Zimbabwe, where Zimbabweans often flock to buy goods and services. Francistown is the nearest town on the border between Zimbabwe and Botswana, and in Chin'ono's view, the deal was going to benefit Botswana because Zimbabwe depended on its neighbours for 'basic things like toothpicks and toilet paper'. That Zimbabwe depended on its neighbours for basic things such as toothpicks and toilet paper highlighted its dire economic situation, which left citizens with no option but to migrate.

The 'agreement' was a 'shrewd business' decision on the part of Botswana which would benefit financially as Zimbabweans flocked to Botswana to buy goods and services. In Chin'ono view, South Africa had done a similar business transaction when it decided to renew permits of nearly 200,000 Zimbabweans living and working in South Africa. Chin'ono considered South Africa's decision to extend the Zimbabwe Exemption Permit as a business move because Zimbabweans were 'doing jobs that many South Africans [did not] want to do for the low wage paid'. The implication was that both Botswana and South Africa were making decisions that benefited their economies while Zimbabwe continued to present itself as a consumer of goods and services produced in other countries. Zimbabwe would, in Chin'ono's view, benefit nothing from the deal because citizens of Botswana only came to Zimbabwe to 'visit family and not to buy anything'. Botswana was thus the 'big winner' in the deal because it would collect 'trade dollars' from Zimbabweans flocking to Botswana for basic goods and services. In this post, Chin'ono exposed not only Zimbabwe's pariah status in the region but also the way in which migration and cross-border business had become survival strategies for Zimbabweans.

On 17 December 2023, Chin'ono posted a message in which he reported that members of parliament in Botswana had rejected the Zimbabwe-Botswana migration deal. In fact, although President Mnangagwa had announced the deal as if it was 'imminent', President Masisi of Botswana 'told his parliament that that there was no agreement [and the so-called agreement] was just a concept'. The implication was that President Mnangagwa was probably too desperate for the deal to go through, to alleviate the crisis in his country, yet Botswana's parliamentarians were concerned that if the deal went through, Zimbabweans would flock into their country in numbers, putting pressure on their health system. In this post, Chin'ono described Zimbabwe as a failed state which had become a liability to other countries in the region.

Chin'ono used his Facebook Page to highlight Zimbabwe's collapsed health system which had been destroyed by what he described as 'massive corruption and incompetence'. Although President Mnangagwa and President Masisi of Botswana postured as close friends, this 'friendship' could not influence the deal because Zimbabwe was an economic liability. Botswana had a similar deal with Namibia in which citizens of both countries could travel using identity cards instead of passports, however, a similar deal with Zimbabwe would have been problematic because the latter depended on other countries in the region for jobs, public goods, and services. Reflecting on the failed Botswana-Zimbabwe 'migration' deal, Chin'ono described Zimbabwe as 'the troublesome sick man of the region' ruled by a corrupt party, ZANU-PF, which did not seem to understand how bad politics influenced economics.

Zimbabwe had become, in Chin'ono's words, 'a regional leper' because of its perennial economic problems. In biblical times, lepers were often kept outside the city because they were considered unclean and if they came into the city, they would be stoned to death. The metaphor of Zimbabwe as a 'regional leper' is an apt description that captures the country's status regionally and globally, and the ways in which Zimbabwean citizens were treated in neighbouring countries such as Botswana and South Africa. The impression that Chin'ono created through this post was that Zimbabwe was a burden not only for those living within it but also for its neighbours. In this post, Chin'ono saw the failed deal as an embarrassment to Zimbabwe and confirmation that the 'corrupt and incompetent' political elite in Zimbabwe did not seem to understand that countries often prioritised national interests and that deals between countries required 'careful political and economic consideration of the practical implications on both sides'.

The motif of Zimbabwe as an economic 'leper' is also evident in a message which Chin'ono posted on 22 December 2023, reflecting on the experiences of Zimbabwean migrants in Uzbekistan. The message demonstrated how Zimbabwe had become a pariah state, not only to other countries around the world but also to its citizens. Chin'ono used the experiences of three Zimbabwean teachers employed by an international school in Tashkent (the capital city of Uzbekistan) to demonstrate that migration was an economically viable option for Zimbabweans who wanted to transform their lives for the better. The teachers told Chin'ono that life in Uzbekistan was 'far much better than back home in Zimbabwe' because 'the starting salary was around US$1400' going up to 'around US$2,500 per month after one year' through gradual increments. By contrast, teachers in Zimbabwe 'earned around US$100' which was not enough to buy basic goods. The post also highlighted the affordable accommodation in Uzbekistan (US$600 per month) and internet data ('only US$13 a month'). Some social media users who responded to this message did not even know there was such a country as Uzbekistan. In the message, Chin'ono pointed out that Uzbekistan, like many Arab countries in the region, did not offer permanent residency to migrant workers and in Africa, it had only one embassy in Egypt. Given that Zimbabwe is in Southern Africa, the presence of Zimbabwean migrant workers in Uzbekistan (a country that had one embassy in Africa) only served to highlight the extent to which the Zimbabwean crisis had affected citizens.

While the economic crisis, particularly the high inflation and lack of employment opportunities, pushed Zimbabweans out of Zimbabwe, the better living conditions and economic opportunities in Uzbekistan were pull factors. In his message, Chin'ono stated that in Uzbekistan, one could get 'a mobile phone line with 1500 minutes, 8gb internet and 1500 text messages' for only US$5. Transport was also affordable, public buses cost 25 cents per trip and private taxis US$50 per month. The Zimbabwean teachers that Chin'ono met lived 'a comfortable life' in Uzbekistan because of 'favourable working conditions, affordable living expenses, and the absence of racism'. They also had access to a functional health system which they did not have in Zimbabwe. In addition, one Zimbabwean family told Chin'ono that when they had a baby 'the paediatrician [would come] home to check up on their child'. Zimbabwe, on the other hand, has a dysfunctional health system which has no capacity to provide basic health services. Chin'ono's migration narratives suggest that those who migrated from Zimbabwe benefited from better economic conditions in destination countries such as Uzbekistan. The Zimbabwean teachers could not only afford to take care of themselves but also buy properties back home in preparation for retirement given that Uzbekstan did not offer permanent residency to foreign workers.

On 23 December 2023, Chin'ono shared the story of Njabulo, a Zimbabwean aviation engineer who worked for the airliner, Emirates, in Dubai. Chin'ono met Njabulo on a flight from Dubai to Harare (Zimbabwe). Njabulo was one among many Zimbabwean professionals who were forced to seek economic opportunities elsewhere in the aftermath of Zimbabwe's economic collapse. What Chin'ono highlighted in the post was not only the 'green pastures narrative' but also the extent to which the mass exodus of Zimbabwean professionals had affected Zimbabwe's economy and benefited economies of other countries. Chin'ono mused that professionals such as Njabulo 'could have been working on Boeing passenger planes at Air Zimbabwe had it not been driven into the ground by the ZANUPF rulership'. In Chin'ono's view, Njabulo's story demonstrated how corrupt and incompetent leadership, which he called 'ZANU-PF rulership' had ruined the country, forcing the skilled workforce to migrate to other countries.

Professionals such as Njabulo left Zimbabwe because of a lack of employment opportunities and bad governance. Zimbabwe has only one airline company,

Air Zimbabwe, and one flying plane. Chin'ono used the example of Emirates to show how corrupt rule is responsible for migration in Zimbabwe. He argued that 'Emirates started with two borrowed planes from Pakistan Airlines in 1985, but through good leadership, it now has over 200 planes'. On the other hand, 'Air Zimbabwe had 21 planes and a cargo airline called Affretair left by Ian Smith [in 1980] but [was] bankrupted by the ZANUPF regime'. Skilled professionals such as Njabulo opted to leave Zimbabwe because it had 'only ONE plane flying', and thus no employment opportunities. By putting 'one' in capital letters, Chin'ono emphasised not only the economic ruin caused by bad governance but also the limited economic opportunities for skilled professionals in Zimbabwe.

Most of Chin'ono's posts depicted Zimbabwe as a risky country for economic investment because of political instability and bad governance. In this post, he advised Njabulo to invest in South Africa because the latter had 'political stability, rule of law and [...] a health care system that [was] medical aid based'. Unlike Zimbabwe, where one could easily lose property to 'politically connected land baron[s]', in South African one could 'earn money through Airbnb, [and] on a property worth US$75,000, [one] c[ould] get an average return of US$1,315 a month'.[5] The implication was that it made sense to leave Zimbabwe because it was a risky economic destination where the political elite and the politically connected did whatever they wanted without following due process or observing the rule of law.

On 11 January 2024, Chin'ono posted another message in which he reflected on the story of Godfrey Tsenengamu, a former ZANU-PF youth leader who migrated from Zimbabwe to the UK in search of better economic opportunities. For Chin'ono, Tsenengamu's migration to the UK demonstrated that there was 'no future in this broken Zimbabwe' and the only option for those who wanted to improve their lives was to migrate to other countries. Again, as in previous posts, Chin'ono encouraged young people to leave Zimbabwe because 'they will get old saying that things will get better'. He also gave a hypothetical example of someone who was 30 years old in 2003 who was 'now 50 years old and things have gotten worse'. The underlying logic of Chin'ono's messaging was that those who wanted to improve their lives had no other option but to leave the country. If they did not migrate, their lives would most likely worsen. Zimbabwe's economic indicators such as inflation (over 1,000% at the beginning of 2024) and unemployment showed that the situation was getting worse.

Chin'ono's posts encouraged young people to leave Zimbabwe so that they could work, save, and invest as they prepared for old age. This was necessary because, in Chin'ono's view, citizens were on their own in Zimbabwe, 'pensioners ha[d] lost everything and [were] dying miserable deaths without income or access to basic healthcare'. Therefore, migration was one way to avoid miserable death in old age. In this post, Chin'ono used his own story of working as a cleaner in 'Planet Hollywood in London's Piccadilly Circus' to encourage young Zimbabweans to migrate and seek better economic opportunities. Migration was not only about

---

[5]https://twitter.com/daddyhope/status/1738463302726955117

looking for opportunities to improve one's life, but also about improving the lives of generations to come. Chin'ono ended his message by encouraging those who were unemployed and could leave to 'please do so for the sake of your children'. The implication here was that the Zimbabwean crisis had deprived citizens of the ability to accumulate wealth, thus setting in motion a cycle of generational poverty.

Most of Chin'ono's posts on the ongoing Zimbabwean crisis suggested that poor governance, incompetence, and corruption in Zimbabwe affected not only the welfare of citizens but also the image of the country globally. On 12 January 2024, Chin'ono posted a message in which he commented on a decision by the British government to reject Zimbabwean academic and professional documents because they were not verifiable. The British government also claimed that they had information to the effect that some of the documents were acquired fraudulently. This decision affected many Zimbabweans who intended to migrate to the UK to seek better opportunities, especially in its health and care work sector. Chin'ono took this incident as an opportunity to explain how bad governance at home affected the country's image on the international arena and how Zimbabwean citizens were perceived and treated in other countries. The Zimbabwean state had, in Chin'ono's words, lost 'the underpinnings of a respectable state' which included 'trust, competence, rule of law, transparency, accountability and good governance'. Although most of Chin'ono's messages advocated migration as a solution to the Zimbabwean crisis, at least at individual level, the British government's decision to reject Zimbabwean documents suggested that the problems in Zimbabwe also compromised the ability of Zimbabweans to move around the world and secure economic opportunities.

Responding to Chin'ono's Migration Narratives: Views from Zimbabwean Social Media Users

In this section, I reflect on how Zimbabwean social media users responded to Hopewell Chin'ono's messages which encouraged young Zimbabweans to migrate and seek better economic opportunities in other countries. While some social media users agreed with Chin'ono's migration option, and even provided testimonies about how migration had improved their lives, I am particularly interested in posts that offered alternatives views on migration vis-a-viz the Zimbabwean crisis. One of the issues raised by social media users is that not all Zimbabweans had the relevant connections and financial means to migrate to other countries. Responding to Chin'ono's post of 5 November 2023 in which he encouraged young people to 'leave the Republic of Kwachustan', one social media user (LK) questioned Chin'ono's migration option through the message 'Running away? I ran away am in SA but am still suffering'. LK's post suggested that running way from the Zimbabwean crisis was not a solution because some of those who ran away were suffering in destination countries, in this case South Africa (SA).

In recent years, South Africa has experienced serious socio-economic challenges that range from unemployment, poor service delivery to rolling power cuts. South African citizens have responded to these challenges by, among other things, blaming migrants from different part of the continent, including Zimbabwe. South Africa is thus no longer an attractive destination for African migrants. One social media user, BM, asked Chin'ono to give advice to those who could not leave 'because not all of us can afford or are connected'. In his posts, Chin'ono encouraged those who could leave to leave 'now' but he did not seem to have any words of advice for those who could not leave either because they had no means or were not connected. One of the problems with success stories of migration, at least as pointed out by social media users who responded to Chino's posts, is that they lack sufficient detail about how to succeed in a foreign land. An example is a story by one Kumbirai, a Zimbabwean who migrated to Germany '7 years ago' 'with nothing and no plan' but ended up owning a 7-figure company in Germany. Instead of providing information about how he managed to build a 7-figure company with no plan, Kumbirai waxed into a moralistic tirade about how his story was a 'testament to the power of perseverance and the strength of the human spirit'. Social media users queried Kumbirai's claim that he had no plan because to travel to Germany, one needed a visa and a flight ticket, and one could not get these with 'nothing and no plan'.

The problem with migration narratives, including Chin'ono's pro-migration posts, is that they lack sufficient information about how to navigate unfamiliar worlds. Some social media users such as JS and TM expressed interest in leaving Zimbabwe, but they did not know how to do it. In fact, JS stated that he had been 'scammed' perhaps because he did not have proper guidance on where to go and how to go there. On the other hand, TM appealed to Chin'ono to provide information on how to travel abroad, saying in Shona '*tatsvuka ropa muno muZim*'. The phrase '*tasvuka ropa*' literally means 'we have been battered' and it paints the image of a bloodied boxer on the losing side of a boxing match, as if Zimbabweans were boxers wrestling with the economic crisis.

People usually need connections to migrate, either in the form of friends and relatives who live in destination countries or reliable travel agents. Those without those connections often find it difficult, if not impossible, to migrate. This probably explains why most Zimbabweans migrate to neighbouring countries such as South Africa and Botswana. One social media user, BM, described Botswana and South Africa as 'our only glory' suggesting that these were the only countries that were easily accessible, although he was aware that they had their 'own challenges'. Other social media users such as LT and SPM described Chin'ono's 'gospel' of migration as 'poisonous' because running away was, for them, not a solution to the problem of dictatorship in Zimbabwe. They advocated 'going back to the bush' to 'reclaim and free our country from detractors'. In fact, SPM appealed to those who were connected such as Hopewell Chin'ono to 'organize us weaponry and ammunition, *kunyiwe* once'. The word '*kunyiwe*' is Ndebele for 'to defecate' and in this context it refers to the suffering associated with war. Another social media user, IN, intimated that Zimbabweans had only two options 'either they stay and launch an armed struggle against the corrupt and oppressive regime, or they get out'. The comment corroborated Chin'ono's view of Zimbabwe as Kwachustan, a broken country that had no hope especially for young people. While Chin'ono's posts were interested in offering practical solutions that could transform individual lives for the better, social media users such as LT and SPM were concerned about long-term solutions.

The Problematics of Migration: Is the Grass Green on the Other Side?

In most of his posts, Chin'ono portrayed migration as a liberating experience that opened economic opportunities and possibilities of a better life for the migrant. However, some social media users contested this view, arguing that addressing the economic challenges in Zimbabwe was the only viable solution in the long term. DG posted a lengthy message in which he pointed out that countries such as South Africa were now doing everything possible 'to protect their workspace from foreign nationals'. He gave the example of Home Affairs Minister, Aaron Motsoaledi, who tried to terminate the Zimbabwean Exemption permit because of South Africa's growing unemployment rates. The rise of vigilante groups that moved 'door to door closing down and sabotaging the foreign owned spaza shops' such as Operation Dudula was also evidence that moving to South Africa was, in DG's words like 'jumping into the sea while trying to get out of the rain'. The metaphor of jumping into the sea to escape a storm foregrounds the futility of migrating to a country that has its own problems.

Although DG claimed that 'fixing the country [was] the only way to go', he did not explain how this could be done. He was, however, convinced that migrating to countries such as South Africa was not a solution because of rising anti-immigration sentiment and the country's growing socio-economic problems. Another social media user supported DG's view, arguing that 'people are suffering here [in South Africa] living for rent'. Unlike Chin'ono's posts which focused on the experiences of Zimbabwean migrants in Western countries such as Netherlands and Britain, posts by migrants in South Africa showed that they were suffering and 'living for rent'. Living for rent is a metaphor for earning little money which cannot cover one's basic needs. Another social media user, MM, noted that most Zimbabweans wanted to escape the economic crisis, but they did not have the means to do so. As a result, they 'end[ed] up crossing Limpopo on foot to mzansi where they suffer[ed] worse'. A close look at Chin'ono's posts and responses from his followers reveal that better economic opportunities tend to be far afield, especially in Western countries, hence they were inaccessible to those with limited or no financial resources. Most Zimbabweans ended up migrating to neighbouring countries where they could walk on foot.

Some social media users were sceptical about the liberating potential of migration. Responding to Chin'ono's post about former ZANU-PF youth leader, Godfrey Tsenengamu who had left Zimbabwe for the UK, one social media user, JM, pointed out that Tsenengamu had 'left it until too late' because 'the UK [was] no longer the same place it was 10/15 years ago'. JM noted that most African migrants who were migrating to the UK using Certificates of Sponsorship (COS) were 'struggling to get work and make ends meet'. The problem with the UK, JM agued, was that there were fewer employment opportunities, and migrants often found it hard to find work. Unlike Hopewell Chin'ono who advised young

Zimbabweans to migrate, JM advised those who had something to do back home to 'stay put'.

In JM's view, migration could worsen someone's life. He pointed out several challenges that migrant labourers faced in the UK such as exploitation by employers, lack of enough working hours to earn a living, high costs of living and expensive accommodation. Based on his experience of living in the UK for over 20 years, JM advised potential migrants to think carefully about migrating to the UK because, in his words, 'UK can be a very lonely place especially when you don't get enough work'. Unlike other countries, especially in Africa, where a family of four can live in a 2 bedroomed house, JM also warned potential migrants that landlords in the UK were strict about the number of people who could live in a house. While Chin'ono encouraged young people to leave Zimbabwe when, and if, they can, JM insisted on caution arguing that the UK was 'no longer a garden of roses' and that it was 'now tough out here'. JM's comments show that migrating to countries that have their own challenges may worse as opposed to improve migrant lives.

This chapter has reflected on narratives and counter-narratives of migration in Zimbabwe, drawing on data from Zimbabwean journalist, Hopewell Chin'ono's posts between December 2023 and January 2024. We read Chin'ono's Facebook as a transnational public sphere that brought together followers from different parts of the world to deliberate about the post-August 2023 election impasse in Zimbabwe. The Page constituted a digital diaspora which 'capture[d] the different material and affective dimensions of mediated displacement and loss (Candidatu & Ponzanesi, 2022, p. 264).

Most of the posts described Zimbabwe as an economic desert that had no economic opportunities, especially for young people who were not politically connected. Chin'ono's posts were mainly based on his own travel experiences around the world and the experiences of other Zimbabweans living abroad, particularly in countries in the West. In his posts, Chin'ono used the success stories of Zimbabweans migrants abroad to encourage the youth to leave the country and explore opportunities elsewhere. Migration, for Chin'ono, was a liberating experience both economically and discursively. Those who migrated and escaped the economic turmoil in Zimbabwe often gained economic and discursive freedom. Apart from the stories of successful Zimbabweans living abroad which he leveraged to encourage migration among the youths, Chin'ono also used his own story of humble beginnings in the United Kingdom where he worked as a cleaner to encourage young people to migrate. While Chin'ono viewed migration as an adventure with potential for economic liberation, some followers on his Facebook page had different views. They expressed scepticism about the liberating potential of migration, citing the harsh conditions in destination countries. Those who lived (or had once lived) in South Africa believed the country was no longer a viable destination for migrants because of limited economic opportunities and hostile government policy towards migrants. Another issue of concern for some social media users was the rising anti-migrant sentiment expressed by vigilante groups such as Operation Dudula. While most of Chin'ono posts painted a rosy picture of life outside Zimbabwe, some social media users argued that the situation was not as attractive because migrants in countries such as the UK struggled to find employment. Considering the above, it suffices to conclude that while Chin'ono portrayed migration as capable of unlocking economic opportunities, other social media texts analysed in this chapter show that experiences of migration are different. While some discover new opportunities and live better lives post-migration, others face many challenges like those that they would have escaped in their countries of origin.

References

AfricaNews. (2022, March 28). Zimbabwean opposition party wins majority in by-elections. *Africanews*. https://www.africanews.com/2022/03/28/zimbabwean-opposition-party-wins-majority-in-by-elections/

Anderson, B. (1983). *Imagined communities. Reflections on the origin and spread of nationalism*. Verso.

Bainbridge, W. S. (2000). Religious ethnography on the World Wide Web. In K. Hadden & D. E. Cowan (Eds.), *Religion on the internet: Research prospects and promises* (pp. 55–80). Elsevier.

Bernal, V. (2020). African digital diasporas: Technologies, tactics, and trends: Introduction. *African Diaspora, 12*(1–2), 1–10. https://doi.org/10.1163/18725465-bja10007

Bhabha, H. (1990). *Nation and narration*. Routledge.

Boehmer, E. (2005a). *Colonial and postcolonial literature*. Oxford University Press.

Boehmer, E. (2005b). *Stories of women: Gender and narrative in the postcolonial nation: Gender and narrative in the postcolonial nation*. Manchester University Press.

Candidatu, L., & Ponzanesi, S. (2022). Digital Diasporas: Staying with the Trouble. *Communication, Culture and Critique, 15*, 261–268.

Eastmond, M. (2007). Stories as lived experience: Narratives in forced migration research. *Journal of Refugee Studies, 20*(2), 248–264.

Fraser, N. (2007). Transnationalizing the public sphere: On the legitimacy and efficacy of public opinion in a post-Westphalian World. *Theory, Culture & Society, 24*(4), 7–30

Makombe, R. (2021). *Cultural texts of resistance in Zimbabwe: Music, memes, media*. Rowman and Littlefield.

Mumba, N., & SADC Electoral Observation Mission. (2023). *Preliminary statement by his excellency Dr. Nevers Mumba, Former Vice President of the Republic of Zambia and Head of the Sadc Electoral Observation Mission (SEOM) to the 2023 Harmonised Elections in the Republic of Zimbabwe held on 23–24 August 2023*. https://www.sadc.int/sites/default/files/2023-08/ZIMBABWE%20SEOM%20-2023%20PRELIMINARY_STATEMENT-Revised%20adopted-25%20August%202023%2012pt.pdf

Ndlovu-Gatsheni, S., & Ruhanya, P. (2020). Introduction: Transition in Zimbabwe: From Robert Gabriel Mugabe to Emmerson Dambudzo Mnangagwa: A repetition without change. In S. J. Ndlovu-Gatsheni & P. Ruhanya (Eds.), *The history and political transition of Zimbabwe* (pp. 1–22). Palgrave Macmillan.

Nedelcu, M. (2018). Digital diasporas. In R. Cohen & C. Fischer (Eds.), *Routledge handbook of diaspora studies* (pp. 241–250). Routledge.

Nyambi, O. (2019). *Life-writing from the margins in Zimbabwe versions and subversions of crisis*. Routledge.

Sahin-Mencutek, Z. (2020). *Migration narratives in policy and politics*. Working paper produced jointly by the Ryerson Centre for Immigration and Settlement (RCIS) and the CERC in Migration and Integration.

Witteborn, S. (2019). Digital diaspora. In R. Tsagarousianou & J. Retis (Eds.), *The handbook of diasporas, media & culture* (pp. 179–192). Wiley Blackwell.

Chapter 5

Discourse of Politics and Security in Migration

Keywords: (In)security; politics; governance; ethnicity; bigotry

Matamanda and Mphambukeli (2022) state that the overall crime rate in Zimbabwe increased between 10% and 15% across most sectors in 2016 with Harare (the country's capital) also becoming an environment where robbers and criminals thrive and prey on innocent citizens. In a similar view, Zubairu (2020) intimates that insecurity is on the verge of becoming Nigeria's heritage since not a single day goes by without incidents which are turning into an unending challenge in the country. Drawing on the literature, Nigeria and Zimbabwe are two countries ravaged by seemingly unending insecurities. Nigeria's volatile political environment has also contributed to the migration of many Nigerians. Entrenched heavily in Nigerian politics are ethnic and religious tensions that often pitch Nigerians against one other and in some cases result in physical and verbal violence. Nigerians thus leave for countries they consider more politically stable. Igwe and Amadi (2021) recognise the entrenched nature of political violence in Nigeria caused by widespread marginalisation, violation of democratic norms, and relative deprivation leading to frustration among a substantial number of individuals and groups. In both countries, political violence creates socio-political tensions which lead to thoughts of migration. Having established these facts in both Nigeria and Zimbabwe, the focus of this chapter explores how concerns about security in Nigeria result in migration-motivated discourse. Insecurity challenges in Nigeria have taken on a different character in the last few years. Cases of militancy, terrorism, gangsterism, abductions/kidnapping, and robbery have permeated the country. For many Nigerians, the answer to the prevalent security problems in the country is migrating to countries with fewer security issues especially since the Nigerian government does not appear to be tackling these security matters.

Viewing migration through political and security lenses, this chapter focuses on social media posts and stories in Nigeria to assess how migration narratives

---

Social Constructions of Migration in Nigeria and Zimbabwe
Discourse, Rhetoric, and Identity, 65–81
Copyright © 2024 by Kunle Musbaudeen Oparinde and Rodwell Makombe
Published under exclusive licence by Emerald Publishing Limited
doi:10.1108/978-1-83549-168-320241005

are created in response to the security and political situation in Nigeria. We entrench this chapter in the theoretical concept of human security which Persaud (2022) argues that the United Nations Development Programme (UNDP) proposed would involve critical areas such as economic, health, food, environmental, community, personal, and political security with a further inclusion of human dignity. In the view of Siloko (2024), the human security concept brings together the elements of human rights and development in a new approach to security. In essence, human security can be understood as the protection and preservation of human survival and daily living (Siloko, 2024). Applying the human security theory to the situation of Nigeria allows us to provide a more nuanced understanding of how political and security concerns drive migration. In its most basic form, security involves protection from harm (Andersen-Rodgers & Crawford, 2022). As such, from a national perspective, they contend that national security must focus on the protection of the individual state from external harm or internal challenges or instability. Quoting the UNDP (1994), Andersen-Rodgers and Crawford (2022) state identified human security as a twofold concept: first, safety from constant threats of hunger, disease, crime, and repression, and second, protection from sudden and hurtful disruptions in the pattern of our daily lives – whether in our homes, in our jobs, in our communities, or in our environment.

Method

Like other chapters, netnography has again been used to gather information for this chapter since Bainbridge (2000, p. 57) observes the concept to mean 'a relatively passive examination of websites, without full interaction with the people who created them'. We purposely selected data that speak to issues of politics and security in Nigeria from the context of migration in order to achieve the aim of this chapter. As discussed in the introduction, social media data possess limitations pertaining to their veracity. Despite this challenge, the recurrent nature of similar narratives, supported by news media, indicates popular discourse that we find worthy of academic investigation. To maintain anonymity, the names of the authors of these posts have been redacted. In the next section, we examined narratives pertaining to politics while in the following one, we focused on discourses concerning (in)security in Nigeria. With Facebook and X (formerly Twitter) being popular for migration conversations in Nigeria, we gathered relevant data from these two platforms for this chapter by searching through keywords such as ethnicity, bigotry, governance, Fulani herdsmen, government, Nigeria, APC, PDP, PDAPC, LP, kidnappers, police, and bandits. Also, we retrieved some data from the *Vanguard Newspaper*. Several Nigerians revealed how the political tensions in the country ignited their migration interests while many others cited the widespread security problems in the country as their reasons.

Political Narratives in Nigerian Migration Discourse

This section discusses how political narratives in Nigeria impact citizens' decisions to migrate considering Van Dijk's (2018) views on politics and discourse.

In view of the proliferation of social media in the last few years, Nigerians have used social media platforms for a variety of purposes. One such purpose is to deliberate on politics. In these political discussions, the issue of migration arises in response to the political atmosphere of the country. Political views also extend into governance since the latter is often a result of the former. Political activities over the last 10 years have produced enough concerns for Nigerians to consider outmigration. Electioneering moments in Nigeria have produced tense and violent atmospheres; it is therefore no surprise that many Nigerians choose to escape from the country. Bad governance, especially over the last 10 years has intensified the desire for migration in many citizens.

Nigerian politics has become more intolerant with ethnic and religious undertones. In a Facebook post, WA states:

> Nigeria is divided because of three major criteria: religion, ethnicity and diversity of language. If the north don't rise to protest for a working NIGERIA then we all will continue suffer from Generation to Generation. So please Japa if you have the means. I rest my case. (WA, Facebook)

Since Nigeria is a multicultural and heterogenous society, politics in the country is often disharmonious. Politicians tend to weaponise socio-cultural differences for political gain. The example above gives credence to the widespread belief that the country is divided along religious and ethnic lines, and if caution is not taken, the suffering of Nigerians will not end. WA advises Nigerians to migrate if they have the means since there seems to be no hope of improvement. The post suggests that political decisions based on ethnicity and religion, and not on merit, can only produce bad governance. Umotong (2020) admits that ethnic politics has ripple effects in all spheres of the polity, creating difficulties in achieving national integration. He further argues that the diverse cultures, languages, and other factors that ought to have been the country's source of strength have become the major causes of disenchantment. Umotong (2020) claims that the fragmentary nature of the Nigerian political space is caused by ethnocentrism which has generated social conflict, distrust, and withered patriotism across the country. He concludes that unguided ethnocentrism in Nigeria greatly undermines the common good and overall well-being of members of the society who are affected by marginalisation and conflicts of interest. This instance particularly presents a challenge for national security which Andersen-Rodgers and Crawford (2022) should focus on internal challenges and instability. Currently, unending ethnic tensions in Nigeria could potentially lead to instability.

In another social media post, JO on X states that:

> Our points of discussion in Nigeria should be different. Not fighting over religion/ethnicity/geographical locations and other mundane things that add zero values to national development. How long will Nigerians continue to 'JAPA'? We are too blessed a nation for us to be running. (JO, X)

The post decries Nigerian politics which lacks substance because attention is diverted towards immaterial issues. JO is particularly concerned that Nigerians have been placed in a position where *japa* is the only option; thinking and fighting over issues such as religion, ethnicity, and land adds nothing to the country's national development. The author further observes that as a nation, Nigeria is blessed with resources that, if managed properly, would guarantee economic prosperity for everyone. In another example, DB on X posted that:

> Nigeria has become a cursed nation. Those who can JAPA should explore that option because the rot is gargantuan and irredeemable. So many people, having been fed with the chalice of religion and ethnicity, can't wake up from slumber to rescue themselves. Pitiable. (DB, X)

This example by DB shows that Nigerians tend to discuss political issues in association with migration. While some Nigerians decry the situation, many encourage *japa* as the only feasible way out. DB perceives Nigeria as a hopeless country with no chance of redemption. For this social media user, the advice is to flee before the political tensions consume the country. The political situation of the country is deeply rooted in ethnicity, and everyday politics is underscored by ethnic and religious discord. According to AO on X,

> You people make everything in Nigeria about ethnicity. I'm glad I don't live there, even more happy my family doesn't live there. That y'all choose that over security, good governance, infrastructure and a working economy still baffles me. Last last all una go find place to japa. (AO, X)

The above example encapsulates the intentions of many Nigerians. AO condemns the fact that everyday politics in Nigeria is laced with ethnicity. Although the author is Nigerian, she is happy that she and her family do not reside in the country. This sentiment stems from her observation that many Nigerians tend to favour ethnicity over basic and essential amenities. Translating directly, the author states that 'at the long run, all of you Nigerians will relocate elsewhere'. AO is also happy that she and her family do not have to witness the decay in the political system. This represents the reality for many Nigerians who have migrated. It is the expectation of many Nigerians that once a family member migrates, such a person can open the doors of migration for others in the family. The author insinuates that once the country collapses due to everyday ethnocentric discord, there would be no home for Nigerians any longer prompting them to all relocate elsewhere. In essence, the view of the author suggests that the heavy presence of ethnocentric views in Nigerian's polity is a concern that could drive the country into a major crisis. The thought of potential instability in the country (Andersen-Rodgers & Crawford, 2022) has thus become a major concern for many Nigerians many of whom have resorted to migration.

Suffice it to say that brazen ethnocentrism in Nigerian political discourse is a concern for many Nigerians that may erupt into civil war. The seeds of division planted through politics continue to germinate with the disturbing result that migration is considered the only alternative. Several countries in Africa have witnessed and are currently witnessing violent repercussions stemming from ethnocentrism. Ethnic intolerances have been inflamed by politics in several parts of the continent and have resulted in civil wars, genocides, and ethnic cleansing. The most recent case is the Democratic Republic of Congo where ethnic tensions became heated resulting in several years of internal conflicts. Hoffmann et al. (2021) contend that the way political competition has unfolded all over the country in the immediate post-independence period in the Congo indicates the degree to which political discourse was laden with ethnicity. As a result, ethnic associations, particularly in urban centres, encouraged members of ethnic groups to provide each other with mutual support and unify against those they perceive as adversaries. At the same time, tensions have also increased in rural areas over ethnic boundaries, political power, and resources. In the case of the Congo, Hoffmann et al. (2021) argue that leaders claim to protect local ethnic communities from 'ethnic' others encroaching on their ancestral lands for which in return, they demand loyalty, sacrifice, and material support. Although the system allows for the production of solidarity and mutual support along ethnic lines, Hoffmann et al. (2021) stress that there is ample historical evidence, both recent and distant, to show that the ethnicisation of the competition over power and resources in the Congo has contributed to the emergence of an unstable, centrifugal, and fragmentary political order.

Like the Congo, available evidence in Nigeria also suggests that ethnicity has been and continues to be built into the country's political system in a dangerous manner. The fear for many Nigerians who have migrated is that the situation in the country might one day degenerate into a Congo-like situation. It is worth noting, however, that ethno-religious concerns are not the only migration factors brought about by politics. Bigotry and nepotism are also significant factors in the Nigerian political environment where everyday affairs have become politicised. Since the country is burdened with corruption, issues such as partisanship, cronyism, and chauvinism remain the concerns of many Nigerians who observe that the country does not provide equal rights and treatment for everyone. It is the views of Eme-Uche and Eme (2023) that unless Nigerian leaders eschew ethnic, religious, and partisan politics in governance, the disintegration and crises caused by ethnic divisions will continue to incite unnecessary distractions that will lead to disunity and underdevelopment in the country. In a Facebook post, DD writes:

> As a youth, as a patriotic citizen, I want to see a better Nigeria I wake up with so much zeal and passion, then I come here and listen to the people speak and I get discouraged I suddenly understand why people Japa. So much bigotry and nepotism, it make me sick. (DD, Facebook)

In the above example, the young author's hope for Nigeria is undermined by the chronic bigotry and nepotism in the country. DD is not only discouraged by this reality but also extremely tired of the sad state of affairs making her identify with people who decide to migrate from the country rather than hope for improvements. In a post that went viral on X (formerly Twitter), a user is seen discouraging Nigerians from migrating stating that the process of migration is money-consuming. He states that if he had the money, he would invest it in a business in Nigeria or use the money to buy (lobby) a government job with a stable salary. This mentality permeates the Nigerian political system where ordinary Nigerians cannot have equal opportunities without money and connections. A response to the post by another user (JA) reads:

> Nothing tarnishes Nigeria's image than u advising people to buy govt job for 5M. Nevertheless, it's the order of d day. But I'd rather japa to a working country than buy a govt job coming with packages like nepotism, insecurity, inflation, human rights abuses etc. I'm tired pls. (JA, X)

JA condemns the original tweeter for tarnishing the image of the country while also admitting that 'it is the order of the day'. In other words, it is a popular practice in Nigeria to use one's nepotistic connections to achieve one's goals. For JA, migrating to a 'working country' with such money is considered more ideal than remaining in Nigeria to endure a myriad of social vices. He goes on to say 'I am tired please' at the end of the post signifying his lack of hope in Nigeria. Nepotism has become so entrenched in Nigeria's daily affairs that the mere thought of residing in a country that presents equal opportunities for Nigerians instantly presents them with hope. Since governance is the dividend of politics, bad governance in Nigeria is a direct result of politics which is further underscored by the following X post by EF:

> Everybody won Japa! Wht kind of nation is that, all the youths won Japa cos of bad Government! If #Nigeria good no body go won Japa! Sold crude oil for 60yrs, use nepotism, religions, & corruption steal money finish! Many European countries Neva see D kind money Nigeria see for their life. (EF, X)

The above post written in Nigerian Pidgin can be translated as:

> Everybody wants to flee from Nigeria! What kind of country is this, the youths want to flee because of bad governance. If Nigeria is good, citizens won't attempt to flee. Nigeria sold exported crude oil for 60 years yet, we used nepotism, religion and corruption to loot the money. Many European countries did not even have access to as much funds as Nigeria did.

Since politics produces (mis)governance, it would be conceptually faulty to discuss politicking without discussing how it affects governance. The above post explains the intricacies of Nigerian politics and by extension, governance. It establishes that a large part of the population intends to migrate especially because of bad governance which the author finds highly disturbing in a country such as Nigeria. It also reflects on the country's current reality which has been made awful by ingrained corruption and nepotism. The saddest realisation for the author of the post is the mismanagement of Nigerian resources by the leaders because of nepotism, religion, and corruption which has driven the country into poverty despite its natural resources. The popularly referred to 'oil boom era' was a period when the country's economy grew exponentially by exporting crude oil. For many Nigerians, responsible management of the country's resources during this period should have provided long-term economic prosperity. However, the mismanagement of the resources resulted in disturbing levels of corruption which the country has continued to suffer.

In a narration by AA, an X user, we retrieved a post which reads:

> I got talking with some white Canadian, then we talked about the cold weather. He was curious asked me why I left Nigeria since our weather is a lot friendlier. I told him we've had successive bad govts he was like come on, we have a terrible govt here. Em never see bulaba. (AA, X)

This post reveals a lot about Nigerians outmigration. First, it reveals certain perceived misunderstandings about why Nigerians migrate. It also discloses one of the main reasons for outmigration. The example relates to a discussion between a Nigerian who presumably now resides in Canada, and a Canadian citizen. Since it is common knowledge that Canada has extreme weather conditions while Nigeria is blessed with a naturally friendly weather, the Canadian wonders why the Nigerian left the warm weather in Nigeria for the cold weather in Canada. The Nigerian proceeds to explain that the migration factor is more about successive bad governance in Nigeria than about the weather. The Canadian tries to draw a parallel stating that Canada also experiences bad governance while the Nigerian laments 'Em never see bulaba'. Translated, this means 'you have not seen bulaba' which is the Nigerian's attempt to describe that bad governance is worse in Nigeria than it is in Canada. 'Bulaba' is a popular coinage in Nigeria used to refer to the current President of the country – Bola Ahmed Tinubu. The President is believed by many Nigerians to be unhealthy especially due to his old age and incessant medical travels to Europe. In one of his presidential campaigns, the President failed to pronounce the word 'hullabaloo' correctly, which resulted in several variations such as: 'balablu', 'bulaba', and 'blublu'. Many people assumed that his inability to pronounce the word confirmed his unhealthy state while some of his supporters believed it was a mere mistake. Notwithstanding which side one belongs to, the wrong variations of the word have been deployed by common Nigerians to mock and ridicule the President especially since the Nigerian social media political space is replete with political rhetoric meant to bully, mock, and laugh at political opponents. References to 'bulaba' continue to resurface after elections to reflect Bola Ahmed Tinubu's bad performance even as President. The examples analysed in this chapter already suggests that bad governance is indeed one of the major concerns for many Nigerians who leave the country.

Further exacerbating the distress of many Nigerians is the lack of perceived hope in the governance of the country especially since the leading political party as well as the leading opposition party are often accused of connivance and colluding for their own political interests. The two most popular political parties have lost the trust of the people since they appear to have an amicable relationship rather than an uncongenial one which is expected from opposing political parties. The All Progressives Congress (APC) and the People's Democratic Party (PDP) are the two leading political parties that have had the most influence since 1999 when Nigeria returned to democracy.[1] While it is expected that the opposition party should be a voice against the misdemeanours of the government, the PDP has been the opposition party since 2015 and has performed underwhelmingly in its duties. With members of both parties notorious for switching from one to the other for electoral selfishness, it has become crystal clear that Nigerians can expect little by way of systemic changes in governance. The former Independent National Electoral Chairman (INEC) in the country, Professor Attahiru Jega, has referred to the two leading political parties as the 'Siamese twins of corruption' while encouraging Nigerians to eliminate them in the next general elections. The excerpt below from Professor Jega's interview with BBC Hausa in 2021 was adapted from the *Vanguard Newspaper*:

> Nigerians should dump the two parties because of their bad antecedents over the last 20 years. They've destroyed everything. Looking at their inability to change the economic fortunes of Nigeria for 20 years now, it is now apparently clear that they would not do anything even if Nigerians vote for any of the two parties again. The APC and PDP have formed governments; we were all witnesses. They did not come with good intentions to make amends. If you look at the fight against corruption, all these corrupt people that were supposed to be prosecuted sneaked into the APC. That is why we believe now is the time to establish a platform which every good Nigerian should join and contribute towards building the nation on the right path.

In the above piece, Professor Jega, who witnessed the 2015 general elections in Nigeria warns the citizens to do away with both political parties since their alliance would render it challenging to make any positive impact in Nigeria. Professor Jega urges the citizens to reject the two parties completely for the country to develop. He further states that it is 'lack of good leadership in the country that threw the nation into its current problems, which had led to the series of agitations for the country to be balkanised'. Jega finally called on Nigerians to direct their focus towards new political parties other than the APC and the PDP.

To further highlight the alleged alliance between the two political parties, a statement made by the current Nigerian president, Bola Ahmed Tinubu, who

---

[1] https://africaelects.com/nigeria/

erroneously almost said 'God bless PDP' instead of 'God bless APC', became an item of ridicule on Nigerian social media platforms (Shibayan, 2022). Tinubu was a presidential candidate at the time when he said, 'God bless PD... APC' and realised that the PDP was an opposition party. The compounded acronym, PDAPC, has been used several times on Nigerian social media to make a mockery of the Nigerian political system as one which is irredeemable. Below are some examples of posts that reflected on this issue on Twitter and Facebook:

i. *There's no way u will find good leaders in pdapc. They are transactional leaders. That is why I don't have hope in this country. The best is to leave (SJ, X).*
ii. *Just remember there's an amalgam known as PDAPC in your decision to japa from this country (PE, X).*
iii. *When Tinubu said PDAPC, people were laughing him thinking he made a mistake. From the recent development in River's state, PDP chairman resigned to take a FG in Abuja (JAM, Facebook).*
iv. *PDAPC is doing well, because I have carefully observed that the master Election riggers of the PDP are now APC member. Enjoy your victories while it last (FA, X).*
v. *Jagaban agenda is to make all opposition parties to be one under him. Like PDAPC but LP said no. I don't even know of NNPP. That is why people don't have hope in this country and just want to escape (MM, X).*

The first example by SJ ridicules the current political situation in Nigeria since the standard of governance has appeared to deteriorate following the policies introduced by Bola Ahmed Tinubu inaugurated as president on 29 May 2023. SJ reminds Nigerians that good leadership cannot be expected from either the PDP or the APC since politicians from both parties are transactional leaders. The alliance between the two parties which PE refers to as an amalgam is confirmation that these parties are incapable of producing well-meaning leaders. The current Bola Ahmed Tinubu presidency, despite him being an APC party stalwart, has seen the appointment of some key members of the PDP into the cabinet due to the roles they played in Tinubu's election victory. This point is alluded to by the FA who refers to a PDP state chairman who took an appointment in an APC government, as well as the fifth author who alleges that PDP election manipulators are now members of the APC. President Tinubu, who is fondly referred to as Jagaban by his supporters, is perceived to have an agenda that allows him to control all the opposition parties although the alliance between PDAPC seems to be the most obvious so far.

Drawing conclusions from the above, the negative political atmosphere in Nigeria coupled with the appalling situation of its governance are key factors in the decisions made by citizens to flee from the country. We have established that sociopolitical conditions in a country are key factors that contribute to outmigration. In the case of Nigeria, as the citizens become distressed and despondent because of the country's governance, recourse is made to outmigration to countries perceived to be better alternatives.

Security Concerns in Nigerian Migration Discourse

Political governance failures in the country cause security concerns. Put differently, it would be impossible to separate the security issues in the country from its political instability and bad governance. The insecurity in the country is largely a consequence of bad governance since security is perceived as the primary responsibility of any government. From a global perspective, human security has been a matter of concern since the 1994 Human Development Report by the United Nations Development Programme (UNDP) which attempted to broaden the meaning of security and perhaps, most importantly, challenge the state-centric notion of national security (Lau, 2023). According to Lau (2023), the United Nations (UN) General Assembly in 2012 formally recognised human security as a necessary approach to 'assist Member States in identifying and addressing widespread and cross-cutting challenges to the survival, livelihood and dignity of their people'. Consequently, the UN's attention is focused on the responsibility to protect (R2P) which is a drive against mass atrocities, genocide, war crimes, ethnic cleansing, and all other forms of crimes. In essence, security concerns often receive global attention to avoid the re-occurrence of war-like and criminal situations that have ravaged many parts of the world. With issues of security holding such significant status in the world, the lack of it in one's environment implies a dangerous situation which people must endeavour to evade.

From time immemorial, unrests and disorders have been known to cause migration. Survivors of war-like situations often seek refuge in new environments or countries. In the case of Nigeria, the insecurity in the country is causing strategic outmigration of Nigerian citizens to other countries that seem to value human security more than Nigeria. The last few years have been devastating for many Nigerians in terms of security. For a long time, Boko Haram terrorists continuously killed and maimed people, especially in the northeastern parts of the country. Although political statements in Nigeria tend to claim that Boko Haram has been defeated by the Nigerian government, available evidence does not support these politically motivated assertions. In fact, public discourse in Nigeria now refers to 'bandits' instead of 'terrorists' as a way of implying reduced terrorism in the country despite consistent attempts by the so-called 'bandits' to carry out acts of terrorism. However, a recent catastrophic occurrence in December 2023, when the Nigerian military accidentally killed almost 100 people and injured dozens of several others, saw the Nigerian military admit that they were 'after terrorists', and mistook innocent villagers for terrorists.[2] It can be surmised from the statement that the biggest security challenge in the country is still unsolved. The unintentional killing of innocent civilians by the Nigerian military has occurred for so long that the Nigerian military forces saddled with the responsibility of protecting Nigerian lives have become security threats themselves. Insecurity in Nigeria

---

[2]"Tinubu ya yi tir da harin Filato wanda aka kashe 'fiye da mutum 140'"[Tinubu condemns Plateau attack that killed 'more than 140 people']. *BBC News Hausa* (in Hausa). 26 December 2023.

features so often in everyday discourse that it has now become normalised. As such, discourses of insecurity tend to focus less on restoring security but focus more on coping with the insecure situation of the country. Apart from crimes committed by individuals almost daily, Boko Haram, Islamic State's West Africa Province (ISWAP) which split from Boko Haram, the Fulani Herdsmen crisis, are groups that pose a threat to Nigerian citizens. Further, in a mass shooting at the St. Francis Xavier Catholic Church in Owo, Ondo State of Nigeria, more than 40 worshippers were killed with almost another 100 injured in a massacre that has remained an unsolved mystery since it happened.

In 1973, Nigeria introduced the National Youth Service Corps (NYSC), a national programme set up to assist with nation building and national cohesion (Okafor & Ani, 2014). Eligible graduates of universities and polytechnics in the country are required to participate in the National Youth Service Corps programme for one year – the national service year. To develop national cohesion, graduates are deployed to states/provinces other than their own states/provinces and, in many cases, other than their regions as a way of cross-pollinating with people of other ethnic groups and cultures. Through this process, it is believed that Nigeria can foster intercultural tolerance. The intention of this programme has since been defeated due to insecurity. Reported incidents of Corp Members (graduates) being abducted, robbed, and violently attacked have created resistance among Nigerians who now make efforts to prevent being deployed to distant and unfamiliar territories to avoid similar incidents. While commuting to their different states of primary assignments, stories abound of Corp Members being kidnapped for long periods of time until ransoms are paid by family members or the government. To properly understand how insecurity has been normalised in the country, the NYSC handbook lists certain areas as 'high-risk roads' which members should avoid while commuting to their designated locations for national service. The NYSC scenario aptly captures Nigeria's approach towards insecurity: situations that must be avoided rather than resolved. In another instance, the governor of the most popular state (Lagos) in Nigeria, Babajide Sanwo-Olu, while addressing the incessant traffic robberies in the state that have left the citizens distraught, advised the citizens to always 'roll-up' their car windows while in gridlock (Opejobi, 2018). The notoriety of traffic robberies extends way beyond the governor's proposed solution since perpetrators of these acts are often equipped with tools to shatter car windows. This is another instance of the Nigerian government admitting that it is unable to tackle insecurity issues and that citizens must find ways to cope with the situation.

There are no credible signs that the matter will ever be resolved. Eke et al. (2023) argue that insecurity in the country has metamorphosed from pockets of sectional unrest to a national challenge and that Nigeria is in a war-like situation which continues to pose a serious existential threat to Nigerians. As Andersen-Rodgers and Crawford (2022) argue, a threat, either real or imagined, requires protection from a specified actor. It is the lack of such protection that have led several Nigerians to flee the country. Citing dominant types of insecurity in each geographical region of the country, Eke et al. (2023) confirm that these insecurity concerns have worrisome effects on citizens in their everyday lives. The following

X post by MJ is an instance of the everyday psychological impacts that Nigerians face in terms of insecurity:

> Mahn my husband got a call from NYSC camp where his brother is and he freaked out cos he straight up thought he had been kidnapped or something. Turned out it was camp radio station calling to give him a S/O from his brother. He said 'oh?' followed by a long silence. Lmfaooooo!! (MJ, X)

Above, a woman narrates her husband's experience when he received a call from the NYSC camp where his brother was deployed. Given the incessant stories of kidnapping of Corp Members in the country, the unsolicited call signalled to the husband that his brother had been kidnapped. Upon receiving the call, it became apparent that the intention of the caller was to 'give a shoutout' (greeting) to the brother from the NYSC camp. The husband's reaction after realising the reason for the call was described as a long silence which could be interpreted as him being thankful that his brother has not been kidnapped. Ordinary Nigerians are subjected to everyday mental torture propelled by the insecure nature of the country. It must be recognised however that human security is not just about protection from physical harm but about stability, well-being, freedom, and the capacity of individuals to thrive (Andersen-Rodgers & Crawford, 2022). As has already analysed, *japa* is the Nigerian colloquial term for migration which implies fleeing from an unfavourable situation, and references to *japa* in the examples below are made by Nigerians who intend to flee the country. The examples are drawn from X and Facebook:

i. *Sometimes people don't japa because they want to make it big out there, sometimes they relocate for security reasons, for their kids to have a better life and protection. Imagine staying in a country where you can be killed Fulani herdsmen, a police man can even kill you for refusing to give him #50 bribe. Someone can just snatch you and use you for ritual, because they want to make money. If you can, take yourself and your family out of this country (IS, Facebook).*
ii. *Japa is my sure bet cause I'm sure there's no Fulani herdsmen where I'm going. I'm sure there is no police man extortion where I'm going. I'm sure even if I work on my laptop and have a dread, I won't be tagged as yahoo boy. So make I Japa and leave this dream killer country (ME, Facebook).*
iii. *Another reason why you should japa from Nigeria. Imagine bandits having the courage to invade a whole defense academy. I fear who no fear Nigeria o (JJ, X).*
iv. *Japa o, everyone dey leave for govt and ISWAP....make them face themselves, may we not be caught in between (LA, X).*
v. *Hoodlums are taking over the country, kidnapping everyday, insecurity everywhere.... Japa now seems to be the best alternative because the government is not doing anything (PO, X).*

In the first example by IS, the author attempts to create a nuanced view of the Nigerian *japa* syndrome by stating that matters of insecurity are dominant in migration discourse. The author states that for many outmigrants, the motive is not necessarily the desire for sudden economic growth, as many would love to believe, but the insecurity already engrained in Nigeria. Outmigrants choose to also relocate for the purpose of living in a more secure environment where their lives and those of their kids would be better protected. The author cites the Fulani herdsmen violence, police brutality, and ritual killings. The situation surrounding Fulani herdsmen violence in Nigeria has been unresolved for a long time. The Fulani herdsmen from the Fulani tribe have a long-term practice of open grazing: they roam and guide their animals along open fields in search of food, water, and shelter. Cattle farming is a sector dominated by the Fulani tribe, which means that sighting cows feeding in open fields, the immediate assumption is that the herdsman is Fulani. The troubles brought about by this open grazing is therefore instantly construed to be caused by Fulani herdsmen. Since the land spaces used for grazing are random and often belong to other people, owners vehemently started to reject open grazing. Furthermore, the land spaces often used for farming in some cases result in cows feeding on people's agricultural produce. Since Fulani herdsmen find open grazing much affordable than close grazing, they insist on leading their animals across people's farms to feed freely.

Consequently, there is often huge disagreements between farmers/landowners and herdsmen that have resulted in violent killings of several farmers where the herdsmen reverted to violence. According to Akinyetun (2016, p. 94):

> [T]he Fulani in the course of carrying out their pastoral nomadic activities has been seen to have changed tactics from mere land grazing to barrel-induced-land grazing. In short, the spate of killing and kidnappings as perpetuated by the Fulani nomads calls for great concern before this fetus is given birth to and culminates into another sect, or plunges the country into a primitive, primordial and pedestrian state of nastiness, solitary and brute.

The violence on several farmlands has led to reprisal attacks, also resulting in fatalities amongst both the herdsmen and the farmers. Many Nigerians have called on the government to ban open grazing since the crisis also brought about religious undertones. The Fulani herdsmen are predominantly Muslim which has led to the death of many Christians especially where Christian farmers resist the use of their lands for open grazing. This ongoing crisis has existed for so long that Nigerians have given up hope that the situation would ever be resolved while farmers and herders scheme against one another. Duke and Agbaji (2020) note that the herders contaminate water by dragging their cattle into water ponds while farmers poison the water ponds with harmful insecticides meant to kill and prevent the pastoralists from contaminating their only source of water. They further contend that the Fulani herdsmen crisis, deemed only less deadly than Boko Haram, has grievous repercussions that threaten the country's national security. It is not surprising that the Fulani herdsmen crisis is mentioned in the first two examples above; Nigerians are concerned that the deadly Fulani herdsmen crisis in the country, which grows daily, could worsen. The perceived lack of protection from sudden and hurtful disruptions in the pattern of Nigerian daily lives (UNDP, 1994) has put the issue of security at the centre of migration discussions in Nigeria. According to Andersen-Rodgers and Crawford (2022), human security can only exist when individuals and communities are safe from both chronic, long-term threats to their well-being and from more sudden threats to their physical safety.

Also, IS's reference to ritual killings spotlights one of the longstanding barbaric vices in Nigeria where human sacrifice is perceived as a way to sudden wealth and riches. Kidnapping as mentioned in the fifth example takes place for many other reasons as well, for example organ harvesting and ransom demands. The death of the 22-year-old Bamise in December 2022, who was found dead with private organs cut off after boarding a Bus Rapid Transit (BRT) in Lagos, as well as the murder of a young Justina Nkang Otuene who was also dismembered by her boyfriend in October 2023, are a few killings that have been attributed to rituals and organ harvesting. Regardless of the motive, these sad events further underscore the precarious nature of the country and why outmigrants make security a focal factor of their decisions. The reality that ritual killings or organ harvesting are recurrent experiences in the country in itself is concerning. In the first example, IS states clearly that in Nigeria, 'someone can just snatch you and use you for ritual, because they want to make money'.

Salihu et al. (2019) state that thousands of innocent Nigerians across all ages have been killed and their body parts severed for money ritual sacrifices, and although the practice seems to have been suspended in Nigeria for a long time, there has been a recent upsurge in taking people's lives for money ritual sacrifices in the country. Salihu et al. (2019) ascribe the recent surge in this barbaric act to socio-economic challenges in the country. Put differently, the harsh economic reality in the country forces young people especially to consider quicker and illegal approaches to obtain money. Reports suggest that these young people are manipulated to believe that rituals can transform their financial lives while the bodies are in fact being used for organ trafficking. Although this study cannot delve into the potency (or lack of it) of 'money rituals', they remain barbaric acts that have continued to permeate the country. These realities further add to the myriad of security problems already ravaging the country which have become motivating factors for migration. The further realisation that the Nigerian government has paid little attention to this problem despite its frequency is in fact a strong motive to flee from the country. Abidde (2021) confirms that most traffickers and criminal syndicates involved in human trafficking are never arrested and/or prosecuted since the government barely considers this practice a national security challenge. The government still views national security and national interests in terms of power projection: expelling external threats, imprisoning dissidents, and outlawing domestic groups and individuals that challenge or pose a threat to state authority.

Reference is made to police extortion and brutality in the first and second examples. Instances of extra-judicial killings as well as brutality by the Nigerian police have occurred for a long time which has also caused thousands of Nigerians to leave the country. The ENDSARS protests referred to in the third chapter of this book derive directly from cases of police brutality. The corrupt nature of the Nigerian Police is not news; it is an identity they have had for decades. With numerous illegal police checkpoints set up across different areas of the country, many times, within short intervals from one another, the Nigerian police are notorious for receiving bribes on roads from drivers without conducting any actual checking. Adisa et al. (2020) confirm that for a long time in Nigeria, public outcry over the incidence of police corruption in Nigeria has increased despite concerted efforts to reform the police and improve their service delivery. It is expected that individuals should be able to live their lives free from physical violence, as well as systemic deprivation, adversity, inequity, and human rights violations (Andersen-Rodgers & Crawford, 2022).

Reports abound of instances when drivers who resist extortion from triggerhappy Nigerian policemen have resulted in violent reactions from the policemen who have killed innocent citizens for refusing to give unwarranted bribes. The statement 'a police man can even kill you for refusing to give him #50 bribe' in Example 1 above speaks for itself. It is indeed a reality that the refusal of a civilian, who has not committed any offence, to willingly give a policeman a bribe has resulted in the killings of many Nigerians and despite the call by ordinary Nigerians for the police to be reformed, the matter has continued to aggravate. There have been several cases of police wrongful profiling of common Nigerians, threatening them, and in fact, forcing them to make cash transfers or withdraw large amount of money to hand over to the police in order to avoid being arrested. Since it appears that these problems cannot be solved, the need to avoid police brutality by migrating is evident in the second example: 'I'm sure there is no police man extortion where I'm going'. In other words, the reality in the destination country presents the police as a helpful people rather than a party to insecurity which is the situation in Nigeria.

Cases of kidnapping for ransom in Nigeria have been mostly attributed to banditry. 'Bandits', as Nigerians refer to them, have committed many atrocities and have gone unchecked for a long time. Okoli and Abubakar (2021) intimate that armed banditry is prevalent in Nigeria, and it has competed with insurgency for the soul of Nigeria's national security. Reports of bandits kidnapping and seeking hefty ransoms are circulated around Nigeria, and ordinary citizens are fearful to travel along highways. This reflects strongly in PO's post: 'Hoodlums are taking over the country, kidnapping everyday, insecurity everywhere…. Japa now seems to be the best alternative because the government is not doing anything'. The author laments the poor security in Nigeria suggesting that it has become a daily reality where the best alternative is to leave the country since the government is incapable of ensuring human security. JJ also strongly advises Nigerians to flee after an incident that saw bandits invade the Nigerian Defense Academy (NDA) in August 2021. Two officers were killed in the process while the bandits abducted a senior officer. The NDA is an institution where cadet officers are trained to be deployed in the Nigerian Armed Forces. It would be expected that such an institution would be well guarded and secured, but the lack of adequate security at the NDA affirmed to Nigerians that even the military is incapable of protecting its citizens if bandits can successfully invade the academy to kill and abduct officers.

The bandits have also been reported to invade university hostels where they rape and abduct students, especially in the Northern Nigeria. The effrontery of these bandits to attack the NDA, and the possibility of further spreading their camps across Nigeria make many Nigerians feel that security problems in the country have become emboldened rather than mitigated.

In this chapter, we have examined how political issues, as well as security matters, reflect heavily in Nigerian migration discourse. Issues surrounding bad governance, political activities, insecurity among others find their way into Nigerian social media spaces daily with many narrating their experiences as well as commenting on the dreadful state of the nation. The current reality of the country has been vastly attributed to the unending cycle of bad governance which has now been exacerbated by the lack of adequate security in the country especially in recent years. Since migration discourse carries with it the lived realities of the participants, the experiences of many Nigerians regarding politics and security, as portrayed on social media platforms, have thus been reproduced in this chapter vis-à-vis how they concern migration. Generally, migration discourse in Nigeria might feature less security concerns if people feel that basic needs are being met today, and will continue to be met for the foreseeable future (Andersen-Rodgers & Crawford, 2022). By and large, the failure of the Nigerian government to be responsible for the protection of the Nigerian citizens is a concern for many Nigerians that has warranted migration.

References

Abidde, S. O. (2021). Trafficking in body parts and human organs for commercial and non-commercial purposes in Africa. In A. D. Hoffman & S. O. Abidde (Eds.), *Human trafficking in Africa: New paradigms, new perspectives* (pp. 205–214). Cham.

Adisa, W. B., Alabi, T., & Adejoh, S. (2020). Corruption on the road: A test of commercial drivers' encounters with police extortion in Lagos Metropolis. *Journal of Police and Criminal Psychology, 35*, 389–399.

Akintunde, S. M., Okey, O. D., Ahiara, W. C., Olaleye, T. O., & Okewale, O. A. (2023). A sentiment-aware statistical evaluation of Vawulence Tweets for cyberbullying analytics. In M. Lahby, A. K. Pathan, & Y. Maleh (Eds.), *Combatting cyberbullying in digital media with Artificial Intelligence*. CRC Press.

Akinyetun, T. (2016). Staff to gun: Fulani herdsmen in Nigeria. *Asian Journal of Multidisciplinary Studies, 4*(8), 38–44.

Andersen-Rodgers, D., & Crawford, K. F. (2022). *Human security: Theory and action*. Rowman & Littlefield.

Bainbridge, W. S. (2000). Religious ethnography on the World Wide Web. In K. Hadden & D. E. Cowan (Eds.), *Religion on the internet: Research prospects and promises* (pp. 55–80). Elsevier.

BBC News Hausa. (2021, January 22). *Attahiru Jega: Abubuwa uku da tsohon shugaban INEC ya lissafa kan sake fasalin Najeriya*. https://www.bbc.com/hausa/labarai-55755180

Duke, O., & Agbaji, D. D. (2020). Fulani herdsmen crisis and the socioeconomic development of Benue State, Nigeria. *International Journal of Scientific and Research Publications, 10*(8), 343–357.

Eke, C. O., Nsereka, B. G., & Whyte, D. H. (2023). Newspaper coverage of corruption and insecurity during Buhari's administration: A comparative analysis of the nation and the punch editorials. *The International Journal of African Language and Media Studies (IJALMS)*, *3*(1), 142–154.

Eme-Uche, U., & Eme, O. (2023). The politics of exclusion & governance in Nigeria: A thematic analysis of the Buhari Administration. *International Journal of Social Science and Human Research*, *6*(2), 1092–1110.

Hoffmann, K., Vlassenroot, K., Carayannis, T., & Muzalia, G. (2021). Violent conflict and ethnicity in the Congo: Beyond materialism, primordialism and symbolism. *Conflict, Security & Development*, *20*(5), 539–560.

Igwe, P., & Amadi, L. (2021). Democracy and political violence in Nigeria since multi-party politics in 1999: A critical appraisal. *Open Political Science*, *4*(1), 101–119. https://doi.org/10.1515/openps-2021-0011

Lau, R. K. S. (2023). Operationalizing human security: What role for the responsibility to protect? *International Studies*, *60*(1), 29–44.

Matamanda, A. R., & Mphambukeli, T. N. (2022). Urban (in)security in an emerging human settlement: Perspectives from Hopley Farm Settlement, Harare, Zimbabwe. *Frontiers in Sustainable Cities*, *4*, 933869.

Okafor, C., & Ani, J. K. (2014). The National Youth Service Corps programme and growing security threat in Nigeria. *Africa's Public Service Delivery & Performance Review*, *2*(2), 149–164.

Okoli, A. C., & Abubakar, M. (2021). 'Crimelordism': Understanding a new phenomenon in armed banditry in Nigeria. *Journal of Asian and African Studies*, *56*(7), 1724–1737.

Opejobi, S. (2018, October 2). Tinubu 'anointed' candidate, Sanwo-Olu defeats Ambode in Alausa. *Daily Post Nigeria*. https://dailypost.ng/2018/10/02/tinubu-anointed-candidate-sanwo-olu-defeats-ambode-alausa/

Persaud, R. B. (2022). Human security. In A. Collins (Ed.), *Contemporary security studies* (pp. 144–158). Oxford University Press.

Salihu, H. A., Isiaka, M., & Abdulaziz, I. (2019). The growing phenomenon of money rituals-motivated killings in Nigeria: An empirical investigation into the factors responsible. *UKH Journal of Social Sciences*, *3*(2), 32–44.

Shibayan, D. (2022, November 15). EXTRA: Tinubu suffers gaffe, says 'God bless PD… APC' (video) | TheCable. *TheCable*. https://www.thecable.ng/extra-tinubu-suffers-gaffe-says-god-bless-pd-apc-video/

Siloko, B. E. (2024). Human security, sustainable livelihoods, and development: The case of the Niger Delta region in Nigeria. *Global Discourse*, *14*(2–3), 411–432.

Umotong, I. D. (2020). Ethnic politics in nation building: The African perspective. *Ifiok: Journal of Interdisciplinary Studies*, *5*(1), 1–13.

UNDP. (1994). *Human development report 1994*. Oxford University Press.

Van Dijk, T. A. (2018). Discourse and migration. In R. Zapata Barrero & E. Yalaz (Eds.), *Qualitative research in European migration studies. IMISCOE Research Series* (pp. 227–245). Cham.

Vanguard Newspaper. (2021, August 3). APC, PDP've ruined Nigeria, don't vote them again – JEGA. https://www.vanguardngr.com/2021/08/apc-pdpve-ruined-nigeria-dont-vote-them-again-jega/

Zubairu, N. (2020). Rising insecurity in Nigeria: Causes and solution. *Journal of Studies in Social Sciences*, *19*(1), 1–11.

Chapter 6

Co-existence of Power and Powerlessness in Nigerian Migration Discourse

Keywords: Power; powerlessness; financial capacity; migration; myths and misconceptions

Migration discourse in Nigeria has, from generation to generation, espoused dreams of greener pastures in other lands. This chapter focuses on myths and misconceptions in discourses of migration in Nigeria vis-à-vis power and powerlessness. Power and powerlessness in this chapter are rhetorical terms that do not mean physical energy, but in the Nigerian context, they refer to matters of status and privilege (economic, social, occupational). With the proliferation of social media in the current era, migrants share updates about their living conditions abroad although some of these updates are exaggerated. In return, the people back home who have not migrated are given the impression that living in the diaspora yields easy rewards. In these social media conversations, Nigeria can be made to appear powerful or powerless depending on context. This chapter explores the complex interplay of power dynamics within the context of migration narratives from Nigeria, particularly as they are represented and reshaped on social media platforms.

Guccione (2022) contends that globalisation, with its new long-distance communication technologies, has enabled migrants to maintain active communication with their fellow countrymen and to introduce new forms of identity, community establishment and cooperation that have replaced the multiculturalism that characterised early migrations. In the same vein, Guillem (2015) observes that recent research studies emphasise the stronger and more continuous contact that migrants of the internet era often have with their places of origin, including exposure to their native languages, popular culture products, or political and economic debates. Hence, the structure and content of different kinds of social media such as Facebook, Twitter, or YouTube, offer more options for a continuous back-and-forth movement between cultures, which arguably shapes migrants' experiences in new and interesting ways (Guillem 2015). This chapter is entrenched in what Schiller et al. (1992) captured as transnationalism which is used to describe how immigrants live their lives across borders and maintain their ties to home, even when their countries of origin and settlement are geographically distant. Most social media posts tend to portray Nigeria and its residents as powerless while outmigrants and their new countries are considered powerful. It goes without saying that powerful or wealthier people find it easier to migrate since migration is an expensive process. People who have been fortunate enough to be able to migrate often return feeling more powerful or privileged than others who have remained in Nigeria. At the same time, the less wealthy, who have remained in Nigeria, believe that outmigrants gain financial prosperity by merely moving to economically advanced countries. This is where matters of power and powerlessness become critical. This chapter examines interactions between the powerful and the powerless in Nigeria based on popular discussions on social media.

Many countries in the Global North display their power by introducing policies that attract immigrants. These policies are constantly discussed and exploited by Nigerians to serve their migration motives. In fact, Nigerians keep themselves abreast of critical migration policies in migrant-friendly countries as they scheme to find the 'perfect' destinations for themselves and their families. Power and powerlessness are also strongly reflected in the choice of country for migration. For instance, based on social media discourse on migration, African countries do not appeal to many Nigerians. However, many are forced to consider African countries due to budget constraints, which is often a means of plotting onward relocation to another country. In the same vein, not all countries in Europe appeal to Nigerians, but many migrate to less popular European countries as an avenue to migrate to another country with more stable immigrant policies. This represents another sign of power in migration discourse since a path to citizenship or permanent residence is one of the major determinants in the choice of a destination country. The popularity and status of countries according to international standards also relate to power depending on whether a country is a destination country or origin country. For instance, Nigeria is mostly considered an origin country thus making Nigeria powerless. As such, many young Nigerians intending to migrate are attracted to countries such as Canada, the United States of America, the United Kingdom, and Australia as their destination countries which are considered powerful. The popular perception is that living in any of these countries would be beneficial to the migrant and those that remain behind. More importantly, migrating to such countries often reflect power and confidence on the part of the migrants. Power and powerlessness in Nigerian migration discourse are about status and living experiences. A discussion follows below on how power and powerlessness in Nigerian migration discourse draws credence from social media narratives.

Method

As with other chapters, netnography has again been employed to gather relevant data for this chapter. According to Bainbridge (2000, p. 57), netnography is 'a relatively passive examination of web sites, without full interaction with the people who created them'. In gathering relevant information for this chapter, certain keywords were sought on Facebook and Twitter which include: IJGB, goodbye Nigeria, POF, UK, NHS, detty December, Canada, cost of living, health workers, rule of law, ease of doing business, Doctors, nurses, tech sector, japa, policy, and professionals. Discourses produced on Facebook and Twitter relating to these keywords were selected based on their appropriateness to this study. In order to keep the authors of the social media posts anonymous, we have used initials to identify them. The keywords revealed very diverse information which led to the categorisation of the gathered data under several power versus powerlessness themes which include: (i) socio-economic rhetoric in Nigerian migration discourse, (ii) reactions to migration requirements, (iii) comparing Nigeria with the diaspora, and (iv) individual and national implications. These themes present a nuanced understanding of power versus powerlessness in the Nigerian migration context.

Power and Powerlessness: Analysis of Socio-Economic Rhetoric in Nigerian Migration Discourse

Major indications of power demonstrated in Nigerian migration discourse derive from the patriotic views of some citizens who, despite the significant rate of migration, have refused to migrate citing their connection to the country as a major factor. Instances abound on social media of users who disregard the tough socio-economic realities in the country as possible reasons for migration. The examples below are from Twitter and Facebook:

i. *It's been long I saw 'goodbye Nigeria, the evil you have done is enough' on twitter. The ones that went abroad and denigrated the country have told others that the grass is not greener on the other side (DE, X).*
ii. *I cannot understand how people are excited to live their fatherland and live in other countries. It can't be me. We are going to fight it out in Nigeria (EN, X).*
iii. *The cost of living abroad is on the rise daily. If you are earning averagely well in Nigeria, just stay here. No point going anywhere else. This is home and no place can be like home (BA, Facebook).*

Evident in the above examples is patriotism strongly reflected in Nigerian migration discourse as some citizens resist the urge to migrate. The first example captures DE's view who has not recently witnessed the social media usage of the popular phrase discussed in Chapter 3, namely 'Goodbye Nigeria, The Evil You Have Done Is Enough'. Some outmigrants liken the sad living conditions in Nigeria to evil and when they depart from Nigeria, they post the phrase on social media to signify that they are relocating to countries with better living conditions. It is however the view of social media user (i) that such outmigrants are denigrating Nigeria by likening the country to evil. The author states that a decrease in the use of the phrase is an indication that the greener pastures earlier outmigrants were in search of have not been realised, and that the later generation of outmigrants has become aware of the disappointment. For EN, he expressed his lack of interest in living in other countries based on the singular reason that Nigeria is his fatherland, and he is ready to tackle the abundant challenges in his own country. The third example reflects on living expenses abroad which a lot of outmigrants often complain about. It is the belief of BA that people earning decent salaries in Nigeria should remain in the country and shun the idea of relocating to unfamiliar countries. However, as established in the third and fifth chapters, financial growth is not the only reason for Nigerian outmigration.

Notwithstanding the patriotism of Nigerians as demonstrated in the above examples, Uchechukwu (2019) argues that patriotism is fast diminishing in Nigeria due to the failure of the Nigerian state to fulfil its promise of a good life to the people aggravated by the hedonistic lifestyles of the political class. Thus, in contrast to available patriotic evidence that would suggest a certain degree of 'power' in Nigeria, major indications of powerlessness are observable in Nigerian migration discourse signifying the absence of patriotism among despondent citizens. According to ON's post on X (formerly Twitter), *most people still living in Nigeria now, are there, because they can't get visa to run to the country of their dreams. Not because 'home is the best' or that they 'love' Nigeria.*

The author of the post contradicts the perceived patriotism among Nigerians by arguing that their lack of interest in migration is caused by a lack of financial capacity to migrate to their desired countries. The notions that *'home is best'* or that they *'love'* Nigeria are demystified thus implying that with adequate resources, even seemingly patriotic Nigerians would consider migrating to countries with better opportunities. Arguably, the first factor to consider when migrating is the availability of financial resources. Many Nigerian outmigrants explore several means to gather the required funds to migrate. A study conducted by Okeke-Ihejirika and Odimegwu (2023) shows that many Nigerian migrants fell into heavy financial debt in their efforts to travel abroad as some sell their belongings, including landed property, in a bid to raise enough funds. They further observe that in some cases, financial responsibilities are often distributed across family members with the assumption that their investments will yield a substantial return once the beneficiary arrives abroad. In few cases, beneficiaries are even warned by family members not to return to Nigeria until all debts incurred in the process of migration have been repaid. The financial commitment associated with migration is so exorbitant that only Nigerians with means can successfully migrate. This is the contextual background to the position of the author in the X post, namely that for many, the lack of interest in leaving, although masquerading as patriotism, can in fact be attributed to the absence of finance.

For many Nigerians, migration-friendly countries are those that have friendly policies, particularly in relation to the funds that they require from potential migrants. Available migration routes to countries such as Canada, the USA, the UK, and Australia for instance are often dependent on a certain amount of funds required from potential migrants. This reality further entrenches the power versus powerlessness argument in Nigerian migration discourse. Taking these countries as case studies, migrant-friendly countries are first-world countries which are assumed to be more industrialised and have better economies, which sharply contrast with Nigeria, a third-world country with a poor economy. Migration discourses often depict first-world countries as powerful and Nigeria as powerless due to its harsh economic status. According to the World Data Lab (2023), over 70 million people in Nigeria are living in extreme poverty which represents 32% of the country's population. As Obi-Ani et al. (2020) put it, Nigeria has regressed to become the new poverty capital of the world, displacing India in the inglorious top spot. Canada, the USA, the UK, and Australia all have 0% of their populations living in extreme poverty. Otekunrin et al. (2019) also stress that the poverty situation in Nigeria is escalating with a huge percentage of the population now living in abject poverty with no signs of improvement. Ironically, the first-world countries invite migrants from countries with severe poverty pandemics. Ironically, the poor remain in Nigeria, while the wealthy relocate from the already poor Nigerian economy to countries with blossoming economies. Migration policies from these countries often put emphasis on financial capacities of the potential migrants.

Power and Powerlessness: Analysis of Reactions to Migration Requirements

In the final months of 2023, Canada and the UK revised their immigration policies for international students which is one of the routes that Nigerians have explored to relocate and settle abroad (Immigration, Refugees and Citizenship Canada Departmental Plan 2023-2024, 2024; Office, 2023). While Canada increased proof of living expenses required from each applicant by more than a hundred percent, the UK increased the compulsory National Health Service (NHS) Surcharge by above 65% per year for each applicant. Over time, the fastest migration route for many Nigerians has been through the study abroad channel since this process mainly requires seeking admission and demonstrating the required proof of funds. The updated required funds by Canada and the UK have thus elicited a variety of social media responses from Nigerians. Some of the reactions on X (formerly Twitter) include:

i. *On this immigration journey, procrastination is dangerous. It is now or never (DW, X).*
ii. *Na wa oh! But we must move to this Canada. The POF will not deter us (AY, X).*
iii. *Canada has increased POF, naira is losing the battle. Which way japa? (AD, X).*
iv. *Canada is really frustrating young Nigerians with this their new POF policy (DD, X).*
v. *Those planning to go to UK are in trouble. Una money go long o. UK increasing visa application and NHS fees. Una go need break bank to meet up (FO, X).*

Through satirical lamentations, Nigerians display their concerns over the increment of required funds for migration. The first example confirms the popular saying that 'procrastination is the thief of time' from Edward Young's poem to imply that people must be prompt in taking necessary actions lest opportunities slip away. Thus, Nigerians are being encouraged to hasten their migration processes. This is in response to the increment of required funds as well as more stringent measures constantly being adopted by migrant-friendly countries. As such, Nigeria is perceived as the powerless country where the citizens must do all they can to move to the powerful countries before they shut their doors or before the processes become even more cumbersome. The second example by AY clarifies this further. The term *na wa oh!* derives from Nigerian pidgin to represent sighs, lamentations, and tiredness. As such, the author of the post could be said to have exhaled loudly after reading the new finance requirements for Canada. The POF in the post signifies 'proof of funds' which implies the amount of money required to travel to Canada. And with over a hundred percent increment in the required POF as announced in December 2023 for international students, the author's desire to relocate to Canada remains active; he will not be discouraged. The author is determined to move to Canada and will not be deterred by increased financial requirements.

The author of the third example, AD, demonstrates a sense of confusion with the rhetorical question – *which way japa?* Translated, which way in the Nigerian context implies *what next?* In other words, what are the chances we are presented with in this migration adventure especially given the increase of financial requirements in Canadian Dollars compared to Naira which is on a steady decline. The impression created is that a vast majority of Nigerians are already struggling to achieve the existing proof of funds and that the increment presents even more obstacles for Nigerians who rely on their weak currency to prove their financial status. The increment results in frustration for many Nigerians, so the fourth example accuses Canada of frustrating Nigerians with their new proof of funds policy. In reality, the new policy does not target Nigerians as it applies to everyone across the world who intend to travel to Canada for study purposes. However, Nigerians believe they are being targeted due to the high number of Nigerians who harbour migration plans. In the last example, FO envisages financial challenges for people planning to relocate to the UK. Due to the increment in the cost of visa applications as well as NHS fees, the author, using Nigerian pidgin makes direct reference to financial requirements stating that *'Una money go long o'* and *'Una go need break bank to meet up'*. Translated, this means *'you will need a lot of money'* while the latter means that *'it will cost a fortune to meet up with the financial requirements'*. Since most Nigerians explore travel opportunities as a means to relocate their families, travelling to first-world countries is even more exorbitant for Nigerians as adequate funds also need to be demonstrated for dependents.

The reality is that for most Nigerians, the challenges brought by these increments are severe. The almost everyday decline in the value of the Nigerian Naira against the strong currencies of first-world countries aggravates the financial positions of migrants. Okeke-Ihejirika and Odimegwu (2023) also intimate that the Naira is highly unstable, and its steady decline has radically decimated its purchasing power thus leaving average Nigerians hovering on the poverty line.

Co-existence of Power and Powerlessness in Nigerian Migration Discourse   89

This further exacerbates the powerlessness in Nigeria. The dwindling currency is in fact one of the reasons for migrating according to the findings of Okeke-Ihejirika and Odimegwu (2023) who argue that the prospects of escaping or sending a relative to the West is a temptation many Nigerians cannot resist.

Another significant example of the co-existence of power and powerlessness in Nigerian migration discourse is reflected in the choice of countries considered in migration plans. This is reflected in the example below by DW, a popular Nigerian X user who specialises in producing migration contents (see Fig. 1):

> If you cannot afford USA🇺🇸 or Canada🇨🇦, I can always recommend Portugal 🇵🇹, Finland🇫🇮, Malta🇲🇹, Austria🇦🇹, Czech Republic🇨🇿, Luxembourg🇱🇺, Italy🇮🇹, France 🇫🇷
>
> Start from somewhere first, atleast in a country where you are sure of constant electricity, data, water and fresh air.

Fig. 1.   Information Regarding Migration Opportunities for Nigerians (DW, X).

The tone of the X post points to an existing preference for the USA and Canada. Since funding is becoming a bigger challenge due to increased financial requirements and the depreciating Naira, migrating to these countries is becoming harder for Nigerians. As such, other countries such as Portugal and Finland become alternatives to consider. The countries suggested in the post are all in Europe. And like this post, other similar migration posts on Nigerian social media rarely feature African or Asian countries although many feature Australia and New Zealand. The author of the post advises Nigerians not to be deterred by the cost of moving to Canada or the USA and to also consider other countries with better living conditions than Nigeria. Advising Nigerians to 'start somewhere' presupposes that the USA and Canada are long-term ambitions but that the journey can begin in countries where they can save enough to afford this dream. Nigerian migration discourse thus categorises certain destination countries as more powerful than others. In a Facebook post, ABI states that *'everyone is sleeping on these small countries in the EU because they all want UK, Canada, US and Australia. You all need to wake up and try these other countries as ladders to go to your dream destination before it is too late. They are even cheaper. Many of the countries even allow you to move with your family members as a student. Don't waste all your time in Nigeria abeg'*. In this post, the author encourages Nigerians to attempt European Union (EU) countries in their migration plans as a means to proceed to their dream countries. Affordable migration costs as well as family unification factors are highlighted as significant reasons to relocate to EU countries although these are not the final goal. In another X post by DW, the difference in the financial requirements of some countries is represented as follows (see Fig. 2):

90 Social Constructions of Migration in Nigeria and Zimbabwe

> JAPA Education budget for one person with this NAIRA inflation:
>
> -UK🇬🇧: Atleast 25M (1 yr Msc)
>
> -Canada🇨🇦: Atleast 30M
>
> -USA🇺🇸: Atleast 30M
>
> -Finland🇫🇮: Around 7M (scholarship) and 15M (Paid)
>
> -Austria🇦🇹, Czech Republic🇨🇿, Portugal🇵🇹: 5-6M
>
> -Malta🇲🇹 -12-13M

Fig. 2. Rough Estimates of Migration Expenses for Nigerians (DW, X).

While EU countries are indeed less expensive, a large population of Nigerians would still be unable to afford the seemingly reasonable options. Many have nevertheless successfully migrated, and these people can be considered powerful while those who fail are considered powerless in the context of Nigerian migration. Here is where issues of status appear robustly in discussions surrounding power and powerlessness in Nigerian migration discourse.

Power and Powerlessness: Comparing Nigeria with the Diaspora

Several Nigerians attribute living abroad to being privileged while everything Nigerian is viewed from a negative lens. Some Nigerians who have lived abroad for short periods return to Nigeria with altered accents from speaking British or American English. Some invest a lot of energy in demonstrating to people living in Nigeria that they have just returned from the UK, the USA, Canada, or Australia and use phrases in conversations such as *'I just got back'* which has been acronymised as IJGB in popular parlance across the country. For a long time, IJGB has been deployed to make sarcastic references to people returning temporarily to Nigeria during festive seasons to display their wealth and boast about their better living conditions.

It is common practice in Nigeria for citizens living in the diaspora to return to the country every December to celebrate the festive season with families. The discourse surrounding this practice has demonstrated the interplay between power and powerlessness; those who reside abroad are regarded as powerful, while those in Nigeria are perceived as powerless. In fact, there is the general perception that Nigerians living abroad are wealthier than Nigerians living at home, resulting in an attempt by the latter to exploit this by making demands for financial assistance.

Below, we reproduce selected social media posts from X and Facebook that best depict the co-existence of power and powerlessness from the perspective of status in Nigerian migration discourse:

i. *If you go out enough in Lagos, you'd know detty December isn't for you and sit at home. It is for the tourists and IJGB (OB, X).*
ii. *The way IJGB snatch people's girlfriends in this Nigeria is alarming ... (DD, X).*
iii. *IJGB routine. Visit Nigeria in December after a year away and complain about everything like they've never been familiar with it. 'This heat is crazy. How do you people cope?' 'Why are these roads bad? Don't you guys complain to the leaders?' (FR, X).*
iv. *I have just relocated and would have joined these batch of IJGB in Lagos but I need to practice my accent well first. So next year please (MO, X).*
v. *People in Nigeria often overlook the fact that Nigerians abroad have their own financial responsibilities, focusing solely on the money sent back. Even if someone is earning $140k per annum, it is still not sufficient to clear the accumulated debts the person owes (FR, Facebook).*
vi. *Nigeria is so broke. Most of us rely on the money sent to us by friends and families living abroad. This is my motivation to get out of this terrible country (FB, Facebook).*

As already mentioned, IJGBs are temporary returnees who visit Nigeria and spend lavishly during December periods. Since the Nigerian currency is weak, returnees often expend their funds in flamboyant ways compared to citizens who reside and earn in the country. To fully enjoy their experiences, IJGBs in Nigeria, often return to Lagos which is the most exciting city in the country. During December, services tend to be more expensive since the locals are aware that IJGBs as well as tourists visit the country with hard currencies. This is what OB refers to in the first example while advising people who reside in Lagos to reduce their recreational activities as the period is dominated by a group of people who can afford to spend more money than Nigerians living in Nigeria. To further emphasise his point, the author refers to the period as *'detty December'* which can be interpreted as *'spending December'*.

The term *'detty'* is borrowed from the word *'dirty'* to imply a period of the year when IJGBs spend a significant amount of money in the country without restraint. Thus, the author warns those who earn in local currency to recuse themselves from *'detty December'* while allowing IJGBs and tourists to do the spending. It is not news that in many parts of the world, the December period is marked by celebrations and festivities. However, the powerlessness of the Nigerian state is made evident by the fact that festivities are enabled by income earned from other countries considered more powerful. The December period, spearheaded by IJGBs, is characterised with a variety of social dynamics which include behavioural changes in some Nigerians, as the author of the second example highlights. The author laments the way IJGBs deploy their wealth to destroy relationships; heart-wrenchingly described as the *snatching of girlfriends*. The use of heartbreak emojis emphasises the message. Since IJGBs are believed to be privileged and wealthy, many returning IJGBs (mostly men), deploy their savings to sway young women thus influencing the women to leave their partners. The display of wealth by IJGBs for a short period in December illustrates the interplay between power and powerlessness in the discourse of migration. People, gifts, and funds from abroad tend to assume more powerful status over everything Nigerian in what has been a recurrent cycle of powerlessness on the part of Nigeria.

Not only do IJGBs portray Nigeria as powerless, but also emphasise the powerlessness in Nigeria by drawing comparisons with their new countries. This point is affirmed in the second post by DD where the author makes a mockery of common statements made by IJGBs. In what the author terms IJGB routine, he berates the pride demonstrated by Nigerians who can live abroad. According to him, IJGBs visit Nigeria after living abroad for only a year, then complain excessively about Nigeria as though they are not already familiar with the country. For instance, IJGBs complain about the heat, the poor roads, and the bad leaders. The intention of the IJGBs here is to demonstrate power in a way that suggests they live in more developed countries with fewer governance problems. Often present in such discussions are comparisons with Global North countries with excellent road networks, good electricity supply, as well as leaders who are more responsible and accountable. For many IJGBs, merely living in the diaspora is a sign of status upgrade and this is reflected in their communication. In the fourth example, MO sarcastically refers to accent as one of the characteristics of the IJGBs. The author who has recently relocated abroad according to the post is unable to join the current batch of IJGBs who have returned to Nigeria in December 2023 since she has not perfected her British or American accents. Thus, the author intends to learn to understand European and American accents ahead of the following year to join the IJGBs.

That many Nigerians abroad alter their accents to sound American or British is not new. Discarding the Nigerian or perhaps African accent is seen as a sign of status upgrade since it presents an obvious distinction in the mannerisms of Nigerians at home, and the Nigerians who live abroad. Since the American and European accents are considered by many Nigerians abroad as superior to the Nigerian accent, speaking in a foreign accent is perceived as a sign of power. A study by Ugwuanyi and Oyebola (2022) investigated the attitudes of Nigerian expatriates towards the English accent. They found that as Nigerians settle in new communities, they enter new linguistic ecologies, which tend to influence their linguistic behaviours, and they found that this significantly impacts on attitudes towards the new (varieties of) languages to which they are exposed. Their results indicate that compared to the Nigerian English, British English is rated more positively for both status and solidarity. The prestige ascribed to British as well as American accents over the Nigerian accent again shows the interplay between power and powerlessness in Nigerian migration discourse. Even in Nigeria, the local accent is reduced to powerlessness while foreign accents are uplifted and extolled.

Another critical aspect of Nigerian migration discourse is the issue of misconstrued perception. For instance, many Nigerians at home have the overrated impression that Nigerians living abroad are wealthier and more financially stable. As a result, Nigerians living abroad carry a huge financial burden owing to demands from family members and friends back home. This is akin to what is referred to as 'black tax' in South Africa which is widely regarded as the financial burden borne by Black people who have achieved some success and who provide support to less privileged family members, and at times, friends. The situation is quite dire in the Nigerian context as for many, there is a sense of entitlement towards family members living abroad. The notion that the few family members living abroad should be financially responsible for the multitude of family members living in Nigeria has long permeated the country where lack of such financial support has bred hatred, jealousy, and resentment in some families. This is the case of the fifth example where the author condemns some Nigerians for being selfish. Those who remain in Nigeria often perceive people abroad as without their own financial responsibilities and expected to service 'black taxes'. The author proceeds to argue that being a high earner abroad does not mean one has no financial responsibilities. The high earner is also responsible for bills and debts which should be prioritised. In many parts of the world, migration remittances are indeed a popular practice. Chukwudi (2022) notes that it is a long-term practice for migrants to send remittances to their home countries where they are used to develop communities as well as to improve the living standards of family members. Migration remittances can be perceived as benevolent acts. However, when regarded from a perspective of entitlement, as reflected in the example under discussion, Nigerian expatriates who do not help family back home are perceived as oppressing powerless family members.

Finally, FB states that *'Nigeria is so broke. Most of us rely on the money sent to us by friends and families living abroad. This is my motivation to get out of this terrible country'*. The point the author makes is that Nigeria is financially deprived, and the major source of income for many people is migration remittances. Adeseye (2021) notes that remittance inflows have increased significantly in Nigeria and have become one of the most constant sources of economic growth and development. Adeseye (2021) further links remittances to growth in Nigeria's GDP (Gross Domestic Product) establishing that the money sent back by diasporans has a positive impact on the country's development. We have established earlier that for Nigerians, migration to developed countries is a financially challenging process. Despite coming from a poor country, Nigerians are required to convert a significant amount of local currency into foreign currencies to actualise their travel goals. However, the migration remittances, although they make Nigeria a recipient of foreign currencies, surprisingly do not make Nigeria powerful. In fact, it further renders Nigeria powerless as a country whose citizens must constantly rely on financial returns from abroad to ensure good living standards.

Power and Powerlessness: Individual and National Implications

Deeply rooted in migration studies, as well as migration conversations in Nigeria, is the concern around brain drain. Globally, skilled professionals are known for migrating from one country to another for many reasons among which are wage differentials, employment, better earning, and family life (Bhardwaj & Sharma, 2023). The authors use Maslow's hierarchy of needs to demonstrate human needs as enablers of skilled migration. They found that previous studies have focused on the attempts made by developed countries to attract skilled professionals from developing countries to meet their human resource needs. Furthermore, they argue that less developed countries have often viewed economic measures as the main reason for migration by skilled professionals while neglecting other important factors such as adequate rules, strong property rights, and infrastructures – all of which play important roles in the decision-making process. It is the view of Bhardwaj and Sharma (2023) that developing countries have paid inadequate attention to the multiple factors that trigger the exodus of professionals. This lack of understanding has led to brain drain in the Nigerian context as well. Other extrinsic factors often neglected by developing nations include opportunities for research, growth (to satisfy self-esteem and self-actualisation needs), technological advancements, standards of living, and quality of work life. So, for us to understand the brain drain in Nigerian migration discourse from the perspective of skilled professionals, it is important that we delve beyond economic measures. The following are selected examples Facebook and X examples on Nigerian migration discourse that focus on brain drain:

i. *Nigeria is in the middle of a brain drain. We miss Drs, nurses, tech sector and other people on a daily basis (OO, X).*
ii. *Nigeria has impoverished & frustrated hardworking intelligent professionals, intellectuals & entrepreneurs leading to massive brain drain. The brain drain in the health sector is even worse. Despite Nigeria being endowed with remarkable healthcare professionals, we are witnessing a concerning trend of brain drain in the health sector (TA, Facebook).*
iii. *It is now about time to improve the facilities across all the hospitals in Nigeria and the welfare of the health workers to stop the brain drain (EF, X).*
iv. *The Minister of Education was busy lamenting about the shortfall of staff in Nigerian Universities as a result of the japa syndrome. I wonder what he was expecting after long strikes with no payment. We have just started (FF, Facebook).*
v. *The truth is all financial institutions in Nigeria are feeling the heat. The brain drain in the Tech sector in the last 3 years is heavy. Whole technical department wiped out in weeks. The telecom industry is facing the same issue! (YF, X).*
vi. *Nigeria is experiencing a brain drain, with some of its most talented and educated individuals leaving in search of more favorable conditions elsewhere. This loss of human capital is a significant issue, as the country's brightest minds are essential for its growth and development (SA, X).*

In the first post, OO states authoritatively that Nigeria is currently in a brain drain crisis as a large percentage of the country's skilled professionals such as medical doctors, nurses, and technological experts are leaving in droves. According to Michael Nnachi, the President of the National Association of Nigeria Nurses and Midwives, more than fifty-seven thousand (57,000) nurses have migrated from Nigeria for greener pastures abroad within a period of five years spanning from 2017 to 2022 (Nigeria, 2023). This point is reinforced by TA who insinuates that the socio-economic situation of the country has impoverished professionals, intellectuals, and entrepreneurs who, out of frustration, have emigrated. A sector that has been heavily impacted by the brain drain is health since many doctors and nurses have migrated to developed countries with promising wage structures as well as health infrastructures. TA further states that although Nigeria produces great healthcare professionals, the country has lost many of them. For instance, many Nigerians have exploited the United Kingdom healthcare system to assume healthcare roles.

In December 2023, Nigerian President, Bola Ahmed Tinubu, appealed to Nigerian health workers practising abroad to *'sacrifice their time to come back home and serve their people'* (Angbulu, 2023). He begged Nigerian healthcare professionals abroad to contribute their knowledge to the Nigerian healthcare system saying that *'charity begins at home'*. This statement clearly underscores the urgency of healthcare professionals brain drain in the country. As expected, the statement elicited many reactions from Nigerians on social media such as: *(a) Return to where to do what exactly; (b) What kind of expensive joke is this; (c) Stop begging them. begging them does not pay their bills, provide good salary and enabling work environment for them and they will return; (d) I am sure they know better not to return; (e) If teachers have their way, they will leave too.* Most of the thousands of reactions on social media mocked the President's appeal suggesting that healthcare workers would not consider returning to the country in its current situation. While some citizens find the president's remark laughable, others find it disturbing that he is so removed from the reality that he fails to realise the gravity of the Nigerian economic situation. Other responses to the president included references to poor salary structures and the negative work environments that healthcare workers are subjected to. Unless these issues are resolved, appeals by the president will not address the deep-rooted problems in Nigerian healthcare.

The author of the third example, EF, states that *'it is now about time to improve the facilities across all the hospitals in Nigeria and the welfare of the health workers to stop the brain drain'*. To resolve the issue of brain drain in Nigeria, the health sector requires governmental upgrades in hospital facilities as well as paying attention to the welfare of health workers who often feel undervalued in Nigeria. In 2019, the then Minister of Labour and Employment, Dr Chris Ngige, was quoted saying *'doctors are free to leave Nigeria, we have enough'*.[1] It can be assumed that healthcare professionals took the statement literally, which has led the current president to appeal for their return barely five years later. Okafor and Chimereze (2020) attribute the brain drain in the health sector to both 'push' and 'pull' factors which implies that unfavourable conditions in the home country 'push' healthcare professionals out of Nigerian to developed countries. The latter 'pull' Nigerian health professionals by offering them favourable and attractive conditions. Ogaboh et al. (2020) add that other key factors for the migration of healthcare workers are poor remuneration, unsafe work environments and poor working equipment and facilities.

---

[1]Doctors Free to Leave Nigeria, We Have Enough - Minister. (2019, April 26). allAfrica.com. https://allafrica.com/view/group/main/main/id/00067484.html

Professor Tahir Mamman, the Minister of Education, recently lamented the brain drain in Nigerian higher education institutions as both young and old academics are also migrating to developed countries (Erezi, 2023). Even more concerning is the fact that those who have not yet migrated are in the process of doing so. The Nigerian higher education sector has for a long time been plagued with industrial actions that have seen universities closed indefinitely and as a result academics have not received salaries for a long time. This situation has prompted experienced academics to flee the country. This has also made Nigerian academia less attractive to emerging academics who currently are now also considering careers abroad. The author of the fourth post, FF, insinuates that the minister should have expected brain drain in higher education since academics have been unfairly treated in higher learning institutions. In the fifth post, YF bemoans the brain drain in the technology sector where many technological experts have also fled the country. The author states that the recent technological problems faced by financial institutions (banks) whose online services have been catastrophic, as well as the poor network services provided by the telecommunications companies have mostly been the result of departing technological experts.

From the examples above, SA is concerned that Nigeria is losing most of its talented and educated citizens to developed countries. This loss of human capital is disastrous for the country especially since growth and development may not be achieved when the brightest minds continue to flee. However, it does not appear that the problem of emigration in the country is receiving proper and urgent attention. Anetoh and Onwudinjo (2020) argue that for Nigeria to retain her best brains, there must be good structures in place, quality education delivery, career opportunities and job prospects as well as an enabling and conducive environment that allows intellectual excellence and innovation to thrive. The problem of leadership in the country needs to be addressed to enable citizens to actualise their individual goals. Since this is a rather long-term solution, one might expect the exodus of skilled professionals from Nigeria to continue and to take up significant space in Nigerian migration discourse for the next few years.

Among the other implications of the co-existence between power and powerlessness in Nigerian migration discourse is the citizens' disposition towards the rule of law. For Adamolekun (2016), the rule of law helps to ensure respect for property rights and contracts, while preventing the government and influential individuals from acting capriciously. Rule of law suggests that every individual is bound by and accountable to the law regardless of position or authority in society. Rule of law should guide daily activities in a country, and all citizens are expected to obey. The view of many Nigerians on social media is that the lack of regard for rule of law is another motivating factor for emigrating. Some social media reactions to this topic include the following:

i. *There is no RULE OF LAW in NIGERIA, zero human rights for citizens. Only when Nigerians are in diaspora do they demand constitutional rights (FO, X).*
ii. *The only way an average Nigerian can enjoy the rule of law is to live in better countries. The rule of law in Nigeria is only for the poor people so the rich can continue to oppress them We have serious concerns over the rule of law in Nigeria. No way anyone is convincing me not to japa if I can (RD, X).*

iii. *The only way to de-market going abroad or the 'Japa Syndrome' is to Market Nigeria in every form possible starting with the rule of law (AA, Facebook).*
iv. *The abortion of the justice by the judiciary defined how the rule of law in Nigeria can be traced to the politicians pocket. As it's now, japa seems to be a good choice. Japa is loading...... (SI, X).*

Over the years, there have been recurrent and sustained arguments in Nigeria about the lack of the rule of law which is supposed to be applicable to all citizens. In the first post, FO emphasises the absence of the rule of law in Nigeria using capital letters. The author's position is that in Nigeria, citizens cannot enjoy the rule of law as the government does not respect basic human rights. The author further states that Nigerians are only able to claim their constitutional rights when they live in other countries. Recent events in Nigeria regarding the position of the law have been extremely fuzzy; implementation and consequences tend to depend on the financial state of the involved parties. This reality has forced many Nigerians to flee the country since poor people cannot expect justice against the rich. Many citizens perceive that the law is treated and applied differently based on socio-economic factors which overrule provisions of the law in the country. This is a point also stressed by RD who argues that an average Nigerian can only attain justice in other countries where the rule prevails. The author is fully convinced that fleeing the country is the only option for a Nigerian to enjoy the rule of law. In this regard, Nigeria as a country is considered powerless while countries abroad are considered powerful.

To further explore the power versus powerlessness argument, the same Nigerians who are made powerless in their own country are made powerful in other countries through the rule of law that allows them to claim their constitutional rights. It is thus the view of AA that the *japa* syndrome that permeates Nigerian society can be combatted if the country embraces the rule of law. This implies that power can be restored when the rule of law becomes an integral aspect of the development of a country. Many Nigerians who flee the country may consider returning if the country has the rule of law which they tend to look for elsewhere. The author of the fourth post, SI, also believes that fleeing from Nigeria is the answer to the lack of the rule of law. He blames politicians for the absence of the rule of law in Nigeria. Instances abound of several successful attempts by politicians as well as powerful people in the country to circumvent the rule of law. Thus, the fourth author believes that getting justice through the judiciary in the country is challenging especially since the author perceives this arm of government to be corrupt because of interference from political leaders. Yagboyaju and Akinola (2019) found that the judiciary, which is responsible for overseeing the rule of law, has often acted contrary to Adamolekun's (2016) observation above. They argue that there is ample evidence of the not-so-tidy relationship between the government and the judiciary especially with the judiciary, in several instances, appearing partisan. Drawing on the findings of Yagboyaju and Akinola (2019), one can conclude that in most parts of the advanced democratic world, the rule of law is an important asset whereas the Nigerian judiciary has often failed integrity and morality tests which have rendered advanced countries more powerful than Nigeria.

Finally, doing business in Nigeria is another sector filled with the dynamics of power and powerlessness. Citizens often complain about the difficulty of doing business especially since many Nigerians have resorted to entrepreneurship due to the lack of job opportunities. Some X reactions to this subject include:

i. *There is nothing like 'ease of doing business' in Nigeria. You can do business o, but it will NEVER be easy. Except it's illegal. If you want ease in your business, try other countries (TF, X).*
ii. *The ease of doing business in Nigeria is non-existent. There are so many things plaguing Nigeria and sadly it won't change, at least, not in our lifetime. A major reason I'm vocal about people leaving. Everyone deserves the sanity of a working system (AB, X).*
iii. *There is no single ease of doing business in Nigeria. Let's face the fact. Agencies of govt are not helping, they frustrate businesses every now and then. I may just have to japa at this point (DA, X).*

Consistent across the three posts above is the notion that 'ease of doing business' is fictional. Young Nigerians are frustrated by societal, governmental, and financial challenges, which means that businesses barely survive in the country. The author of the first post, TF, agrees that the prospect of starting a new business is possible but uses the word 'never' to stress the fact that it will not be accompanied by ease. The author further implies that the only form of business that can be productive given the state of the country would be illegitimate ventures. What is strongly inferred from this is that the genuine intentions of Nigerians to initiate a business are met with challenges and demands that render the process difficult. As for AB, the author's lack of hope in the Nigerian state is also clear and a further confirmation that the country is challenged by systemic bottlenecks that prevent doing businesses effectively thus encouraging talented Nigerians to flee the country. In the third example, DA decries the tough situation imposed on Nigerians by government agencies responsible for overseeing and regulating businesses. The author stresses that these agencies endlessly frustrate business efforts. Power and powerlessness therefore also co-exist in entrepreneurship; where Nigerians who should be powerful by virtue of their talent and innovations are rendered powerless by the socio-economic realities of their own country.

Power and powerless reside in migration discourse especially in the Nigerian milieu as we have demonstrated in this chapter. To this end, we have discussed how Nigerians in the diaspora tend to show the disparity between their resident countries and Nigeria through several means which are often reflected in economic, social, and political matters. We have also demonstrated that aspects of power versus powerlessness are not only reflected in interpersonal relations, but also exist even in inter-country observations where some global north countries tend to appear powerful based on the development in their countries while Nigeria appears powerless. In fact, power versus powerlessness also extends to how the Nigerian currency is perceived as weak while currencies of the global north countries appear strong. Considering the above, one can conclude that discourses are capable of reflecting power or powerlessness in the context of migration.

References

Adamolekun, L. (2016). *The idea of Nigeria: Two challenges – Unity in diversity and prosperity*. Convocation lecture delivered on November 14 at Lead City University, Ibadan, Nigeria.

Adeseye, A. (2021). The effect of migrants remittance on economy growth in Nigeria: An empirical study. *Open Journal of Political Science, 11*, 99–122.

Anetoh, B. C., & Onwudinjo, V. G. (2020). Emigration and the problem of brain drain in Nigeria: a philosophical evaluation. *Journal of African Studies and Sustainable Development, 3*(1), 86–98.

Angbulu, S. (2023, December 12). Tinubu begs Nigerian doctors abroad to return. *Punch Newspapers*. https://punchng.com/tinubu-begs-nigerian-doctors-abroad-to-return/

Bainbridge, W. S. (2000). Religious ethnography on the World Wide Web. In K. Hadden & D. E. Cowan (Eds.), *Religion on the internet: Research prospects and promises* (pp. 55–80). Elsevier.

Bhardwaj, B., & Sharma, D. (2023). Migration of skilled professionals across the border: Brain drain or brain gain? *European Management Journal, 41*(6), 1021–1033.

Chukwudi, E. C. (2022). Migration and dynamics of modern slavery in Nigeria. *Migration, 1*(4), 18–27.

Erezi, D. (2023, December 26). Education minister blames 'Japa' as varsities face a dearth of lecturers. *The Guardian Nigeria News – Nigeria and World News*. https://guardian.ng/news/education-minister-blames-japa-as-varsities-face-a-dearth-of-lecturers/

Guccione, C. (2022). Migration discourse and the new socially constructed meanings of the English Lingua Franca. *European Scientific Journal, 18*(18), 33–49.

Guillem, S. M. (2015). Migration discourse. In K. Tracy & T. Sandel (Eds.), *The international encyclopedia of language and social interaction* (pp. 1–10). John Wiley & Sons.

Immigration, Refugees and Citizenship Canada Departmental Plan 2023-2024. (2024, February 6). Canada.ca. https://www.canada.ca/en/immigration-refugees-citizenship/corporate/publications-manuals/departmental-plan-2023-2024/departmental-plan.html

Nigeria, G. (2023, May 12). Over 75,000 nurses, midwives left Nigeria in five years. *The Guardian Nigeria News – Nigeria and World News*. https://guardian.ng/news/over-75000-nurses-midwives-left-nigeria-in-five-years/

Obi-Ani, P., Anthonia Obi-Ani, N., & Isiani, M. C. (2020). A historical perspective of Nigerian immigrants in Europe. *Cogent Arts & Humanities, 7*(1), 1–15.

Office, H. (2023, December 7). *Statement of changes to the Immigration Rules: HC 246*. GOV.UK. https://www.gov.uk/government/publications/statement-of-changes-to-the-immigration-rules-hc-246-7-december-2023

Ogaboh, A. A., Udom, H. T., & Eke, I. T. (2020). Why brain drain in the Nigerian health sector. *Asian Journal of Applied Science, 8*(2), 95–104.

Okafor, C., & Chimereze, C. (2020). Brain drain among Nigerian nurses: Implications to the migrating nurse and the home country. *International Journal of Research and Scientific Innovation, 7*(1), 15–21.

Okeke-Ihejirika, P., & Odimegwu, I. (2023). Managing the rising tide of Nigerian migrants to the West – A policy vacuum or a structural challenge? *International Migration, 61*(1), 10–22.

Otekunrin, O. A., Otekunrin, O. A., Momoh, S., & Ayinde, I. A. (2019). How far has Africa gone in achieving the zero-hunger target? Evidence from Nigeria. *Global Food Security, 22*, 1–12.

Schiller, N. G., Basch, L., & Blanc-Szanton, C. (1992). Towards a definition of transnationalism. *Annals of the New York Academy of Sciences, 645*(1), ix–xiv.

Uchechukwu, O. (2019). Mental harmony and patriotism in Nigeria: A philosophical extension of Plato's Tripartite Soul. In A. M. Okolie, H. Saliu, & G. Ezirim (Eds.), *State, governance and regional integration in Africa* (pp. 966–974). Nigerian Political Science Association.

Ugwuanyi, K. O., & Oyebola, F. (2022). Attitudes of Nigerian expatriates towards accents of English. *Poznan Studies in Contemporary Linguistics*, *58*(3), 541–572.

World Data Lab. (2023). *World poverty clock*. https://worldpoverty.io/

Yagboyaju, D. A., & Akinola, A. O. (2019). Nigerian state and the crisis of governance: A critical exposition. *Sage Open*, *9*(3), 1–10.

Chapter 7

Discourse, Zimbabwean Migrants in South Africa and the Politics of Viscerality: The Case of the Zimbabwe Exemption Permit (ZEP)

Keywords: Viscerality; foreign national; Operation Dudula; illegal; anti-immigrant

If anything characterises the contemporary world, it is the question of the border and the figure of the migrant both of which have become subjects of contentious debate around the world. In recent years, the border and the migrants have become political tools in the hands of those seeking political office and sites of all kinds of violence. In the United Kingdom, for example, the Brexit vote of 2016 was driven mainly by the question of how to regain control of the border. Following the migration crisis of 2015/2016, the whole of Europe has been confronted with the question of how to keep unwanted 'others' outside the borders of the European Union. Migrants to the United States and Europe have also been met with high walls, detention centres, camps, and waiting zones. The neoliberal idea of the nation-state as a closed space that belongs to some (citizens) and not to others (non-citizens) is, however, not only limited to Europe and America. Since the end of apartheid in 1994, South Africa has witnessed a steady increase in the number of African migrants flocking into the country from different parts of the continent, resulting in violent tension between migrants and citizens. This chapter deploys Achille Mbembe's ideas on the border and the politics of viscerality to analyse migration discourses in contemporary South Africa, with a particular focus on Zimbabwean migrants and the controversial Zimbabwe Exemption Permit. We explore how South Africans perceive Zimbabwean migrants and migration in the context of debates about whether the Department of Home Affairs should terminate or extend the Zimbabwe Exemption Permit (ZEP) which allowed Zimbabwean migrants to live and work in South Africa. We examine

---

Social Constructions of Migration in Nigeria and Zimbabwe
Discourse, Rhetoric, and Identity, 101–122
Copyright © 2024 by Kunle Musbaudeen Oparinde and Rodwell Makombe
Published under exclusive licence by Emerald Publishing Limited
doi:10.1108/978-1-83549-168-320241007

how the anger, frustration, and disappointment associated with contemporary South Africa influence the ways in which South Africans perceive Zimbabwean migrants. We argue that Zimbabwean migrants have become scapegoats in South Africa not only because they are perceived as responsible for aggravating black pain but also because they are seen as outsiders who can never understand the pain and suffering that South Africans are experiencing.

In a BBC documentary titled 'Loathing and Fear in South Africa', a South African middle-aged woman confesses, 'to tell you the truth, I hate foreigners'.[1] She can hardly contain her anger. She breaks down into tears, looking up and repeating 'I hate foreigners'. The hatred that the woman feels against foreigners is deep. It seems to come not only from her mind (reason) but also from her insides (visceral). She feels it with the vital parts of her body organs, and for a moment, she is one with her pain. She is her pain. In *Black Skin White Masks*, Frantz Fanon discusses a similar experience in what he calls 'the North African Syndrome' (Fanon, 1952). Fanon tells the story of a patient who goes to a doctor and when the doctor asks what is wrong with her, the patient explains that she feels pain everywhere, every part of her body hurts – the back, the abdomen, the head, the limbs, everything. Finally, the patient says 'I am my pain. Doctor, I am dying'. The woman in the BBC documentary hates foreigners, but unlike Frantz Fanon's patient who eventually dies because of the overwhelming pain, the woman in the BBC film has found purpose in her pain. She has lost a son to the drug epidemic in her neighbourhood and she blames this on foreign migrants. Foreigners sell drugs. She knows it. Her son tells her. The foreigners have killed her son. They have robbed him of his future. The woman is a member of an anti-immigrants group called Operation Dudula. Dudula is a Zulu word which means 'to force out', as one would do to vermin. When she talks about Operation Dudula, the woman's eyes lighten up. Operation Dudula will rid South Africa of these foreigners – she says, with a smile on her face. She will have her son back. She will have her life back. What kind of hatred is this that gives one a sense of purpose? We are interested in this hatred, the hatred that makes one cry, that makes one wish to drive out or even kill the other.

In a separate incident in August 2022, the South African MEC for health in Limpopo province, Dr Popi Ramathuba made the headlines for chastising a Zimbabwean patient who had crossed the border illegally to seek medical attention in South Africa. Ramathuba first addressed the patient in her language, but the later could not respond because she did not understand the language. In response to the woman's failure to understand a South African language, Ramathuba charged:

> You speak Shona? Then how do you find yourself in Bela-Bela when you are supposed to be with Mnangagwa... you're killing my health system.[2]

---

[1] https://www.youtube.com/watch?v=rogZ8BYg-kM
[2] https://www.bbc.co.uk/news/world-africa-62677577, Phophi Ramathuba: South African official's hospital rant at Zimbabwean goes viral.

Ramathuba's reasoning, as expressed in the quotation above, is that the patient should not be in Bela-Bela (a town in the Limpopo province, South Africa) because she does not speak the local language of that area. She belongs *elsewhere* with Mnangagwa (the President of Zimbabwe) not *here*. The distinction between *here* (where Ramathuba belongs) and *elsewhere* (where the woman belongs) creates what Achille Mbembe calls a virtual border that divides bodies as opposed to the geographical border that divides territories. The woman is 'othered' because she does not speak *our* language. The transition from 'You speak Shona?' to '*then* how do you find yourself in Belal Bela' presupposes a correlation between language and place. You cannot be in a place if you cannot speak the language of that place. To Ramathuba, the woman is not only a patient seeking medical attention (albeit illegally) but also a killer of a whole health system. In seeking her own health, the sick woman becomes an agent of death to others. She is killing the health system. Again, one can see a border between 'you' and 'my' – the woman-patient-cum-killer and Ramathuba whose health system is being killed. A far as Ramathuba is concerned, the woman is 'supposed to be with Mnangagwa' because 'you know, he doesn't give me money to operate on you guys, and I'm operating with my limited budget'.[3] The sick woman is not only 'killing' the health system to the detriment of deserving South African citizens who may die as a result but also straining the South African fiscus. Ramathuba has no option but to stretch her 'limited' budget which is meant to serve citizens to cater for 'you guys' – the 'others' who have no right to benefit from the South African health system. The woman has morphed from an alien who does not speak *our* language to a murderer, who is killing *our* health system, to a robber, breaking into the South African fiscus. Interestingly, Ramathuba sees a direct correlation between what the woman has done (seeking medical attention in a South African hospital) and the healthcare crisis in South Africa. Thus, in her conclusion, she says:

> That is *why* when *my* people want health services, they can't get [them]. And that is endangering the community… this is unfair.

In Ramathuba's logic, there is a direct causal relationship between the woman's pilfering of health services and failure by her people to access the same. An article published by the BBC titled 'South African official's hospital rant at Zimbabwean goes viral' notes that Ramathuba's rant was accompanied by 'laughter and murmurs of agreeance from onlookers in the ward'.[4] Ramathuba is clearly not acting in a vacuum because there are people who approve of her behaviour. In the eyes of Ramathuba (and her cheerleaders), the Zimbabwean woman is not only a victim of circumstances (a car accident in Harare) but also a danger to the community because she is depriving South Africans (the insiders/citizens)

---

[3] https://www.bbc.co.uk/news/world-africa-62677577, Phophi Ramathuba: South African official's hospital rant at Zimbabwean goes viral.
[4] https://www.bbc.co.uk/news/world-africa-62677577, Phophi Ramathuba: South African official's hospital rant at Zimbabwean goes viral.

of health services. Perhaps, Ramathuba is not only addressing this one woman at this point because there is no way one surgical operation can collapse the whole health system. The woman represents a group of outsiders, those real and imagined Zimbabweans who have been flocking into the border province to seek medical attention.

Achille Mbembe has argued that discourses of othering are not interested in facts or truthfulness of issues, in fact, the less factual the allegation, the better. The woman does not have to be the one causing the collapse of the health system. In any case, she is not alone but part of an 'invading' mass. Ramathuba also makes a value judgement, 'this is unfair' suggesting that the woman's act of seeking medical help in a South African hospital is unjust – a self-serving act that has no regard for others. In the South African context, the discourse of fairness resonates with constitutionalism and notions of equality and fairness enshrined in the constitution. If what the woman has done is not fair, the question is what she should have done. Was she supposed to stay in Harare and die to ensure fairness in South Africa? When Popi Ramathuba embarrassed the patient, the onlookers in the hospital did not think she was doing anything wrong because we are told that they laughed and murmured in agreeance. What logic would justify laughing at a sick woman being insulted in hospital? This, to us, is an ontological question. The woman is not one of *us*. She is probably not human like us because she is a Zimbabwean woman. Moreover, she is different. She does not speak *our* language. She is killing *our* health system. She is responsible for all South Africans who are dying in a poorly funded health system.

When the incident went viral on various social media platforms, some people both in Zimbabwe and South Africa, blamed Ramathuba for being opportunistic and insensitive to the helpless Zimbabwean woman. Others praised her for highlighting the impact of Zimbabwean migration on South Africa's health sector. In the aftermath of the media fallout and the negative media publicity that the incident attracted, Ramathuba did not back down. She insisted that the 'influx of foreign nationals [was] choking the province's health system, resulting in doctors often working under pressure'.[5] Achille Mbembe's idea of the politics of viscerality identifies a particular physiological experience associated with viscerality, an experience of choking and pain that seems to have no outlet. In the Algerian colonial context that Frantz Fanon analysed, it was colonial oppression that caused this choking effect. In contemporary South Africa, it is Zimbabwean migrants that are choking the health system, triggering a ripple effect of doctors that must work under pressure and South Africans who cannot breathe because of the strained health system.

Achille Mbembe's notion of the politics of viscerality comes from Frantz Fanon's theorisation of the experiences of the colonised. Fanon argues that the colonial system creates conditions that suffocate the colonised in all areas of life, leading to all kinds of mental disorders. During a workshop at the Franklin

---

[5]https://www.bbc.co.uk/news/world-africa-62677577, Phophi Ramathuba: South African official's hospital rant at Zimbabwean goes viral.

Humanities Institute (FHI) at Duke University in 2016, Achille Mbembe described 'the politics of viscerality' as a politics that characterises academic and activist discourses in contemporary South Africa. This politics is associated with a form of defiance against the establishment and a quest for a new form of social and political existence. It is premised on individual experiences of anger, frustration, and disappointment that emanate from what is often seen as the sluggish pace of transformation in post-apartheid South Africa. It is these feelings that produce an acute desire for something radical. This new form of radical academic and activist politics rejects all modes of social and political organisation that prioritise negotiation, reconciliation, forgiveness, and constitutionalism – the premises on which post-apartheid South Africa was founded. In the BBC film alluded to earlier, members of Operation Dudula say they have run out of patience because 'the government is doing nothing about it [the influx of foreigners]'. Mbembe argues that contemporary radical groups such as Operation Dudula do not trust democratic processes to bring about the change that they envisage. Democracy is seen as a way of suspending the revolution and protecting what was obtained through conquest. For such radical groups, change can only come, not through following democratic processes, but through direct human action or what one activist called 'taking back our country by force'.[6]

Academic discourses associated with the politics of viscerality, as Mbembe (2016) argues, are black feminist theory with its focus on intersectionality, and decolonial theory, with its focus on dismantling apartheid institutions and structures that perpetuate the marginalisation of black people. In the same way that black feminism constructs the experiences of black women as unique, this radical school of thought constructs the black South African experience as shot through with various intersecting experiences. The visceral politics of this new radical politics draws inspiration from the works of Steve Biko and Frantz Fanon, particularly the privileging of radical (read as violent) ways of addressing problems. Mbembe (2016) adds that this group privileges new modes of reading (or misreading) that are non-exegetical, non-contextual, non-historical, and anti-method. Although Mbembe (2016) singles out groups such as the student movements of 2015/2016 which demanded free decolonised education, one can also see the politics of viscerality in anti-immigrant groups such as #PutSouthAfricaFirst and Operation Dudula. #PutSouthAfricaFirst and Operation Dudula are radical anti-immigrant movements that seek to address South Africa's migration crisis by physically evicting foreigners. These groups speak the language of confrontation and protagonism as opposed to negotiation and compromise. They are visceral as much as they rely on emotions to articulate their political positions, sometimes in ways that render old emotions inaudible. In this new politics, the sacrifices of yesterday do not matter anymore, what matters is the pain that one feels today. This means that those who fought against apartheid no longer have the moral authority to speak or make claims, because at worst, they are seen as sell outs.

---

[6]https://www.youtube.com/watch?v=8y0vTkTV7JI, #PutSouthAfricaFirst marches against foreign nationals.

Mbembe (2016) argues that this new radical politics rejects conventional notions of reason, preferring to use pain and suffering as yardstick to grant membership to the community of those who have the right to speak. Those who have not suffered as *we* have suffered (outsiders/foreigners) cannot be members of this group. It is pain, located in the vital organs (liver, heart, intestines, etc.), that legitimises one's claims to certain privileges. Visceral reason is not necessarily interested in dismantling or even challenging the system that causes suffering and pain. It focuses its attention on figures of evil (such as African immigrants and/or foreigners). The term 'viscerality' as Mbembe defines it, refers to that which is located among, or draws its energies and powers from, the visceral, that is the internal organs located in the large cavity of the trunk such as the liver, intestines, and the heart among others. The politics of viscerality is organ-based, bodily politics. It is that which is felt as if it touches the vital organs – one's very life within. The woman that Ramathuba chastises in the hospital is an enemy par-excellence because her actions have touched the vital organs of the South African body. She is a danger to the community, an existential threat. Because the visceral refers to those vital organs among the visceral (without which we cannot live), viscerality resides at the border of that which we can and that which we cannot dispense of. Frantz Fanon describes the visceral as that which is instinctive, that which is felt in the internal organs of the body. Mbembe (2016) notes that when the visceral is touched in a particular way, it elicits a response suggesting that some vital processes are at stake. Since visceral organs are connected to the trunk, anything that affects the visceral may lead to suffocation or feelings of being choked. Thus, in both the Ramathuba incident and the case of the woman in the BBC film, the presence of the Zimbabwean foreigner elicits feelings of choking because it threatens the very existence of the South African citizen.

Mbembe (2016) has also told us that the politics of viscerality privileges motifs of the body, pain, anger, suffering, outrage, grief, and fear. It is as if one is in a state of delirium, of intense pain, like Fanon's patient whose whole body is painful. Those that engage in the politics of viscerality do not make claims based on a shared humanity. In *Black Skin White Masks*, Fanon submits that the colonised demand freedom based on the fact that they are human like any other. The visceral subject, on the other hand, makes claims based on a certain kind of pain that he/she has experienced. In the South African context, this is black pain – the pain that only disenfranchised black people can understand. Mbembe (2016) describes a visceral body as a body that cannot breathe, a body that has been abused so much that the subject cannot reclaim it. This is the figure of the black body in contemporary South Africa, full of anger and wishing to inflict on the oppressor, the same kind of pain that was inflicted on her. Mbembe (2016) gives the example of RhodesMustFall activist, Chumani Maxwele, who threw human excrement at Cecil John Rhodes' statue to signify 'the filthy way in which Rhodes mistreated our people in the past'.[7] One can see a connection between Chumani Maxwele's desire to see Rhodes suffer (even in his death) and the woman in the BBC film's desire to see the foreigner suffer as much as her son has suffered. The

---

[7]https://www.youtube.com/watch?v=lg_BEodNaEA&t=3389s, Frantz Fanon and the politics of viscerality.

politics of viscerality (like the visceral organs themselves) is associated with the metaphysics of waste, of that which stink – like the everyday experiences of black people who live in informal settlements.

Considering the above, the Zimbabwean immigrant in South Africa can be read as one who touches the visceral, one whose presence elicits feelings of choking for the South African citizen. The general sentiment in South Africa is that the large numbers of Zimbabweans pose an existential crisis to South African citizens, akin to an experience of suffocation. The politics of viscerality privileges emotions such as anger, fear, frustration, and experiences that one has undergone (injuries, wounds) as opposed to reason. Thus, for groups such as Operation Dudula and #PutSouthAfricaFirst, the question of Zimbabwean migrants is not debatable because it touches those vital organs that sustain the lives and livelihoods of South Africans. Hence, South African public discourse on Zimbabwean migrants is characterised by anger and the desire to inflict pain on the migrant who is seen as causing *our* suffering. It does not matter what the circumstances of the individual migrant are, as is the case with Popi Ramathuba and the Zimbabwean migrant woman. The migrant must simply go back to his or her country. Period.

Zimbabwean Migration Discourse in South Africa: A Review of Literature

In a study of representations of Zimbabwean migrants in South African media, Banda and Mawadza (2015) argue that South African media depicts Zimbabweans as threats to the socioeconomic fabric of South African society. Oftentimes, media representations promote moral panic by supplying unsubstantiated statistics that create the impression that Zimbabwean migrants are overrunning South African communities, they are everywhere like cockroaches.[8] Anti-immigration content posted on social media tends to 'heighten anxiety and miseducate more than it enlightens readers on migration issues' (Banda & Mawadza, 2015, p. 47). Media organisations often have an agenda other than providing information to the public. Banda and Mawadza (2015) note that South African newspapers such as *The Sunday Times* and *The Daily Sun* usually publish sensational stories that do not reflect the views of migrants, thus creating a narrative that correlates Zimbabwean migration with all kinds of social and economic problems in South Africa. The highly generalised language of the media fails to recognise the complexity of the migration phenomenon and the manifold distinctions between different kinds of migrants and immigrants (Banda & Mawadza, 2015, p. 49). The use of the us and them dichotomy in anti-immigration discourse 'depict the other as outsiders who endanger the national social order' (Banda & Mawadza, 2015, p. 53). Zimbabwean immigrants in particular are identified as the source of concern and fear for South Africa's well-being (Banda & Mawadza, 2015, p. 53).

---

[8]In the BBC documentary, Fear and Loathing, one South African activist characterises migrants as cockroaches as they run away from Operation Dudula militants, 'Look at how they are running, its like they are cockroaches'.

Ordinary South Africans and media organisations have accused Zimbabweans of engaging in criminal activities. Muzondidya reports that South African national newspapers such as *The Sunday Times* and *The Daily Sun* have published sensationalised stories that suggest that Zimbabweans were engaging in high profile criminal activities such as bank robberies and cash-on-transit heists. Muzondidya (2010, p. 42) further argues that 'Zimbabweans and migrants from other African countries are also accused of queue jumping, fraudulently taking state welfare, and occupying government houses built for South African low-income earners'. Discourse, whether in the media or in everyday communication, has played an important role in casting the image of Zimbabweans as threats to the social and economic health of the South African polity. Some studies, such as Norma Kriger (2010, p. 87) show that some South African citizens have in fact 'sold or rented out low-cost government-built homes that they had been allocated to foreigners, while they went back to live in shacks and placed their names again on waiting lists for housing'. As a result, the popular image of a Zimbabwean everyday discourse is that of 'a murderous criminal, also responsible for a host of other vices such as prostitution, drug abuse, spreading HIV-AIDS, impregnating young girls and leaving them to raise the children alone' (Muzondidya, 2010, p. 42). There is no attempt to distinguish migrants in terms of their legal status (documented or undocumented) because, in the South African popular imaginary, the term Zimbabwean is synonymous with illegality and criminality – a code-name for foreigners. Borrowing from colonial racist discourses and notions of South African exceptionalism, South Africans have sought to exclude foreigners, Zimbabweans included, castigating them as 'inferior human beings, […] despicable and filthy subjects with smelly bodies' (Muzondidya, 2010, p. 42). Given that race remains one of the unresolved issues in post-apartheid South Africa, 'Zimbabweans in South Africa, like other African migrants, also have to deal with being black in a country where categories of race and ethnicity are still used to mark boundaries of social location and status' (Muzondidya, 2010, p. 44).

Since the beginning of the political/economic crisis in Zimbabwe, many Zimbabweans have migrated to South Africa in search of better economic opportunities. Nyandoro (2010, p. 10) speculates that 'the South African government's decision in May 2009 to scrap off visa requirements for Zimbabwean visitors' may have compounded the situation by encouraging Zimbabweans to live and work in South Africa. The impact of the scrapping of visa requirements between Zimbabwe and South Africa was evident in the flood of undocumented Zimbabweans who crossed into the Republic through dubious channels (Nyandoro, 2010, p. 123). In fact, Nyandoro (2010, p. 124) observes that xenophobic attacks occurred against the backdrop of the huge influx of Zimbabweans who were blamed by South Africans for crime and 'stealing jobs' from locals. Although South Africa is home to migrants from different parts of the world, including Asian countries such as Bangladesh, Pakistan, and India, Zimbabweans have increasingly become objects of popular hate because of their numbers.

Dube (2017) claims that Zimbabweans are 'the most disliked foreigners in South Africa'. Official statistics put the number of Zimbabweans living and working in South Africa at 1.5 million, although others claim that the numbers could be higher because of illegal migration. 'As the largest group of foreigners in South

Africa', Dube (2017, p. 392) argues, 'Zimbabweans are now the archetypical other, often viewed as dirty, smelly criminals – the untouchables of South Africa' (Dube, 2017, p. 392). Reflecting on the precariousness of being Zimbabwean in South Africa, Norma Kriger (2010, p. 85) submits that 'the interplay of foreign policy support for the Zimbabwe regime and xenophobia and the imploding situation in Zimbabwe have combined to make the situation of Zimbabwean migrants both distinctive and precarious'. South Africa's foreign policy towards Zimbabwe, which Kriger refers to, has been of support for the governing regime, which ironically, is responsible for the migration crisis. Muzondidya (2010, p. 41) concurs that 'Zimbabweans have often been particular targets in the rising xenophobia in South Africa, alongside Nigerians, Mozambicans and others, and are accused of overwhelming South Africa by their large numbers'. Apart from the fear of the other, Dube argues that xenophobic/Afrophobic tendencies in South Africa are also fuelled by the notion of South African exceptionalism. Being the last country on the continent to gain independence in 1994, South Africa is regarded as different from the rest of Africa. Given their imagined exceptionalism (or difference with the rest of other Africans on the continent) 'blacks in South Africa have also ended up imagining themselves to be more civilized and "closer" to white people both culturally and in terms of skin color (that is, having lighter skin complexions than *makwerekwere*)' (Dube, 2017, p. 392). *Makwerekwere* is a derogatory term used to refer to African migrants in South Africa. South Africans often identify foreigners through skin colour based on the assumption that migrants from other parts of the continent are darker than South Africans. This marker of difference has led to the deaths of some South Africans, after having been mistaken for foreigners because of their complexion. The obsession with skin colour as a marker of difference reminds us of Franz Fanon's analysis of colonial relations in *Black Skin White Masks*. Fanon argued that 'the stigma attached to being black in colonial societies results in self-loathing among blacks, with lighter skinned blacks viewing their darker kin as ugly and inferior' (Dube, 2017, p. 396).

The notion of South African exceptionalism intertwines with apartheid's isolationist policy and racist attitude towards the rest of the African continent'. Francis Nyamnjoh (2006) argues that contemporary South African society replays the racial hierarchies of apartheid, 'with white South Africans at the helm as superiors, black South Africans in the middle as superior inferiors and the *makwerekwere* as the scum of humanity'. In this formulation, African migrants (Zimbabweans included) are constructed in colonial terms, as 'primitive and uncivilised'. In fact, in black townships, migrants are stereotyped as 'sorcerers who use witchcraft to succeed in business, gain employment ahead of South Africans and snatch other people's wives, husbands, girlfriends or boyfriends' (Muzondidya, 2010, p. 43). Most of these negative perceptions are not based on facts but they go a long way in inciting public discontent among ordinary South Africans, especially in poor communities.

Some scholars have argued that the end of apartheid has created new hierarchies in South African society based on a new understanding of citizenship. During apartheid, Black South Africans lived in independent black states called Bantustans, effectively making them foreigners in their own country. The dawn of democracy in 1994 conferred rights of citizenship on black South Africans, which they could use to make claims on the state and access rights and privileges. In the minds of many South Africans, citizenship is therefore something to be defended because it is through citizenship that they have access to social, economic, and political rights. Dube (2017) argues that some South Africans believe that foreigners (Zimbabweans in particular) do not have a legitimate claim to an inch of South African space – geographical, social, and economic. Speaking from her experience, a Zimbabwean participant in Dube's (2017) study explains that some Zulu-speaking South Africans would not assist one if one addressed them in English. They would insist on being addressed in Zulu and if one told them they were not South African, they would simply say 'So what do you want here' (Dube, 2017, p. 404). This response emanates from a nativist position that constructs South Africa as the preserve of citizens and not outsiders/intruders. What is interesting, however, is that this exclusionary attitude only applies to African/Zimbabwean nationals and not to Europeans. Muzondidya (2010, p. 47) points out that 'it is rare to find white Zimbabweans singled out for criticism or hear of xenophobic-inspired violence against them'. One participant in Dube's (2017, p. 407) study, an academic at a university in South Africa, reported that white academics from Europe in his department were called expatriates, while he was called a foreigner.

Angu (2023) concurs that the xenophobic and Afrophobic violence that has engulfed South African communities in recent years is linked to the perpetuation of racism and attempts to protect white privilege in post-apartheid South Africa. The pain, anger, and frustration that black people feel because of limited transformation is directed at foreign nationals, who are also struggling to eke out a living in a difficult economic environment. Those who seek to promote white privilege, including the emerging black middle class, blame most of South Africa's socioeconomic problems on African migrants. Angu (2023, p. 1) concurs with Achille Mbembe (2016) in arguing that 'post-apartheid South Africa is characterized by growing feelings of pain, anger and frustration amongst black communities triggered by pervasive social inequalities'. This anger has given birth to 'new forms of political and social activism shaped by crude violence, vandalism, destruction, brutal killings of women and children as well as thuggery in different black communities' (Angu, 2023, p. 1). By engaging in violence against African migrants, South Africans are responding to systemic violence that has kept black people in perpetual poverty since the demise of apartheid. Angu (2023, p. 2) intimates that 'black anger, pain and frustration are triggered by the "pervasive material inequality between whites and blacks"'. The anger and pain that pervades black communicates intricately intertwines with 'a global political economy of racial inequalities' (Angu, 2023, p. 3) that keeps black lives in limbo and redirects black anger to other blacks who are also victims of the same system. The general message that the privileged in South Africa, both black and white, want to disseminate to the disenfranchised is that 'the black-led government is prioritizing the wellbeing of illegal migrants at the expense of its own citizens' (Angu, 2023, p. 5). This is the underlying message behind anti-immigrant groupings such as #PutSouthAfricaFirst and Operation Dudula, as implied in the BBC film where the woman whose son has become a drug addict says, 'the government is doing nothing about it'.

Tella (2016) identifies three theories that have been used to explain the prevalence of xenophobia in South Africa. The first is the isolationist theory that explains xenophobia in terms of South Africa's history of apartheid, which isolated black South Africans from other Africans on the continent. The notion of South African exceptionalism is considered a product of this apartheid-era isolationism. The second is the scapegoating theory wherein South Africans blame foreigners for their socio-economic problems such as unemployment, poverty, and crime. The anger that South Africans must direct at those who have failed to transform society and improve the lives of ordinary citizens is directed at foreigners. The last is the biocultural hypothesis which claims that cultural and physiological differences between South Africans and African migrants make it easy for South Africans to identify and victimise foreigners.

Klotz (2016) discusses the centrality of borders in anti-immigration discourses. However, one cannot talk about borders in Africa without talking about colonialism and how it used borders to control and regulate black people. Communities living around the Zimbabwe-South Africa border have relatives and families on either side of the border. In the past, these communities could easily visit each other but today they cannot easily do so because they are deemed to belong to different countries. Mbembe (2019) understands the borderisation of the world in terms of the fears that govern the global present, particularly the fear of the 'other' whether in the form of the migrant or the so-called 'terrorist'. 'Wherever we look', Mbembe argues (2019, p. 8), 'the drive is simultaneously and decisively towards contraction, towards containment, towards enclosure and various forms of encampment, detention, and incarceration'. In the contemporary world, the border has become 'the name we should use to describe the organised violence that underpins both contemporary capitalism and our world order in general' (Mbembe, 2019, p. 9). If one takes Mbembe's argument to its logical conclusion, one will argue that South Africa has embraced the idea of the border not as a line of demarcation but of exclusion. Mbembe (2019) characterises the contemporary neoliberal world as one that is obsessed with the idea of apartheid, of separation, of living without others. In this world, it is believed that 'a separation wall [will] resolve a problem of excess numbers, a surplus of presence that some see as the primary reason for conditions of unbearable suffering' (Mbembe, 2016, p. 23). The migrant is conceptualised as the other par excellence, one who is so different it is not possible, even desirable, to reconcile and live with her.

A Note on Methodology

Data for this chapter were collected from three online sites, namely the *Daily Maverick* online, *Newsroom Africa* and South African Broadcasting Corporation (*SABC*) YouTube channels. The *Daily Maverick* is a South African independent newspaper, while Newsroom Africa and SABC are independent and government-controlled television channels respectively. Each of the selected sites carried a story about the Zimbabwe Exemption Permit which the Minister of Home Affairs wanted to terminate. Although we also reflected on the stories themselves, we were mainly interested in the comments posted by readers and/or viewers in response to the stories. We used netnography as a data collection method and tool. Netnography is a research method that seeks to transfer ethnographic research methods such as observation and document analysis to the online platform (Makombe, 2022, p. 160). Bainbridge (2000, p. 57) defines netnography as a 'relatively passive examination of web sites, without full interaction with the people who created them'. Data were purposively selected in line with the research objectives and categorised into themes. Purposive sampling is the selection of groups or categories to study based on their relevance to the research questions, the theoretical position and, most importantly, the explanation or account that one is developing (Yin, 2011). The themes emerged from the data through thematic analysis, a form of pattern recognition within the data, where emerging themes become the categories for analysis' (Fereday & Muir-Cochrane, 2006, p. 4). Seven (7) themes, ranging from economics to issues of governance emerged from the data. Participants were identified with their initials to ensure confidentiality. Since there were two stories by the *Daily Maverick*, one by Hwacha 'Kicking the can down the road' and another by Ndongo 'Zimbabwe Exemption permit termination', we identified the two stories as DM1 and DM2 respectively.

Discourses of the Zimbabwean Exemption Permit

The history of the Zimbabwean Exemption permit begins in April 2009 when the South African government decided to regularise Zimbabwean migrants through a special program called the Zimbabwe Dispensation Permit (ZDP) (Department of Home Affairs - Gazetted extension of ZEP, n.d.). At the time, many Zimbabweans had flocked into South Africa to escape the economic and political crisis that was arguably at its climax in Zimbabwe. Although the history of Zimbabwean migration to South Africa goes back to the 1880s, with the establishment of gold mines in Witwatersrand and Kimberley, the years 2007 and 2008 saw a significant increase in Zimbabwean migration particularly because of the deepening economic crisis and the violent elections of 2008. When South Africa's Department of Home Affairs announced the ZDP programme, it also requested those who held fraudulent documents and asylum permits to surrender them to the department to facilitate the regularisation process. By the end of the programme, about 200,000 Zimbabweans had been issued with the new permit which the Department went on to renew at regular intervals for several years. However, the Department was careful not to allow the permit to run for over five years because the South African constitution stipulates that if someone held a permit continuously for five years, they would be eligible for permanent residence. As a result, most of the permits were valid for four years in each cycle and would be renewed periodically. In 2017, the Zimbabwean Dispensation Permit, which was given a new name, the Zimbabwe Special Permit in 2014, had morphed into the Zimbabwe Exemption Permit (ZEP).

In 2021, South Africa's Minister of Home Affairs, Aaron Motsoaledi, decided to termite the Zimbabwe Exemption Permit, directing beneficiaries of the permit to other mainstream permits that were available under the Immigration Act (Department of Home Affairs, 2024). This decision caused a lot of panic among Zimbabweans and Human Rights groups who saw the decision as an attempt to implement mass deportation of Zimbabweans, most of whom had lived in South Africa for over 10 years. The main problem with the decision, at least from the perspective of most Zimbabwean immigrants, was that the mainstream permits that the Minister wanted them to apply for had stringent requirements which were waived under the special dispensation programme. Human Rights groups such as the Helen Suzman Foundation and the Zimbabwe Immigration Federation took the matter to court challenging the Minister's decision which they claimed was unfair because the affected parties had not been granted an opportunity to make representations as stipulated in the constitution. They also argued that the decision was unfair because most of the affected migrants had established themselves in South Africa and they knew no other home. In fact, the Zimbabwe Immigration Federation, led by Luke Dzviti, argued that the migrants deserved to be granted permanent residence because they were law abiding and were contributing to the South African economy.

Narratives of the Zimbabwean Exemption Permit:
Daily Maverick, Newsroom Africa, and *SABC News*

Following the decision by the high court, which ruled against the Minister's decision to terminate the ZEP, the three South African news channels, the *Daily Maverick* (newspaper), *Newsroom Africa*, and *SABC* news (television channels) ran stories that reflected on the court decision and its impact on the affected parties. The *Daily Maverick* published two opinion pieces on 8 August and 5 December 2023, one by Muchengeti Hwacha titled 'Kicking the can down the road – the Zimbabwean Exemption Permit saga continues' and another by Gaby Ndongo titled 'Zimbabwean Exemption Permit termination "is pushing people towards undocumented migration"' (Hwacha, 2023; Ndongo, 2023). Hwacha's piece argued that terminating the ZEP was an irresponsible decision on the part of the Department of Home Affairs because it did not solve the migration crisis. By refusing to extend the ZEP permits, the department was 'kicking the can down the road' or transferring the problem of Zimbabwean migration to someone else without addressing it. The article was accompanied by an image of a man displaying a ragged, dog-eared Zimbabwean passport. The old-looking passport spoke not only of the many years that Zimbabweans had lived (and continue to live) in South Africa but also about how Zimbabwean livelihoods have become entangled with ownership of a travel document.

The article put the number of ZEP holders living in South Africa at 178,000 although it also speculated that this number 'could easily swell' if one considered the children and other dependants of the permit holders. The word 'swell' is associated with an injured body; hence it conjured images of an expansion that caused pain. The article was generally critical of the minister's decision to terminate the ZEP, arguing that the decision had far-reaching consequences. The Minister's decision was described as 'baffling' because it went against the legalisation of Zimbabwean migrants, which the writer thought was the most rational way to deal with the migration crisis. In fact, the story suggested that Zimbabweans were being treated unfairly because they had not been afforded an opportunity to make representations as prescribed by the constitution. The writer also argued that there was no justification for deporting Zimbabweans back to Zimbabwe because the crisis which had made them migrate to South Africa was still ongoing.

Gaby Ngongo's piece titled 'Zimbabwean Exemption Permit termination is pushing people towards undocumented migration' relied on a report which was published by the Centre for Sociological Research and Practice (CSRP) which stated that the Department of Home Affairs was 'pushing people towards undocumented migration by making permits scarcer at a time when people can ill-afford to leave'. As in the previous article, the CSRP argued that deporting Zimbabweans back to a country in the throes of an economic crisis would only breed 'pockets of corruption' because migrants would have to look for alternative ways of remaining in South Africa. The article also argued that the minister's decision was unfair because most ZEP holders would not qualify for other permits such as work visas which required applicants to demonstrate that they had 'critical skills' that the South African economy needed. Quoting the CSRP report, the article argued that the Home Affairs Department was making it difficult for 'people to document themselves'. The article also suggested that terminating the permit was unfair because other migrants from developed countries were often granted the opportunity to apply for permanent residence after holding a valid permit for 5 years. The writer insinuated that South Africa had turned its back on the pan-African dream by enforcing colonial borders and neoliberal values that saw human beings as objects of capital who only had value when they contributed to the economy.

Newsroom Africa and *SABC* ran two separate stories in which they interviewed the Chief Executive Officer of the Zimbabwe Immigration Federation, Luke Dzviti and Nicole Fritz of the Helen Suzman Foundation, two organisations that represented Zimbabwean migrants (Newzroom Afrika, 2023; SABC News, 2023). In the Newsroom Africa interview, Luke Dzviti argued that the decision by Home Affairs was unfair because Zimbabweans had been asked to submit their documents in 2009 in the hope that they would get a better deal. Apart from the fact that Zimbabweans had already established themselves in South Africa and that they were contributing to the economy, Dzviti also pointed out that Zimbabweans were being scapegoated for the effects of the COVID-19 crisis. South Africans lost jobs during Covid, and the government was trying to address that problem by deporting Zimbabweans who had secured jobs before the crisis. Similarly, in the SABC story, the CEO of the Helen Suzman Foundation argued that the minister had flouted the constitution by failing to consult all those who were likely to be affected by his decision. The latter was therefore 'unlawful, unconstitutional and invalid' because it left migrants vulnerable to arrest and deportation.

In the following section, we analyse public responses to the four stories discussed above, in terms of firstly, how South Africans perceived Zimbabwean migration and secondly how they deployed the politics of viscerality to express anger, frustration, and disappointment about the multiple socio-economic challenges facing South Africa, including the migration crisis.

The Migration Crisis as a Crisis of Bad Governance

Some of the discussants who participated in the different discussion forums represented the migration crisis in South Africa as a crisis of governance on both sides of the Limpopo River. Responding to the *Daily Maverick* story 'Kicking the can down the road' MT saw the Zimbabwean migration crisis as emanating from 'an uncaring [ANC] government' which he believed should have 'exerted pressure on Mugabe' to fix the economic crisis in Zimbabwe during his tenure as president. MT was probably blaming South Africa, particularly Thabo Mbeki's government, for adopting the policy of quiet diplomacy which was not helpful in addressing the Zimbabwean crisis. He speculated that if the political elite had acted in time, 'we probably would not have seen that many Zim refugees'. MT sympathised with Zimbabwean migrants, describing them as 'poor Zimbabweans, some [of whom] have been here for 15 years and they are still on temp permits'. The question of the legal status of Zimbabwean migrants is a bone of contention in South Africa as we have discussed above. Some, like MT, believe that 'any other country would have given [the migrants] permanent residency by now'. Human Rights organisations such as the Helen Suzman Foundation have also argued that Zimbabweans deserve to be given permanent residence, not only because the constitution says so but also because they have lived in South Africa, abiding by its laws like any other citizen for many years. Concluding his comment, MT confessed that he had a Zimbabwean employee whom he characterised as 'good, honest, intelligent and hard working […] An asset to the economy'. While some have accused Zimbabweans, almost indiscriminately, of being criminal elements, MT recognised them as assets to the economy because of their work ethic and good attitude, thus suggesting that they have earned the right live in South Africa.

Another participant, SL, blamed the 'economic and political instability' in Zimbabwe for the illegal migration crisis. However, she/he did not understand why the South African government was giving 'unconditional support to the Zimbabwean government that is causing the problem'. Following the contested election of August 2023 in Zimbabwe, which the South African government endorsed although it was condemned by many observers including the regional body, SADC, some Zimbabweans felt that they had a right to stay in South Africa because the latter was complicit in the Zimbabwean crisis. One Zimbabwean participant, TM, quipped that Zimbabweans will 'stay here in South Africa until further notice, as long President Ramaphosa still standing with ZANUPf'. The implication was that South Africa had a responsibility to take care of Zimbabweans as pay back for supporting the governing regime in Zimbabwe. Commenting on DM2, RP also stated that 'it's just payback time [for South Africa] since Mugabe allowed the 'Freedom Fighters' right of passage in the fight for freedom'. This is quite interesting because some South Africans tend to think that South Africa owes Zimbabwe nothing. Other commentators such as JC believe that the problem is that Zimbabwe has a legitimacy crisis that probably emanates from the coup of November 2017 and the subsequent contested elections of 2018 and 2023. JC noted that if the ANC intervened to ensure that there was a legitimate government in Zimbabwe then 'the problem will go away by itself'. Unlike some South Africans who believed that South Africa owed Zimbabwe nothing, JC believed that South Africans should in fact 'hold the Anc accountable for propping up an illegitimate regime'.

Responding to the *Daily Maverick* story, DM1, PB argued, without providing any substantive evidence, that the decision by the Minister of Home Affairs to terminate the ZEP was motivated by a corrupt deal which had gone wrong. In recent years, both Zimbabwe and South Africa have had challenges with corruption especially among government officials. PB described the Minister of Home Affairs, Aaron Motsoaledi, as 'perpetually greedy Aaron' because of his alleged involvement in COVID-19 primary protection procurement deals. The minister's decision, as PB argued, was an attempt to 'threaten Emerson (the President of Zimbabwe) that unless he got a big fat slice of Marange diamonds, he would send 200k angry Zims back to Harare just before the elections'. The Zimbabwean election took place on 23 August 2023, a few months before the Minister's decision to terminate the permits. PB's source for this incriminating information is 'an Uber driver' whom he claims, 'never lie[s]'. The politics of viscerality, as Achille Mbembe (2016) has told us, privileges personal experience, sometimes at the expense of reason.

The foregoing arguments also resonate with Achille Mbembe's notion of 'planetary entanglement' which suggests that the contemporary world is so intricately connected that it is impossible for insiders to live alone without outsiders. The advent of globalisation has created a situation whereby a problem *here* is also a problem *elsewhere* because, as Mbembe argues, the *here* and the *elsewhere* have become so entangled that it is difficult (if not impossible) to distinguish one from the other. Zimbabwe and South Africa maybe two sovereign countries but they are inextricably interconnected.

Neo-Revisionist Discourses: We Owe Zimbabweans Nothing

In theorising the politics of viscerality, Mbembe argues that the new generation of South African activists does not seem to have any regard for the past or past sacrifices. Even those who spent years in prison fighting the apartheid system no longer have the moral authority to make any claims. For this group, what matters is the pain and suffering of the present and not stories about what happened in the past. In the context of this analysis, this group believes that Zimbabwe has nothing on South Africa. Responding to the *Daily Maverick* story (DM1), VM did not understand how 'one [can] blame another country for how it governs it's people'. VM believed that since Zimbabwe was 'a sovereign country with its own laws' its problems should not affect South Africa, another sovereign country with its own laws. This argument does not hold water because globalisation has seriously undermined the neoliberal idea of sovereignty. VM invoked sovereignty to justify the exclusion of outsiders from South Africa's territorial space which he believed was reserved for citizens. Interestingly, VM also argued in the spirit of the new generation of anti-establishment activists in South Africa that:

> South Africans never crossed boarders in droves even in the height of apartheid, we stayed and participated in fighting apartheid, Zimbabweans must do the same. It amazes me seeing that it is only white South Africans who are fighting for the creation of a Zimbabweans province in South Africa.

VM might be correct to say that South Africans never crossed borders 'in droves', however, his argument is somewhat revisionist in that it creates the impression that South Africa fought and defeated apartheid without outside assistance.

Unlike Zimbabweans who left their country 'in droves', South Africans stayed in the country and participated in the fight against apartheid. Based on this revised historical position, VM urged Zimbabweans to do the same. Responding to DM2, SM concurred with VM that 'during apartheid South Africans never flocked to Zimbabwe at this rate'. SM also argued that 'South Africans died fighting for the freedom', hence Zimbabweans should also fight for their freedom. Mbembe has told us that for the visceral subject, facts do not really matter. This is evident in SM's insinuation that only South Africans deserve to enjoy their freedom because they fought for it. Some scholars such as Angu (2023) have argued that the anger that South Africans direct towards foreigners is in fact meant for white South Africans who are still largely in control of the economy years after the demise of apartheid. Although it is not clear why VM believed that some white South Africans 'are fighting for the creation of a Zimbabwean province in South Africa', one can only speculate that this is probably because white South Africans are the major beneficiaries of cheap Zimbabwean labour. Another participant, JM, provided a revisionist assessment of the Zimbabwean migration crisis arguing that Zimbabwe created its own problems by removing the colonial government. JM argued that the Zimbabwean crisis was created by 'those who, when they had full bellies and an economy, still took up arms, to liberate themselves from having enough to eat'. Probably, JM is a former Rhodesian harping on 'the good old days' when whites were in charge and the economy was functional. What JM did not say, perhaps because historical facts did not really matter to him, was that the economy that he was referring to, benefited a few whites at the expense of the majority black people. However, as Mbembe has argued, the visceral subject is not driven by reason but by personal experience. JM went on to advise the writer of the story, whom he believes to be Zimbabwean, to 'go back to his country and solve the problem he and his countrymen created'. Because the visceral subject uses pain and suffering to make claims, he has no interest in understanding the pain of those who cannot understand his pain.

Economic Discourses of Zimbabwean Migration

Contemporary neoliberal discourses of migration tend to treat human beings as objects of capital, whose value depend on what they can contribute to the neoliberal economy. Those who cannot add value to the system are often treated as surplus beings who must be discarded, either through imprisonment, long waiting periods in detention centres or deportation. Responding to DM2, NM supported the Minister's decision saying that:

> If we were recruiting people that were adding to the shortage of skills, they would be welcome (However Zim suffers). But we have enough unskilled people. I feel sorry for these immigrants, but South Africa has not got enough money to save the rest of Africa including the accompanying social grants.

NB's comment seems to echo a neoliberal rationality that values only those people that 'add[...] to the shortage of skills' in South Africa. These 'valuable' people can be integrated into the South African economy 'however Zim suffers'. This neoliberal reason does not only treat human beings (Zimbabweans) as pieces in a giant liberal economic jigsaw puzzle but also pursues a zero-sum logic where some lose, and others gain. What matters is that South Africa must get skilled people, it does not matter how much Zimbabwe suffers in the process. NB's logic is reminiscent of Popi Ramathuba's hospital rant discussed before. He claims that he 'feels sorry for these migrants' but he believes that South Africa does not have 'enough money to save the rest of Africa'. The unskilled Zimbabweans, like the sick woman in the Ramathuba case, must suffer and die in their country instead of crossing into South Africa to cause suffering for South Africans.

Most participants on the different discussion platforms made false equivalences between Zimbabwean migration and economic and social problems in South Africa, as if Zimbabwean migration directly led to problems such as unemployment and shortage of medication in hospitals. There is no attempt to recognise that Zimbabwean migrants also benefit the South African economy through skills and tax. Businesses in border towns such as Musina also benefit from Zimbabwean migrants who flock to the city to buy goods and services. Responding to the Newsroom Africa interview in which the leader of the Zimbabwean Immigration Federation, Luke Dzviti, argued that deporting Zimbabwean migrants would lead to a humanitarian crisis, MK quipped:

> he is talking about the 'catastrophe' in Zimbabwe if 178k zimbabweans can be deported, what about the 178k South Africans who will move out of catastrophe? Zimbabweans are selfish, they dont care if South Africans are going to bed hungry.

MK's comment suggests that the deportation of 178,000 Zimbabweans would automatically move 178,000 South Africans out of catastrophe. Apart from the fact that MK does not really care about the catastrophe that would happen on the other side of the border if Zimbabweans were deported, deporting Zimbabweans would not necessarily move South Africans out of catastrophe. MK's reason is problematic because it assumes that South Africans possess the same skills that Zimbabwean migrants possess. Based on this false equivalence, MK concluded that 'Zimbabwean are selfish, they don't care if South Africans are going to bed hungry'. Scholars such as Angu (2023) and Muzondidya (2010) have argued that the anger the South Africans direct at Zimbabweans and other African migrants is an expression of frustration with existing inequalities in the South African economy. That South Africans are 'going to bed hungry' has more to do with structural inequalities in the South African economy than it has to do with Zimbabwean migration, therefore, deporting Zimbabweans may not necessarily put food on the tables of hungry South Africans.

I Am Not My Brother's Keeper: Zimbabwean Migration as a Form of Abuse

The politics of viscerality is the politics of anger, often expressed through some human action targeting the perceived cause of a problem. A good example is that of the RhodesMustFall activist Chumani Maxwele, who expressed his frustration with Rhodes' legacy by emptying poo on his statue at the University of Cape Town. The subheading of this section 'I am not my brother's keeper' aims to capture the logic of contemporary South African radical politics, as expressed on the selected discussion platforms. In response to the Newsroom Africa interview, HM commented that 'the people of Zimbabwe who live in Mzansi are holding us ransom using our constitution and courts and they cannot fix their own country. Its amazing!!'. Here, South Africa is portrayed as a victim of its own democratic institutions and processes. Zimbabwean migrants, like terrorists, have captured South Africa using its own courts to make claims to a space which, in HM's view, does not belong to them. The statement 'its amazing!!' followed by two exclamation marks is probably not a complement but an expression of disgust at the South African court system which has failed to deal with the Zimbabwean migration problem once and for all. Because discourses of viscerality draw on anger and personal experiences of pain, they often degenerate into insults and violence. Mbembe (2016a) has also stated that the politics of viscerality relies on a misreading of the works of Steve Biko and Frantz Fanon, as if these scholars were apostles of wanton violence. This is evident in VF's response to the Newsroom Africa interview:

> These people, you give them a hand, they DEMAND the whole arm. Uproot your established life back to your country, you knew that that permit was temporary.

The language of othering 'these people' identifies Zimbabweans are different, not human like us, and therefore, deserving of deportation without sympathy. The word 'demand' is in capital letters to suggest that VF is angry about this unreasonable demand. One of the arguments that the Zimbabwean Immigration Federation raised in opposing the minister's decision to terminate the ZEP was that Zimbabwean migrants had already established themselves and built their lives in South Africa and their children knew no other home except South Africa. VF's comment was not concerned about the impact that the deportation would have on Zimbabwean migrants settled in South Africa. All that mattered to him was that they should uproot themselves and go back to their country. Similarly, MN described the attempt by Zimbabwean ZEP holders to stay in South Africa as an 'obsession' and 'pure insanity'. He encouraged Zimbabwean migrants, whom he called 'you guys' to cast [their] eyes to the British, [their] colonisers and leave us alone'. In MN's formulation, Zimbabweans should simply be 'neighbours' with no sense of entitlement to the South African state. Interestingly, MN felt that the British were supposed to take responsibility for the Zimbabwean crisis and not South Africa. The logic of MN's comment is difficult to follow especially because Zimbabwe assisted South Africa's fight against apartheid. Other participants such as AO, MT, and MH resorted to insults and name-calling. AO described Zimbabweans as 'lamakwerekwere' who had no right to 'tell us what to do in our country'. In concluding his remark, AO used the vulgar Zulu word, *kunganyiwa*, which means someone will soil himself/herself, thus suggesting that if Zimbabweans refused to go peacefully, South Africans would resort to violence and remove them by force. The common thread behind these comments is frustration with the status quo which manifests using insults and/or vulgar language.

The Visceral Reason: Of Frustration, Anger, and Despair

The visceral subject as Achille Mbembe (2016a) has argued, is one who is in a state of asphyxiation, one who cannot breathe because of the circumstances of his/her life. Because she is facing an existential crisis, the visceral subject tends to act instinctively, sometimes irrationally. The visceral body is overwhelmed with pain, it is a body that has assumed pain as its identity. This is perhaps the reason why the politics of viscerality have no room for negotiation or listening to the other. In the BBC film 'Fear and Loathing' which I have referred to before, a South African activist tells a foreign shop owner, 'if you disrespect us, we will beat you'. The said shop owner was merely trying to understand why they were harassing her but for the activist that was disrespect which could attract a beating. Because the pain that the visceral subject suffers is indescribable, it is all over the body, the latter is more inclined to act instinctively rather than opt for negotiation. Responding to the Newsroom Africa interview, BN felt 'disgusted' and 'sick' by merely 'listening to this guy' who was 'fighting government in a foreign country'. BN's disgust was directed at the leader of the Zimbabwean Immigration Federation who had taken the Minister of Home Affairs to court in defence of Zimbabwean migrants. Similarly, TN characterised the claim by some Zimbabwean migrants that 'their kids know South Africa as their only home' as 'ridiculous'. Responding in Xhosa, NB said 'sidikiwe ngama Zimbabweans' which means 'we are fed up with Zimbabweans'. The use of derogatory and dismissive language suggests that the participants have made up their minds about what needs to be done: Zimbabweans must go back to their country. Other participants such as DN and LM echoed similar sentiments. DN believed that South African TV channels such as Newsroom Africa should not 'continue giving such people a platform to talk rubbish' while LM expressed shock at why the news channel was 'entertaining this guy'. Similarly, FR called Luke Dzviti, the Zimbabwean Immigration Federation representative a 'con artist' arguing that his victory (in the court case) would mean 'disaster for us' in South Africa. JE also expressed the same sentiments calling on the police to arrest 'these people... with no mercy' and 'stop being soft on these migrants'. The use of phrases such as 'these people' and 'these migrants' creates a virtual ontological boundary between the citizen and the outsider, which subsequently justifies deportation without mercy. Since they are not like us, their problems are not our problems. Achille Mbembe (2019) has argued that the neoliberal state sees the migrant as an excess presence that must be ejected out of its borders. KN's question 'why are they not at the centre of the joburg fire demise' is a death wish on the migrant population, which according to neoliberal logic, is justifiable, because in any case, migrants are surplus bodies. The Joburg 'fire demise' that KN refers to happened on the night of 31 August 2023, killing migrants (mostly Zimbabweans) and some South African nationals. KN's wish for the death of the other can be explained in terms of what Mbembe (2016a) characterised as the desire to inflict on the oppressor (read as migrant) the same pain that he/s she has inflicted on me.

This chapter has deployed Achile Mbembe's (2016) notion of the politics of viscerality and his theorisation of the neoliberal obsession with borders, to argue that Zimbabwean migrants in South Africa have become soft targets of the frustration that should be directed at the slow pace of transformation in post-apartheid South Africa. Scholars such as Muzondidya (2010) and Angu (2023) have argued that the violence that South Africans direct at African migrants (including Zimbabweans) is in fact meant to highlight the structural inequalities in contemporary South Africa which continue to keep most black people in conditions of abject poverty. The stories that we have analysed here reflect the entanglement of relations in the contemporary neo-liberal order, which make it difficult to maintain a clear demarcation between the *here* and the *elsewhere*, the inside and the outside. The stories show that Zimbabwe is intricately intertwined with South Africa because of their shared history of the anti-colonial struggle and the general interconnectedness of things in a globalised world. Despite these entangled planetary relations, most participants on the four online discussion platforms advocated the termination of the ZEP and the deportation of Zimbabwean migrants. Their comments exhibit a radical politics of viscerality which privileges violence as a way of dealing with problems. Most of the participants felt that Zimbabwean migrants were holding South Africa at ransom, and the solution for them, was to terminate the Zimbabwe Exemption permit and force them out by force, if necessary. The use of insults and derogatory language by the participants pitted Zimbabwean migrants as 'others' who were not human like us, the singular cause of *our* suffering. For most of the participants, deporting Zimbabweans would, therefore, translate into a better life for South African citizens.

References

Angu, P. (2023). Being black and non-citizen in South Africa: Intersecting race, white privilege and afrophobic violence in contemporary South Africa. *Sociology Compass*, *17*(9), e13123.

Bainbridge, W. S. (2000). Religious ethnography on the World Wide Web. In K. Hadden & D. E. Cowan (Eds.), *Religion on the internet: Research prospects and promises* (pp. 55–80). Elsevier.

Banda, F., & Mawadza, A. (2015). 'Foreigners are stealing our birth right': Moral panics and the discursive construction of Zimbabwean immigrants in South African media. *Discourse and Communication*, *9*(1), 47–64.

Department of Home Affairs - Supreme Court of Appeal grants Minister Motsoaledi leave to appeal the Zimbabwe Immigration Federation (ZIF) matter. (2024, March 14). https://www.dha.gov.za/index.php/statements-speeches/1754-supreme-court-of-appeal-grants-minister-motsoaledi-leave-to-appeal-the-zimbabwe-immigration-federation-zif-matter

Department of Home Affairs - Gazetted extension of ZEP. (n.d.). https://www.dha.gov.za/index.php/immigration-services/gazetted-extension-of-zep

Dube, G. (2017). Levels of othering—The case of Zimbabwean migrants in South Africa, *Nationalism and Ethnic Politics*, *23*(4), 391–412. doi:10.1080/13537113.2017.1380458

Fanon, F. (1952). *Black skin, white masks*. http://ci.nii.ac.jp/ncid/BB11785653

Fereday, J., & Muir-Cochrane, E. (2006). Demonstrating rigor using thematic analysis: A hybrid approach of inductive and a deductive coding and theme development. *International Journal of Qualitative Methods, 5*(1), 1–11. https://doi.org/10.1177/160940690600500107.

Hwacha, M. (2023, December 5). Kicking the can down the road – The Zimbabwean Exemption Permit saga continues. *Daily Maverick*. https://www.dailymaverick.co.za/article/2023-12-05-zimbabwean-exemption-permit-saga-continues/

Klotz, A. (2016). Borders and the roots of Xenophobia in South Africa. *South African Historical Journal, 68*(2), 180–194. https://doi.org/10.1080/02582473.2016.1153708

Kriger, N. (2010). The politics of legal status for Zimbabweans in South Africa. In J. McGregor & R. Primorac (Eds.), *Zimbabwe's new diaspora displacement and the cultural politics of survival* (pp. 77–100). Berghahn Books.

Mbembe, A. (2016a). The society of enmity. *Radical Philosophy, 200*, 23–35.

Mbembe, A. (2016b). *Frantz Fanon and the Politics of Viscerality*. John Hope Franklin Humanities Institute at Duke University. https://www.youtube.com/watch?v=lg_BEodNaEA&t=3389s

Mbembe, A. (2019). Bodies as borders. *From the European South, 4*, 5–18.

Muzondidya, J. (2010). Makwerekwere: Migration, citizenship and identity among Zimbabweans in South Africa. In J. McGregor & R. Primorac (Eds.), *Zimbabwe's new diaspora displacement and the cultural politics of survival*. Berghahn Books.

Ndongo, G. (2023, August 8). Zimbabwean Exemption Permit termination 'is pushing people towards undocumented migration'. *Daily Maverick*. https://www.dailymaverick.co.za/article/2023-08-08-zim-exemption-permit-termination-and-undocumented-migration/

Newzroom Afrika. (2023, November 4). *Zimbabwe Immigration Federation seeks to halt termination of ZEPs*. https://www.youtube.com/watch?v=fmuHnC25B3A

Nyamnjoh, F. (2006). *Insiders and outsiders: Citizenship and Xenophobia in Contemporary Southern Africa*. Zed Books.

Nyandoro, M. (2010). Implications for policy discourse: The influx of Zimbabwean Migrants into South Africa. In E. Guild & S. Mantu (Eds.), *Constructing and imagining labour migration: Perspectives of control from five continents* (pp. 109–134). Routledge.

SABC News. (2023, September 4). *Spotlight on Zimbabwean exemption permit*. https://www.youtube.com/watch?v=xbKdo23W-fY

Tella, O. (2016). Understanding Xenophobia in South Africa: The individual, the state and the international system. *Insight on Africa, 8*(2), 142–158.

Yin, R. K. (2011). *Qualitative research from start to finish*. Guilford Press.

Chapter 8

Post-Migration Discourse and Identity Crisis: The Case of Nigeria

Keywords: Culture; identity crisis; post-migration; patriotism; emigrant population

In discussing post-migration discourse as well as identity crisis, this chapter draws evidence from the Nigerian context considering that Nigeria has the largest emigrant population in Africa (Nwozor et al., 2022). The assumption is that given its long history of migration, Nigeria can offer rich discursive data on post-migration and identity crises. This chapter examines discourses that emerge after migration, whether short- or long-term, vis-à-vis issues of identity crisis to obtain a balanced understanding of migration discourse in Nigeria. Generally, migrating to a new environment is accompanied by challenges of adaptation, homesickness, and lack of a sense of belonging/identity. Communication practices stemming especially from the opinions of people who have migrated are thus the focus of this chapter. The dispositions of migrants after migration as well as their views on conversations surrounding migration are analysed. It is common practice in Nigeria that some migrants encourage migration while others discourage it based on their experiences. In fact, several successful migrants have become popular for offering migration-related content on different social media platforms. They provide information that specifically deals with their diverse experiences of migration.

According to De Fina and Baynham (2012), psychologists regard migration as one of the processes that most profoundly unsettle and reshape people's lives. Matters of identity are significant in the immigration endeavour. Chirongoma (2021), in an exploration of how migration presents many adjustment challenges for Zimbabweans, observes that leaving the comfort of one's home, being uprooted from loved ones and from all that is familiar, and venturing into the unknown all contribute to identity problems. The author adds that some migrants feel they have been stripped of their sense of belonging after living in the diaspora for extended periods. The concern in discourses of migration is that the original identities of people are threatened after relocation to a different society. These discourses extend even beyond the current generation since descendants of migrants eventually assume new identities in host countries. This chapter discusses selected social media content relating to identity crisis since De Fina and Baynham (2012) argue that narratives told by immigrants focus on the construction of identities as scholars investigate how immigrants deal with the 'unsettling' stable notions of self, of place, and how they express and negotiate belonging.

From successful migration stories to many unsuccessful ones, Nigerian migrants experience different realities reproduced in migration discourses through positive and negative innuendos. According to Obi-Ani et al. (2020, p. 11):

> Migrants are attracted to sources of wealth as a moth is to light. Europe is the foremost part of the industrialized world, well-endowed, and better governed. It is its fabled wealth that many migrants are irresistibly drawn to. But Europe is a fortress which only the rich and powerful could easily access. Despite its insurmountable odds, Nigerian migrants, many of them deluded by the grandiose wealth to be attained, stake everything, their patrimony and even life to attain. Many forged travel documents to actualize their quest to partake in this alchemy that would banish excruciating poverty in their lives. Others stow away in ships under turbulent seas to reach their destination – Europe. While a lot more defy the Sahara Desert to cross the perilous Mediterranean Sea Islands of Lampadusa and Spanish Canary Islands to embrace the cherished El Dorado more often in vain. The migrants' attempt to get around this fortress Europe has cost so many lives in recent times.

The quote above represents overt and covert attempts by Nigerians to migrate in search of better economic opportunities. It also explains why many Nigerian migrants tend to portray a positive outlook abroad despite facing enormous challenges in their new countries. These realities, obvious or not, are often inferred in post-migration discourses as matters of identity. Obi-Ani et al. (2020) observe that many medical doctors, engineers, lawyers, accountants are performing demeaning jobs such as cab driving, cleaning, and security jobs in European cities rather than return home. Migration, thus, not only changes social and cultural identities of Nigerians but also their professional identities. In their words, Nigerians are overcome by feelings of shame when they realise that El Dorado is a complete sham and thus portray their living standards abroad as perfect. Below, we examine post-migration discourses on Nigerian social media platforms, with a particular focus on the topic of identity crisis.

Method

This chapter also employed netnography for the purposes of data collection. As already indicated, netnography pertains to passively examining websites, without full interaction with the people who created them (Bainbridge, 2000). We purposively searched for conversations that expressed issues of post-migration as well as identity crisis on X (formerly Twitter) and Facebook platforms specifically from/about Nigerians. The following keywords were used to narrow our search either individually or combined in some cases: challenges of living abroad, japa, Nigerian passport, culture shock, factory worker, UK, Canada, and doctor. The names of the authors have been redacted for anonymity purposes. In the first section, based on the data collected, we started by analysing post-migration drawing on the myriad of challenges faced by and opportunities for Nigerian outmigrants. Then, the fulfilled and unfulfilled dreams of migrants are discussed before examining the context of return migration. In the second section on identity crisis, a broad classification of the data revealed three categories namely: social, cultural, and professional identity.

Post-Migration Discourse in Nigerian Context

Although many Nigerians perceive migration as a path to breakthrough, the reality is distant from common beliefs. Unfortunately for many, the reality only becomes evident after the fact, having invested all their resources in the process. Social media data suggests that challenges as well as opportunities abound for Nigerian emigrants in the diaspora. In Nigerian post-migration discourse, the former is used to discourage other Nigerians from travelling while the latter generally serves the purpose of encouraging Nigerians to migrate. Both challenges and opportunities are represented as a way of controlling migration narratives by drawing comparisons between Nigeria and the diaspora or by creating specific impressions in the minds of those in the process of migrating. In both instances, the discourses produced influence the thinking of Nigerians and either: (a) enlighten them about the factual realities of migration compared to imagined realities, (b) encourage them to migrate by citing many opportunities, (c) discourage them from migrating since Nigeria seems to be better than the diaspora in some regards, or (d) demonstrate a sense of connection with Nigeria emphasising that the mass exodus will not solve Nigeria's problems. Examples of these posts drawn from Facebook and X are below:

i. *Japa isn't the solution to every problem in Nigeria!!! (DW, X)*.
ii. *Japa is not the solution people think it is. Most people abroad are suffering and smiling (OK, X)*.
iii. *Some people think japa will magically help them. I have been here in the UK for over 8 years without going home and Nigeria is still touching me here (JO, Facebook)*.
iv. *These japa crooners are so mean. It's not like you are really enjoying the life over there because some of you are struggling big time. Every time japa, japa, japa as if the cost to japa is that cheap (MA, X)*.
v. *I literally live on peanuts here now and I was way better financially back home, but see, let me continue to manage these peanuts because nothing will change about Nigeria anytime soon. Also, the opportunities here can't be compared to Nigeria. If not for the finance, you can japa for the opportunities at least (OD, Facebook)*.

vi. *To see a doctor in Canada and UK these days is so difficult and expensive. Food is also not cheap here at all. Rent is extremely high. You people in Nigeria don't know what you are enjoying honestly. Not everything is as easy here (MO, X).*

vii. *On this japa matter, many have travelled but the problems didn't fully disappear. Nigerians, we can't run forever. We need a working Nigeria. We need to fight for this country. No place like home (LB, X).*

viii. *I have not fulfilled my japa goals for the past 3 years but at least I don't have to worry so much about all the problems in Nigeria. So, if you have means to japa, please take it serious and ignore all these people wey dey talk say abroad no good. But make sure you have a plan before going abroad o make your eyes no peel (OO, X).*

ix. *Crazy thing about traveling is that you can't come back empty-handed after realising that it is not greener on the other side... if you do that, you would be seen as a failure (PG, X).*

In a bid to discourage Nigerians from considering migration as the answer to the socio-economic realities of the country, DW states that *japa isn't the solution to every problem in Nigeria*. The comments and responses to the post, although mostly hilarious, echo many Nigerian sentiments regarding migration. Other X users reminded the author that they have never considered *japa* as the solution to Nigeria's problems. Instead, they conceived of *japa* as the solution to their own personal problems which Nigeria as a country has exacerbated. In the responses, many Nigerians argued that the intention has never been to resolve Nigeria's problems as that is outside their capacity. For them, the intention has been to provide solutions to their own personal problems. In other words, this discourse exposes a misconception about migration which posits that the mass exodus from Nigeria will not solve its problems. Realistically, many Nigerians emigrate for personal reasons, i.e. the individual desire to provide solutions to personal problems. As such, the attempt to unconsciously manipulate Nigerians to perhaps consider remaining in the country to solve the country's problems, is instantly repelled since this is beyond any individual's capacity.

The second example, by OK, is arguably an extension of the first as the author clearly alludes to the personal factors which the author of the first example neglects. It can be inferred from the view of OK that although Nigerians migrate for the purpose of attending to their personal needs, *most people abroad are suffering and smiling*. The author attempts to advise Nigerians that pastures are not always greener on the other side and that they should desist from assuming that migrating would instantly solve their personal problems. While there might seem to be some truth in the post, reactions from many Nigerians suggest that the sole purpose of such social media posts is to frighten potential migrants. For several years, discourses that frame the diaspora as a difficult environment to live in, have become popular in Nigeria. It is the assumption of many Nigerians that such discourses are deceitful and aim at gatekeeping. However, discouraging views about living abroad have not achieved the aim of preventing Nigerians from migrating since even genuine concerns are perceived as gatekeeping efforts.

A point conceded by Haugen (2012) is that many economically successful Nigerian migrants could be suspected of painting a bleak picture to prevent new people from arriving and copying their achievements. Although social media can be credited for providing daily access to migration information, it is also used as a tool for circulating depressing news by successful emigrants.

In the third example on the topic of post-migration, JO extends the argument made in the first two posts albeit from a different perspective. Like the previous authors, the author of the third post admits that migrating does not solve personal problems. Citing his own experience of living abroad for more than eight years, he admits that he is unable to fully avoid the challenges emanating from Nigeria. The expression *Nigeria is still touching me* is an indication that despite residing abroad, he is still concerned by the happenings in the country. In essence, migration does not fully resolve personal problems since the migrant cannot always pretend not to be unconcerned about the ongoing realities in Nigeria. Considering that migrants maintain social, economic, and family ties with their home country, the perception that migrating solves all the problems of migrants is an exaggeration. From caring about family members and friends in Nigeria to being concerned about the social ills in the country, as reflected daily in news items, it is almost impossible for a migrant to be completely removed from the realities at home. Thus, in Nigerian post-migration discourse, it is evident that migrants are continuously influenced by their home country despite perceiving their new countries as superior.

Often reflected strongly in Nigerian post-migration discourse is the attempt by many emigrants to appear as more privileged than stay-at-home Nigerians, which was discussed in the previous chapter. Notwithstanding the attempts by many Nigerians at gatekeeping through controlling narratives, some have excitedly encouraged other Nigerians to migrate although somewhat arrogant in their approaches. The arrogant ones are referred to by MA as the *'japa crooners'*. *Japa crooners* can be understood as *japa* enthusiasts who constantly present *japa* as a feasible way out of Nigeria's problems thus regarding people who have not migrated as passive in their personal development. In MA's description, *japa* enthusiasts are perceived as 'mean'. The author criticises their living standards abroad suggesting that their quality of life is not entirely in keeping with the degree of arrogance they display on social media. MA is particularly unhappy about the incessant *japa* messages often propagated by migrants who have the resources to migrate thus ignoring the costs involved for people who cannot afford the associated expenses. The view of the author is located in post-migration discourse which tends to portray migration as easily achievable by those who have successfully managed to do so.

The author of the fifth post, OD, partly echoes the sentiments of MA author in terms of living standards abroad. Compared to Nigerian living standards, OD describes his living conditions abroad as living on peanuts, i.e. a small amount of money. According to OD, life in Nigeria was more financially rewarding than living abroad yet the author is content with the 'peanuts' since the situation in Nigeria will unlikely be resolved. In Nigerian post-migration discourse, many migrants lament the conditions of their lives abroad yet discard the possibility of ever returning to Nigeria. It is the understanding of these migrants that although life abroad is not luxurious, the opportunities it presents can never be compared with the realities of Nigeria. OD, although more financially buoyant in Nigeria, prefers to remain where he is for the opportunities it brings which are absent in Nigeria – thus advising Nigerians to overlook the financial aspect in their migration goals and to focus on the avalanche of opportunities. This notion coincides with the view of Okeke-Ihejirika and Odimegwu (2023) that socio-economic opportunities remain significant for Nigerians to persevere abroad since the destination countries are perceived to have better socio-economic conditions and opportunities (pull factors), while the country of origin's situation is comparably much less favourable (push factors).

Nigerian post-migration discourses, especially through the views of emigrants, also reveal areas in which Nigeria is seemingly better than the countries abroad. Many emigrants cite access to healthcare and inflation as factors where Nigeria fares better. For instance, MO believes that access to healthcare is easier and more affordable in Nigeria. MO also believes that the costs associated with procuring food items in Nigeria are affordable. Hence, MO feels that those residing in Nigeria should be appreciative of the affordable living standards. In Nigerian social media discourse, such a post can be easily dismissed as an attempt to discourage out-migration. In essence, the basis for comparison is non-existent since the demands of countries such as Canada and the United Kingdom (UK) mentioned by MO are completely different from the living conditions in Nigeria. The importance of the context cannot be overlooked. While access to medical doctors might be tougher in Canada or the UK, a Nigerian can easily see a medical doctor in private hospitals, but the related costs are expensive for many Nigerians. Additionally, the medical facilities and equipment available in the UK cannot be accessed in Nigeria and this is confirmed by the fact that most wealthy Nigerians prefer to receive healthcare treatments abroad. At the same time, the economic conditions of developed countries cannot be compared with underdeveloped or developing countries.

In the seventh post, like a few others, LB admits that migration does not fully answer all individual problems. The author's perception is that even though many Nigerians have migrated, they cannot fully escape the inherent problems in the country. The alternative would be to create the kind of country that is desired by Nigerians. Post-migration discourse in Nigeria also features patriotic views from some Nigerians. For them, the belief is that remaining in Nigeria and deploying their skills in the development of the country will assist in the growth of the country. The statement *'Nigerians, we can't run forever'* can be considered as an inward reflection meant to encourage Nigerians to build the country since there is *'no place like home'*. The author calls on Nigerians to *'fight for their country'* in a bid to build the country they desire and by so doing reduce the current rate of outmigration. However, as interesting as this might appear, the chances of implementation are extremely low since the concept of *fight* relates to Nigerians' taking active roles in rebuilding the country. The challenges with this view are hydra-headed. On the one hand, such a rebuilding exercise takes time. On the other hand, having established in some of the previous chapters that failed governance is one of the motivating migration drivers, any attempt to rebuild Nigeria requires reforming the political system – an adventure that will be met with resistance and violence given the trajectory of the country's socio-political realities.

Discussions surrounding the need to fulfil one's dreams can also be found in Nigerian post-migration discourse. It can be gleaned from the OO's post that the author set a personal goal for migrating, but the goal has not yet been achieved even after three years. However, OO appreciates the need to detach from Nigeria's enormous problems. Analysing this statement critically gives us an indication that the author's personal goal is to live abroad free from the common problems in Nigeria. Thus, in Nigerian post-migration discourse, Nigerians tend to admit their inability to achieve certain goals which is then overcome by their perceived better living standards. In essence, personal goals are treated with less attention so long as other basic amenities are present. It is for this reason that the author advises Nigerians to pursue their migration goals relentlessly regardless of personal goals, especially since the environment abroad is more enabling and less problematic. According to OO, intending migrants should *'ignore all these people wey dey talk say abroad no good'*. Translated, the statement means that intending migrants should ignore other people who are quick to denigrate living standards abroad to gatekeep out-migracy. The author (OO) however cautions intending migrants to ensure that they plan effectively and efficiently before embarking on migration. *But make sure you have a plan before going abroad o make your eyes no peel* is used to emphasise the need for adequate planning before migrating. The use of the sound 'o' in Nigerian Pidgin, especially when prolonged, is deployed for emphasis which is the author's way of reinforcing proper planning. The phrase *make your eyes no peel* in Nigerian pidgin can also be translated as 'to avoid regrets'. As such, it can be inferred that although migrating comes with several challenges, planning ahead can assist in softening some of the challenges.

The final example by PG captures the pressure associated with migrating. The author of the post states that upon realising that living abroad is not as fruitful as envisaged, the fear of being perceived as a failure prevents migrants from returning to Nigeria. They prefer to remain abroad to avoid being ridiculed; the return of a migrant to Nigeria is supposed to be accompanied by wealth and fortune. Even though living abroad is not as rewarding as expected, it remains the view of many that returning home unwealthy after living abroad is unfortunate. According to Haugen (2012), the misfortune of returning empty-handed to Nigeria may be attributed to laziness, lack of faith and perseverance, or worse: a façade put up to escape from the social obligations to share the acquired wealth. Adeniyi and Onyeukwu (2021) attribute the reasons for return migration to factors such as family reunification, culture shock abroad, and differences in ethics, among others. However, this chapter does not focus on these reasons but on the surrounding discourse regarding return migration. In Nigeria, the rate of return migration is significantly low since many of the reasons that led to migration in the first instance have never been addressed. Notwithstanding this, a few people do return following a successful stint of migration; some to establish businesses in the country after prosperous achievements abroad. Others, although in low numbers, return due to hardships abroad. By and large, post-migration discourses on Nigerian social media also address return migration. Selected instances include:

i. *I was contemplating returning to Nigeria if Obi had won. I know some friends who were ready to return too. But I don't see any hope in this new government honestly. Make I just siddown jejely (MD, X).*
ii. *A working Nigeria will see a mass return of Nigerians in diaspora. Many of us really don't want to be abroad but have no choice (SR, X).*
iii. *This is not a good time for anyone to return to Nigeria to set up businesses. The businesses will suffer and all the money will finish. Doing business in that country is frustrating and I regret it right now. I learnt the hard way (EB, X).*
iv. *The thought of going back to Nigeria does not even occur to me. I commend anyone thinking of such because what will I go and do there. Will I go and look for jobs where there are none or will I go and do business. Nothing is working in that country. Maybe in the future but surely not now (JM, Facebook).*

The first post above by MD captures the position of many Nigerians in the 2023 presidential elections during which time some insinuated that they were ready to return to the country if Peter Obi, one of the presidential candidates, wins the elections. Based on social media observations, the political preference of many Nigerian diasporans was Peter Obi as several citizens, especially youths, were advocating for political change. It is within this context that MD, as well as acquaintances abroad, contemplated a return to Nigeria. However, since the preferred candidate lost, the envisaged beacon of hope in Nigeria was also lost; the opposing candidate became president. *Make I just siddown jejely* can be vaguely translated 'let me just sit down here gently'. Etymologically, the word *siddown* is the pidginised version of 'sit down' while *jejely* in Nigerian parlance refers to 'gently'. Interpreted, this means 'let me just remain here and ignore the thought of returning to Nigeria'. It can therefore be concluded that political outcomes strongly influence return migration decisions. Using Morocco as a case study, Tuccio et al. (2019) establish a strong connection between return migration and political change. In their view, return migration boosts the demand for political and social change as returnees affect general political attitudes. In the case of Nigeria, citizens abroad often remain heavily involved in the country's political outcomes despite being disenfranchised due to a lack of voting facilities or mechanisms for diasporans. They disseminate and engage in political matters in Nigeria, which indicates a genuine interest in the country.

Closely related to the first post is the view of SR who indicates that the lack of return migration is the result of the poor state of the country. A working Nigeria is one in which systems and practices are effective and efficient in comparison with developed countries. The view of SR is that a large percentage of Nigerians will consider return migration if the country's system could be efficient and effective. As we have established in previous chapters, the primary reasons for out-migration in Nigeria revolve predominantly around socio-economic challenges which can be attributed to deficiencies in governance. A point worth noting is that many Nigerians would prefer to live in Nigeria had Nigeria been a 'working country'. The lack of choice referred to by the author is an indication that a decision to reside abroad was propelled by the poor socio-economic situation of the country rather than a desire to be an expatriate. Nwosu et al. (2022) study lends credence to this argument; they found that great numbers of Nigerian youths are willing to migrate abroad, even illegally, despite being aware of the challenges that face them overseas. They argue that poverty is a major factor in the decisions of the youth who are desperate to escape Nigeria by any means. Recognising that the origin of these problems can only be addressed by the government, Nwosu et al. (2022) recommend that the Nigerian government and their agencies manage the economy properly and implement policies to eliminate poverty since it has been identified as the major force that pushes youths into migration and enslavement. If the poor state of the country's economy is not addressed, discourse surrounding return migration will always portray Nigeria as a country that must be avoided.

Over the years, Nigerian emigrants have become popular for bringing wealth into the country to establish businesses which in turn create jobs for others. Drawing on the view of EB, this has become a journey that should not be embarked upon given current realities. The economy of the country has made starting or funding a business a laborious task that the author of the post strongly advises Nigerians in the diaspora to avoid. The statement 'I learnt the hard way' is the author's reference to his own experience of having established a failed business in the country. EB adds that establishing a business in Nigeria is draining and requires endless financial obstacles that could wreck an investor or business owner. In the fourth example, JM argues that returning to Nigeria is not an option and that he is unable to fathom a possible reason for anyone to return to Nigeria after living abroad. His confusion can be gathered from the comment about the lack of jobs and business opportunities in the country. This is enough reason not to return; however, should the situation improve, a future return is possible.

Post-migration discourse in Nigeria reflects the ills that originally caused the departure of several Nigerians. In these conversations, comparisons are often drawn between Nigeria and developed countries which provide for a nuanced understanding of migration. Although many emphasise the benefits of living abroad, emigrants desire a possible return based on a utopian ideal of a better country. Obi-Ani et al. (2020) emphasise the need to restructure the socio-economic organisational sectors of the country and to address the inward-looking leadership by mitigating the systemic problems that drive her citizens to look to Europe for greener pastures. Positive political and social change in Nigeria could lead to changes in social media migration discourses.

Identity Crisis in Nigerian Discourse of Migration

Several studies have examined identity crisis as one of the major consequences of migration. To Viola and Musolff (2019), the socio-discursive landscape surrounding the migration debate is characterised by a growing sense of crisis in both personal and collective identities. Blynova et al. (2020) investigated the social and psychological manifestations of professional identity crisis in labour emigrants and found that changes in professional identities occur in different social and cultural conditions. This study thus adds to previous studies that have addressed identity. Discourses relating to identity crisis in Nigerian migration can be classified under three distinct headings, namely social identity, cultural identity, and professional identity.

Social Identity

As immigrants leave their countries, they are forced to abandon old definitions of who they are and to find new ones while also being confronted with inventories of identities that are imposed on them through public discourses and practices (De Fina & Baynham, 2012). Tajfel's (1974) social identity theory lends credence to the discussion of social identity in the context of Nigerian migration. The theory relies on social interactionism to explain how social identities are formed through intergroup relations of status, legitimacy, and temporality. Tajfel argues that prejudice, conflict between groups, and discrimination are critical aspects which influence the formation of social identity. Wodak (2008) also argues that one way of looking at discourses of difference/discrimination is to examine the ways in which minorities or migrants experience racial discrimination in Europe today. The evolution of social identity theory, according to Raskovic and Takacs-Haynes (2021), started with a focus on out-group degradation then shifted towards in-group distinctiveness. Although the theory is not the focus of this study, it addresses some significant aspects of how social identity is perceived in Nigerian migration discourse. Instances of discrimination, identity validation, self-enhancement, and social categorisation among others, which Raskovic and Takacs-Haynes (2021) alluded to in their study, can be found in Nigerian migration discourse under the concept of social identity. Examples of these include:

i. *Japa is just one step. As a Nigerian passport holder, the outlook internationally is not great, and this is just fact. Ask frequent travellers, they will tell you. Immigration officers profile me almost every time because I have a Nigerian passport. Discrimination everywhere. It's just tiring. Japa can't solve these problems (DM, X).*
ii. *Challenge of living abroad for long is that you never really fit into the new environment abroad. When you return to Nigeria, you are happy to see the familiar environment. However, you have changed as a person. Then you end up not fitting anywhere (SJ, Facebook).*
iii. *Living in the US for so long, I now have two different personalities. One personality abroad and another one in Nigeria. That is the life of a migrant (FO, X).*

The author of the first post, DM, condemns how Nigerians are perceived and addressed internationally. Giorgi and Vitale (2017) also admit that hostility towards immigrants, racism, and xenophobia are all on the rise in Europe. According to the post, *japa* which many Nigerians have resorted to, does not prevent Nigerians from encountering different problems abroad; while they attempt to flee from problems in their home country, they arrive in a new environment with discriminatory atmospheres emanating solely from being Nigerian. The author draws on personal experience to show how Nigerians who travel with Nigerian passports, are wrongly profiled and rudely treated at immigration borders. Olajide (2018) argues that discrimination has remained one of the biggest problems which Nigerian migrants face in host countries. Olajide maintains that this discrimination is generally based on racism as well as religious, gender, and language bias. Sometimes, migrants simply encounter xenophobic attitudes because they are from another country. Olajide (2018), however, neglects the fact that many Nigerians are discriminated against based on an assumption of criminality; a commonly held perception. It is nevertheless the view of DM that Nigerians abroad suffer severe reputational damage that constantly affects their social identities. For DM, fleeing Nigeria does not solve these problems since reputational damage will persist while Nigerians are perceived as 'guilty' simply by association. This represents an identity crisis for Nigerian immigrants.

The discourse of identity crisis dwells on (re)integration problems and disconnectedness. For Tedeschi et al. (2022), living across borders and having hybrid identities, transnationals often feel that they do not fully belong anywhere. In this vein, SJ acknowledges that the Nigerian migrant does not completely integrate into a new environment. At the same time, the migrant is equally unable to reintegrate back into Nigerian society after having lived in a different society for a long period. The concern therefore is that migrants are unable to achieve a full social sense of belonging in either the home country or the host country thus affecting the individual's social identity. To further explain this, the opinion of the author is that while the Nigerian citizen is discriminated against abroad, the society at home does not also fully perceive such a citizen as fully belonging to Nigeria due to their migration experience. The migrant feels disconnected from the home country since what Chirongoma (2021) refers to as the 'communal web of existence' is missing. Across many African countries, members of extended families exist in a web of interrelatedness which is systematically different from the style in the diaspora. Nwozor et al. (2022) observe that the multiple unresolved social dilemmas in Nigeria, which instigate emigration in the first place, also account for the lack of reintegration once emigrants return.

Also reflected in the Nigerian migration discourse on identity crisis is how personalities become altered by differences in societies. Studies have also revealed that transmigrants take actions, make decisions, and feel concerns, and develop identities within social networks that connect them to two or more societies simultaneously (Schiller et al., 1992b). Demonstrating this, FO who has a dual personality is affected by his home and host countries differently. The personality of the author in Nigeria is different from his personality while in the United States of America. In essence, the social identity and perception of the migrant becomes altered based on current realities. A study by Panicacci and Dewaele (2017) also contend that language and culture influence personality which could affect the self-perception of migrants. Considering this view, one can argue that the introduction of Nigerian migrants to different societies with different languages and practices can lead to changes in the personalities of Nigerian migrants. One can even argue that differences in worldviews between Nigerians abroad, and Nigerians at home, can be influenced by the complexities of their current societies.

Cultural Identity

Conceptually, one's culture entails beliefs, knowledge, norms, practices, customs, and behaviours. In essence, evidence of cultural influence is found in almost every stage of human development; it is therefore no surprise that many people form identities based on the customs of their cultures. Jameson (2007, p. 199) defines cultural identity as 'an individual's sense of self derived from formal or informal membership in groups that transmit and inculcate knowledge, beliefs, values, attitudes, traditions, and ways of life'. However, global migration has forced many people into embracing multiculturalism which has led to acculturation for many migrants. Acculturation occurs when one assimilates another culture, especially a dominant one, and it is crucial for migrants to co-exist peacefully with the citizens of host countries. Africa is rich in cultural values, and these values are embedded in individual growth; this also applies in Nigeria. Emigrating Nigerians, however, have had to embrace acculturation in ways that allow their primary and secondary cultures to co-exist, and instances abound of practices in secondary cultures eclipsing the practices of primary cultures. This is what scholars refer to as 'culture shock', and a large body of research exists on the dynamics of culture shock amongst immigrants. Culture shock is a kind of personal disorientation experienced by people who move to a partially or completely different cultural environment (Martinez Guillem, 2015, p. 2). It is worth noting that Nigeria is not monocultural as there are as many cultures as there are people, and the data gathered does not categorically identify a specific culture. Instead, we present long-held popularly accepted practices in Nigeria that cause emigrants to find different practices abroad 'shocking'.

Entrenched cultural identities related to migration are portrayed by Nigerians on X. Some examples include:

i. *Biggest culture shock moving from Nigeria to the UK was being able to call adults by their first names (A, X).*
ii. *Nigeria's culture of respect is rich & worth preserving but e get some excesses wey we suppose scrap. Having & airing your contrary opinion during discussion with your lecturer or manager in this country still feels weird to me. Cannot be Nigeria (OG, X).*
iii. *So many culture shock once you travel abroad. Nigeria has damaged so many of us. In the UK, you will see Ministers and Politicians using the London Underground trains. In Nigeria, an ordinary local government chairman will be driving with 8 cars.........Total madness (LE, X).*
iv. *One of the culture shocks when I got here is saying thank you to bus drivers when you get down at your stop. I was like na abuse we dey abuse ourselves in Nigeria o (FA, X).*

Respect for elders is a cultural attribute endemic to Nigerian society. Young Nigerians are taught to respect elderly people by using honorifics instead of calling them by names. Thus, for A, the first culture shock experienced abroad was the practice of being able to call older people by their first names. In many Nigerian cultures, these honorifics are formal and informal titles, and regardless of the nature of the environment or relationship, younger people are expected to demonstrate respect when addressing elderly people. Ignoring the honorifics is considered disrespectful in many Nigerian cultures. So, according to the author, the practice in the United Kingdom (UK) where a younger person calls an adult by the first name is considered extremely strange. Respect as emphasised by Nigerians also extends beyond reference to older people; younger people are also expected to be docile and not to challenge or contest the views of the elderly or their superiors. This point is also stressed by OG who admits that the culture of respect in Nigeria is significant, however, some elements are excessive. The phrase *e get some excesses wey we suppose scrap* is written in Nigerian pidgin and can be translated as 'there are some excesses in the culture that we should collectively discard'. The author's position is informed by the fact that in the host country, a younger person is allowed to voice an opposing view to one's superior without any adverse reaction. In Nigeria, such an act would often be deemed disrespectful and met with consequences.

The post by LE focuses on the culture of conspicuous consumption in Nigerian society. Nigeria is plagued with an unnecessary display of affluence and status syndrome. Wealthy people or people in positions of power tend to display their riches or status through their means of transportation, the houses they live in, the clothes they wear and so forth. However, the point raised by this author relates to the political leaders in Nigeria who flagrantly display their wealth even though most citizens live in poverty. It is the practice of many political leaders in Nigeria to transport themselves in convoys with large entourages whose only purpose is to show power and affluence. LE was shocked to see ministers as well as other political leaders in the United Kingdom display humility and use public transport. Although Nigerian is a modern society, the culture of displaying of affluence is rooted in ancient cultures where traditional kings and chiefs took pride in status and wealth and in many cases, used it to oppress the less privileged. Wealth and power intoxication in Nigeria are so excessive that the humility shown by powerful and wealthy people abroad is a culture shock for many Nigerians. LE's post sarcastically ridicules the state of Nigeria by drawing a comparison with the United Kingdom where a minister also uses the public train. In Nigeria, an executive of the lowest office such as a local government chairman, also displays affluence using several cars which the author describes as 'total madness'.

In the final post by FA, the author addresses an important issue in human relationships. While many cultures in Nigeria teach respect for adults, they barely teach respect for peers, younger people, less privileged people, or people who render services. Respect is often perceived as one-dimensional; only directed towards older or superior people. Thus, for FA, appreciating the services rendered by a bus driver is considered strange. The use of 'thank you' in Nigeria is often restricted and rarely used in the context of rendered services. In fact, the rendering of services is sometimes followed by hot exchanges of words between the parties involved. This is what the author explains in Nigerian pidgin when he says *I was like na abuse we dey abuse ourselves in Nigeria o*. Put differently, this means 'in Nigeria, bus drivers and passengers often end up insulting one another'. No form of respect or courtesy is culturally expected between the driver and the passenger. In the host country, the author is shocked to discover that a form of courtesy is expected from the passenger. Social media posts suggest that Nigerians experience identity crises when they attempt to assimilate into cultures of their host countries.

Professional Identity

The concept of professional identity is not only fuzzy but also broad. According to Fitzgerald (2020), the concept lacks explicit definition and clarity. It is perceived to be context-dependent, therefore, as work practices and knowledge change, so does one's identity. Nonetheless, Fitzgerald (2020) intimates that popular practice is to define professional identity in terms of what professionals do, their behaviours and activities. Since many Nigerians migrate for the purpose of job prospects, many find themselves in professional crisis that affect their professional identities. In the context of this book, professional identity is related to the nature and characteristics of jobs or professions that Nigerians undertake abroad. The struggle to find employment abroad has significant impact on the professional identities of Nigerians since many are unable to find jobs in their current career trajectories. Some careers are relegated to random jobs; professional desires are toppled by the need to earn and meet financial responsibilities. Gardner and Shulman (2005) find mutuality between professions and society, citing that professionals gain prestige from societal recognition. This inevitably has an impact on identity. Social media examples of posts which contain conversations about professional identities are given below:

i. *Many Nigerians abroad are unable to do what they are really interested in. A friend in the US who was a doctor in Nigeria has not been able find a doctor job for over 5 years now. He is doing something called Medical Data Analyst. He cannot even practice what he learnt in Nigeria (AY, Facebook).*
ii. *A lot of Nigerians come to the UK to do factory work or cleaning. I even know a bank manager who is now a cleaner in the UK. The day I saw her, I felt so sad because her career has basically ended (DO, X).*
iii. *Most people be lying that they are into tech. Everyone is now into tech whereas many of them are doing social work. Small coding, they can't do (YM, X).*

The first post by AY reflects on the general challenges faced by many Nigerian professionals abroad who attempt to secure jobs in their professions. According to the author, many Nigerians abroad resort to other jobs, for example, a medical doctor who was unable to secure a position as a medical doctor in the United States settled for the role of medical analyst. In Nigeria, a medical doctor carries more prestige than a medical data analyst since the latter profession is alien to many Nigerians. While some Nigerian migrants are forced to settle for other jobs entirely, others find related roles and settle for these. The professional identities of many Nigerians have thus witnessed a setback abroad because they are unable to find jobs that align with their original career interests. In some cases, the requirement for positions abroad includes local working experience, which renders the foreign experience of many Nigerians inessential. Using refugees as a case study, MacKenzie-Davey and Jones (2020) explain that the career paths of refugees are not simply the result of their individual choices but responses to encountered barriers and opportunities.

The findings of MacKenzie-Davey and Jones (2020) can be transferred to willing migrants who, because of the obstacles they experience, choose different career paths. For instance, DO laments the rate at which Nigerian migrants are employed in factories and as cleaners in the United Kingdom. Personal reference was made to a bank manager in Nigeria who now works as a cleaner abroad due to the lack of opportunities in the United Kingdom. A managerial job at a bank in Nigeria is perceived as an executive position, but several Nigerians have become resigned to less worthwhile roles abroad because of the *japa* exodus. Oyebamiji and Adekoye (2019) point out that a good number of new Nigerian immigrants in the United States often start with non-professional jobs to meet financial demands from their parents and relatives abroad. However, there appears to be a paucity of research on whether Nigerians starting with non-professional jobs eventually find professional jobs, particularly in their primary line of careers. In fact, to maintain a proper professional identity, YM alleges that many Nigerians deliberately misrepresent their jobs abroad as they tend to avoid disclosing their actual jobs due to the lack of associated prestige. Hence, several Nigerian migrants present themselves as technological gurus whereas upon further investigation, they have no such skills. In the current dispensation, technological jobs are not only prestigious, but also lucrative and professionally identifying with this line of work is highly regarded. This attempt by many Nigerians abroad to hide their actual jobs in some cases can be perceived as an identity crisis from a professional perspective.

As MacKenzie-Davey and Jones (2020) point out, migrants experience multiple losses as they look for opportunities in new countries as many have limited opportunities to prepare for their future careers in the destination country. Many Nigerian migrants lose their professional identities as they find themselves grappling with other challenges abroad that overshadow their career trajectories.

In this chapter, we have examined post-migration discourse as well as the concept of identity crisis drawing mainly on Nigerian migration discourse. The Nigerian post-migration discourses revealed the challenges that many Nigerians face abroad which also point towards the hesitation of some Nigerians to relocate abroad. The data analysed further debunked the misconceived notion that living abroad is easily rewarding without investing time and hard work. In fact, the findings suggest that many Nigerians abroad battle with a lot of challenges among which include economic and social problems.

References

Adeniyi, A. G., & Onyeukwu, P. E. (2021). Return migration, reverse culture shock: A critical analysis of their patterns and particularities amongst migrant Nigerian Elites. *The International Journal of Management Science and Business Administration*, 7(3), 30–36.

Bainbridge, W. S. (2000). Religious ethnography on the World Wide Web. In K. Hadden & D. E. Cowan (Eds.), *Religion on the internet: Research prospects and promises* (pp. 55–80). Elsevier.

Blynova, O., Chervinska, I., Kazibekova, V., Bokshan, H., Yakovleva, S., Zaverukha, O., & Popovych, I. (2020). Social and psychological manifestations of professional identity crisis of labor migrants. *Revista Inclusiones*, 93–105.

Chirongoma, S. (2021). Neither here nor there: The experiences of Zimbabwean migrant children and youth. *Alternation Journal: Interdisciplinary Journal for the Study of the Arts and Humanities in Southern Africa, 33*, 136–154.

De Fina, A., & Baynham, M. (2012). Immigrant discourse. In C. A. Chapelle (Ed.), *The encyclopedia of applied linguistics* (pp. 1–8).

Fitzgerald, A. (2020). Professional identity: A concept analysis. *Nursing Forum, 55*(3), 447–472.

Gardner, H., & Shulman, L. S. (2005). The professions in America today: Crucial but fragile. *Daedalus, 134*(3), 13–18.

Giorgi, A., & Vitale, T. (2017). Migrants in the public discourse: Between media, policy and public opinion. In S. Marino, R. Penninx, & J. Roosblad (Eds.), *Trade unions and migrant workers* (pp. 66–89). Edward Elgar Publishing.

Haugen, H. Ø. (2012). Nigerians in China: A second state of immobility. *International Migration, 50*(2), 65–80.

Jameson, D. A. (2007). Reconceptualizing cultural identity and its role in intercultural business communication. *The Journal of Business Communication (1973), 44*(3), 199–235.

MacKenzie-Davey, K., & Jones, C. (2020). Refugees' narratives of career barriers and professional identity. *Career Development International, 25*(1), 49–66.

Martìnez Guillem, S. (2015). Migration discourse. In K. Tracy, C. Ilie, & T. L. Sandel (Eds.), *Encyclopedia of language and social interaction* (1st ed., pp. 1–10). John Wiley & Sons.

Nwosu, I. A., Eteng, M. J., Ekpechu, J., Nnam, M. U., Ukah, J. A., Eyisi, E., & Orakwe, E. C. (2022). Poverty and youth migration out of Nigeria: Enthronement of modern slavery. *SAGE Open, 12*(1), 21582440221079818.

Nwozor, A., Oshewolo, S., Olanrewaju, J. S., Bosede Ake, M., & Okidu, O. (2022). Return migration and the challenges of diasporic reintegration in Nigeria. *Third World Quarterly, 43*(2), 432–451.

Obi-Ani, P., Anthonia Obi-Ani, N., & Isiani, M. C. (2020). A historical perspective of Nigerian immigrants in Europe. *Cogent Arts & Humanities, 7*(1), 1–15.

Okeke-Ihejirika, P., & Odimegwu, I. (2023). Managing the rising tide of Nigerian migrants to the West – A policy vacuum or a structural challenge? *International Migration, 61*(1), 10–22.

Olajide, O. A. (2018). Migration and poverty among Nigerian youths. *Journal of Nigerian Studies, 1*(2), 2–27.

Oyebamiji, S. I., & Adekoye, A. (2019). Nigerians' migration to the United States of America: A contemporary perspective. *Journal of African Foreign Affairs, 6*(1), 165–180.

Panicacci, A., & Dewaele, J. M. (2017). 'A voice from elsewhere': Acculturation, personality and migrants' self-perceptions across languages and cultures. *International Journal of Multilingualism, 14*(4), 419–436.

Raskovic, M., & Takacs-Haynes, K. (2021). (Re) discovering social identity theory: An agenda for multinational enterprise internalization theory. *Multinational Business Review, 29*(2), 145–165.

Schiller, N. G., Basch, L., & Blanc-Szanton, C. (1992b). Transnationalism: A new analytic framework for understanding migration. *Annals of the New York Academy of Sciences*, *645*(1), 1–24.
Tajfel, H. (1974). Social identity and intergroup behavior. *Social Science Information*, *13*(2), 65–93.
Tedeschi, M., Vorobeva, E., & Jauhiainen, J. S. (2022). Transnationalism: Current debates and new perspectives. *GeoJournal*, *87*(2), 603–619.
Tuccio, M., Wahba, J., & Hamdouch, B. (2019). International migration as a driver of political and social change: Evidence from Morocco. *Journal of Population Economics*, *32*, 1171–1203.
Viola, L., & Musolff, A. (Eds.). (2019). *Migration and media: Discourses about identities in crisis* (Vol. 81). John Benjamins Publishing Company.
Wodak, R. (2008). Us' and 'them': Inclusion and exclusion–Discrimination via discourse. In G. Delanty, R. Wodak, & P. Jones (Eds.), *Identity, belonging and migration* (pp. 54–77). Liverpool University Press.

Chapter 9

Further Thoughts: The Figure of the Migrant in Contemporary Discourse: Reflections and Lived Experiences

We conclude this book in a rather unconventional manner because we believe that every story matters. As migrants ourselves, we cannot reflect on the stories of migrants without reflecting on our own stories. Both of us, the writers of this book, are migrants from Zimbabwe and Nigeria living and working in South Africa. However, before we share our own stories and experiences of migration, we must firstly reflect on and summarise the discourses of migration in Nigeria and Zimbabwe that we analysed in the preceding chapters. The things that people say in everyday communication and the way they say them reveal much about their attitudes, beliefs, and convictions. In the digital age, social media has become a marketplace of ideas where users share views and experiences on different issues, including migration. In the preceding chapters, we argued that one way to understand discourses of migration in the digital age is to evaluate the views that citizens share on social media platforms.

The preceding chapters have demonstrated that both Nigeria and Zimbabwe have a long history of migration. However, in recent years, migration in both countries has happened in the context of serious socio-economic and political problems. Nigeria is the most populous country in Africa, endowed with various mineral resources, including oil, yet it has arguably failed to turn its resources into economic opportunities for its citizens. The same can also be said about Zimbabwe, a country which has, in recent years, seen a significant portion of its population migrating to other countries in search of better economic opportunities. We examined discourses of migration in Nigeria and Zimbabwe for purposes of understanding not only the factors that lead to migration but also prevailing attitudes and perceptions about migration in each country.

Chapter 2 explored global discourses of migration with specific focus on how migrants are perceived and represented around the world. We argued that contemporary migration patterns resemble the migrations of the 19th century, which were inspired by colonialism. While colonial adventures were accompanied by, and justified through, colonialist narratives, contemporary narratives about migration tend to entrench the same age-old stereotypes and misconceptions about 'others' which were developed and rationalised in the crucible of colonialism. While migrants from the Global South flock to the Global North in search of economic opportunities, countries in the Global North have, in recent years, responded by passing stringent immigration policies aimed at preventing South-North migration. Mbembe (2017) has argued in his *A Critique of Black Reason* that the contemporary neoliberal word is built on the logic of race and racism which developed in the slave plantations and in the colonies. It is a world where some move freely while others are told to remain where they are. In the Western imaginary, migrants, especially those from the Global South, are seen as problems. Hence, they must remain sedentary in their respective countries despite the transnational and borderless world that globalisation promises. In most countries in the West (and some countries in the South), African migrants are welcomed, not with economic opportunities as they would expect, but with arrests, detentions, long waiting periods and deportations.

Given the harsh economic conditions prevailing in many African countries, migrants from Africa tend to perceive Western countries as spaces of endless economic opportunities. Chapter 3 explored discourses of migration in Nigeria with particular focus on the 'japa' phenomenon which has caught Nigerian social media by storm. Nigerian discourses of migration depict Nigeria as a broken country with multiple socio-economic challenges. It is a country one must leave one way with no possibility of return. If one must love it, one must do so from a distance. To 'japa' is to leave with no intention of coming back. Those who 'japa' do not wish to come back to Nigeria, not only because they perceive their destination countries as better habitats but also because they believe that Nigeria is beyond redemption, and nothing will transform it into an attractive place for human habitation. The japa phenomenon and the discourses associated with it discussed in this chapter show that most Nigerians consider the ability to leave Nigeria as an achievement. In any case, there is no place on the planet that can be worse than Nigeria.

Nigeria and Zimbabwe are in fact two sides of the same coin. Both countries have experienced unprecedented economic crises for many years although both have educated populations and various natural resources that could be easily harnessed to change their fortunes for the better. Chapter 4 focused on Zimbabwean discourses of migration in the context of the August 2023 elections which dashed the hopes of many Zimbabweans both at home and abroad. If any proof was still needed, these elections proved to many Zimbabweans that change was a dream they would probably not realise in their lifetime. Prominent Zimbabwean journalist, Hopewell Chin'ono took to his Facebook Page to mobilise young Zimbabweans to leave the country and explore opportunities elsewhere. For him, Zimbabwe was a broken country governed by corrupt and incompetent politicians, and if young people wanted to change their lives, they would have to leave the country. We read Chin'ono's social media as a transnational public sphere that not only internationalises the Zimbabwean crisis but also creates opportunities for Zimbabweans to share experiences and ideas on how to migrate. In this chapter, we examined discourses of migration in the context of what scholars such as Fraser (2007) have characterised as transnational public spheres which operate outside the territorial boundaries of the nation state. While Nigerian discourses of migration celebrate the japa phenomenon as an end, Chin'ono' Facebook messages call on those who can leave to do so because there is no hope for Zimbabwe, at least in the foreseeable future.

One of the consequences of corruption and poor governance in many African countries is the breakdown of the rule of law and the proliferation of criminal activity and insecurity. Discourses of migration both in Nigeria and Zimbabwe depict migration as an escape from perpetual conditions of insecurity, be it political or economic. Although Zimbabwe does not have serious security challenges, the ongoing economic crisis has created conditions of precarity compounded by unpredictable government policies and hyperinflation. Chapter 5 focused on discourses of migration in the context of political insecurity in Nigeria. Nigerians who manage to leave the country often see migration as an opportunity to live in peace without having to fear possible abduction or high jacking in a country with a broken criminal justice system.

One of the issues that Chin'ono's posts, discussed in Chapter 4, emphasise is that migration has the potential, not only to liberate the individual from relations of patronage in a corrupt society but also to empower the individual economically. Chapter 6 discussed the theme of power and powerlessness in greater depth with particular emphasis on the Nigerian context. Although migration has its own challenges, such as separation from family and friends and failure to secure desired economic opportunities, it also has its own benefits. Both in Nigeria and in Zimbabwe, discourses of migration depict those who successfully migrate as living better lives regardless of their economic status in destination countries. The assumption in home countries is that no place can be worse than Nigeria/Zimbabwe. In fact, social media platforms in both countries are awash with stories and jokes that compare Nigeria/Zimbabwe with hell. If you have been to Zimbabwe/Nigeria, you have been to hell. Migrants from these countries have thus escaped hell through migration. Since Nigeria/Zimbabwe are abject spaces of no return, migrants often maintain false images of 'success' in destination countries by posting material things (cars, phones, branded clothes, etc.) or places they have visited (hotels, beaches, iconic buildings, etc.). In the Nigerian context, discourses of migration reveal that migration has hierarchies depending on one's destination country. Those who migrate to Europe are often regarded highly because of the global economic status of European countries while those who migrate to African countries are looked down upon. Migration is thus not only about improving one's economic welfare but also about showing off images of success to one's social community.

Although discourses of migration both in Zimbabwe and Nigeria portray destination countries as economic Eldorados, there is always a subtext that suggests that all that glitters in the destination country are not gold. Chapter 7 discussed discourses of migration in the context of the controversy surrounding the Zimbabwe Exemption Permit in South Africa. Drawing on Mbembe's ideas about the migrant, the border, and the politics of viscerality, we argued that discourses of migration in South Africa depict migrants, including Zimbabwean and Nigerian migrants, as problems aggravating the country's numerous socio-economic challenges. In South Africa, the migrant is the unwanted 'other' who exacerbates the pain of those who have suffered the injustices of apartheid. The migrant in South Africa resembles what Mbembe (2016) calls 'excess presence' in his theorisation of superfluous and expendable human bodies in the neoliberal system. We explained xenophobic violence in South Africa's poor communities in terms of the politics of viscerality which designates a bodily response to perceived injustice. Citizens see foreigners as objects of their pain and suffering – those who must leave to ameliorate black pain. The migrant, and the Zimbabwean migrant in particular, is perceived as an excess presence which must be jettisoned from the boundaries of the state because it is this excess presence that has compounded the healthcare crisis, the crime epidemic, poor service delivery, and among many other ills bedevilling the South African polity.

The discourses of migration that we have analysed show that migration is a life-changing experience with numerous challenges. One of the challenges discussed in Chapter 8 is that of managing pre-migration perceptions and post-migration realities. In the popular imaginary, both in Zimbabwe and in Nigeria, to migrate is not only to *seek* a better life but also to *have* a better life. Oftentimes, migrants are bombarded with requests for money, clothes, school fees, etc. a few months after arriving in the destination country. Everywhere, migrants are under pressure to maintain images of success. They do not want to be perceived as 'failed migrants'. The messages and images that they share on social media are not necessarily true, yet it is these messages and images that those back home consume as representations of life in the destination country.

As mentioned earlier, we would like to end this book with a reflection on our own experiences of migration in the hope that our experiences will not only summarise the book but also animate ongoing debates about migration in our contemporary world. Writing about discourses of migration from South Africa is like speaking from the belly of the beast. South Africa has a long history of migration and anti-immigrant violence dating back to the discovery of the rand in the 1880s. Anti-immigration violence in South Africa is not only a historical phenomenon (a thing of the past) but also a reality of everyday life, especially for migrants of African descent. In fact, the question of how to deal with the country's porous borders and migrants in general remains a hot topic that has shaped political discourse for many years. Some political parties such as the ruling African National Congress (ANC) and the Patriotic Alliance (PA) have hyped their anti-immigration rhetoric to attract voters, most of whom blame foreign nationals for the country's numerous socio-economic challenges, ranging from poor service delivery, decaying infrastructure to load shedding. Being a migrant in South Africa is thus a nervous condition. While we acknowledge our positions of relative privilege in the South African academy, we are also very much aware of what it means, and how it feels, to be a foreign national in South Africa.

In fact, Nigerian and Zimbabwean migrants have, in recent years, assumed a special place in discourses of migration in South Africa. For a very long time, Nigerians have been stereotyped as drug lords responsible for supplying drugs to poor black communities. Consequently, businesses owned by Nigerian migrants have been targeted on the pretext that they are 'fronts' for underworld businesses involving drugs. A documentary titled, 'Fear and Loathing in South Africa'[1] by BBC (18 September 2018) shares heart-wrenching stories of migrants living in South Africa and how they are treated. At the beginning of the film, Operation Dudula, an anti-immigrant group has just descended on a second-hand market stall in Johannesburg and migrants who sell clothes at the market run for their lives. In the pursuing crowd, a member of the vigilante group shouts, repeatedly 'look at how they are running! It's like they are cockroaches!'. Operation Dudula is a notorious vigilante group known for its anti-immigration rhetoric and use of violence against foreign nationals. The sight of this group instils fear among African foreign nationals, turning them into 'cockroaches' that must run for their lives. To the members of Operation Dudula, the migrants are not humans like *us* but embodiments of social anomie – cockroaches. Cockroaches are vectors that carry all kinds of diseases. Like vermin, foreign nationals are perceived as vehicles of all kinds of socio-economic problems in South Africa.

One woman in the documentary named Dimakatso Mokoena blames foreign nationals for her son's drug addiction. She believes that foreigners have robbed her son of his future. 'He is an intelligent boy, you know', she says, fighting back tears of anger and hatred. Her boy dropped out of college because of his drug addiction. Dimakatso confesses that she hates foreigners, and she wants them to go back to their countries. When asked whether she thinks deporting foreigners will end the drug problem in South Africa, Dimakatso answers 'this place is full of foreigners, which is not fair really, this is *their* country'. Foreigners are, in Dimakatso's view, like invasive species. They come into a place, displace native species, and lick all the nutrients (economic opportunities), leaving the native species malnourished and emaciated. The problem, as Dimakatso sees it, is that this place (a street in Johannesburg, and by extension South Africa) is 'full of foreigners'. Foreigners are thus, as Mbembe argues, surplus beings (outsiders) that must be ejected out of *our* space to create space for those who belong (citizens/insiders). Dimakatso is being ironic when she says, 'this is *their* country' because migrants are outsiders who should not own anything in the host nation. That they have turned the host country into *their country* is a misnomer. It is not 'fair' for migrants to take over the streets of Johannesburg because by doing so, they suffocate citizens. Dimakatso believes that young people in South Africa, including her own son, are frustrated by the lack of economic opportunities, hence they turn to drugs. The solution, for her, is to evict the foreigners who have 'turned our children into zombies'. Operation Dudula makes no distinction between illegal and legal migrants. When it invades foreign-owned businesses, it does not ask for operating licences or any other legal document. Their dictum is 'foreigners must go'. It does not matter where they must go.

The songs that the vigilante group sings as it attacks foreign-owned businesses construct migrants as bodies with no ontological value. The group imagines itself

---

[1] https://www.youtube.com/watch?v=rogZ8BYg-kM

as a revolutionary movement advocating the rights of citizens. According to one activist in the documentary, members of Operation Dudula should not be apologetic because they are citizens, 'this is [their] country'. One song that the group sang was quite telling not only in terms of how members of the group perceived foreigners but also in terms of the kind of treatment that they believed foreigners deserved. The lyrics of the song are as follows:

> S'zongen' egarage. S'zoteng' ipetrol. Sizotshis' iforeigner. (We will walk into a garage! We will buy petrol! We will burn a foreigner!).

Operation Dudula perceived vigilantism as a revolutionary exercise aimed at ridding South Africa of all socio-economic problems embodied in the figure of the migrant. In post-apartheid South Africa, the body of the African migrant has become a new site of revolutionary violence. As it was during apartheid, where those who were perceived as sellouts were necklaced and set alight, in post-apartheid South Africa, the African migrant is the 'thing' that stands in the way of economic emancipation for the majority of South Africans. To burn a migrant is thus reimagined as part of the 'long walk to freedom'. In the South African popular imaginary, at least as depicted in the documentary, the migrant is perceived as a problem that must be eliminated by any means, including violence and murder.

What is quite interesting for our purposes here is that the documentary 'Fear and Loathing' narrates the stories of two men, one Nigerian, and the other, Zimbabwean. In recent years, Zimbabwean and Nigerian migrants, along with other African migrants, have become scapegoats for most of South Africa's numerous socio-economic problems. In the documentary, a Nigerian man tells the story of how the vigilante group, Operation Dudula, invaded his market stall, destroyed it, and dumped his merchandise in a drain. A coloured woman called Anne Michaels, an immigrants' rights activist, brings the Nigerian man's story to the spotlight when she takes the reporter, Ayanda Charlie, to the destroyed market. Incidentally, the Nigerian man is a naturalised South African, who, in his own words 'votes in this country', suggesting that he has the same rights as other South African citizens. Yet, the vigilante group did not care about his legal status. In fact, they never asked him to prove whether he was a citizen or not. To them, it did not matter that he had lived in South Africa for many years or that he had a South African identity document. He was a Nigerian because they categorised him as such and according to the group, he had one option 'to f**k off' and 'to go back to [his] country'.

A close reading of the Nigerian man's story reveals the multiple challenges that the black African migrant faces, not only in South Africa but also in other countries around the world. The black African migrant is the ultimate other with whom the citizen has nothing in common. Writing about the experience of migrants in Europe, Mbembe (2016b, p. 23) argues that 'the contemporary era is undoubtedly characterized by forms of exclusion, hostility, hate movements, and, above all, by the struggle against an enemy'. While in Europe, the figure of the enemy is that of the Arab 'terrorist', in South Africa, the figure of the enemy is the black African foreign national. Even Anne Michaels, the human rights activist in the documentary, does not seem to believe that the Nigerian man is a 'genuine' South African citizen. Her question, 'Did you have your passport or asylum document on you when you were attacked?' presupposes that the migrant could have done something wrong. When the Nigerian man reveals that he is, in fact, a South African citizen, Anne is visibly surprised. This incident raises questions about citizenship in a globalised world where people move from one country to another, sometimes adopting citizenships of more than one country. How do we distinguish outsiders from insiders?

For the members of Operation Dudula, a citizen is not only someone with legal documents but also an indigene. Since documents can be forged or acquired fraudulently, the group believes that one needs more than a piece of paper to validate one's claim to citizenship. To authenticate himself, the Nigerian man says, 'I vote in this country. I am a citizen' suggesting that his citizenship, and right to live and work in South Africa, derives from his right to vote. To vote is thus, not only to voice one's choice but also to assert citizenship – I vote, therefore I am a citizen. The logic of Operation Dudula is like the logic of the contemporary neoliberal order, which according to Mbembe (2016) divides people into binary categories, of those who belong and those who do not, those who should be here and those who should be elsewhere – in short those who should live and those who should die. 'According to this vision', Mbembe argues, migrants are 'people who, having come from elsewhere, can never be considered our fellow citizens and with whom we can have almost nothing in common' (Mbembe, 2016, p. 30). In the South African context, it does not matter if one acquired South African citizenship or has the right to vote, as we see in the case of the Nigerian, a migrant is an ultimate other who can never be like us. In Europe and America, the Arab immigrant is the opposite other whose beliefs and ways of life pose a threat to *our* way of life. In South Africa, a migrant is a vector of social vice, who sells drugs and engages in all kinds of criminal activities, including impregnating young girls without assuming his fatherly duties.

The documentary also tells the story of one Zimbabwean migrant named Sabelo Ncube who also falls victim to the violence of the vigilante group. His father was a Rhodesian who came to South Africa during apartheid and married a South African woman. Members of Operation Dudula do not ask Sabelo to either explain himself or prove that he is living in South Africa legally. They simply tell him '*k'sasa indaba yakho aiseko*' meaning 'tomorrow your story is over'. Sabelo leaves his house to seek refuge in a shack together with his children. When he reports the matter to the police, the latter tells him not to take any chances because 'those people are heavily armed'. The implication is that the police are either also afraid of the vigilante group, or they sympathise with its cause. Sabelo is thus, like the Nigerian migrant, left to defend himself and his children without the protection of the police. Both Sabelo and the nameless Nigerian migrant are surplus human beings whose death does not matter. They constitute a superfluous excess population that must be thrown away, the way the Nigerian's merchandise is thrown into the gutter, like rubbish.

Although Mbembe (2016) uses Europe as a canvas upon which he sketches his idea of nanoracism, the latter shares similarities with the notion of '*dudula*' in the South African context. The word *dudula* means to force out and/or to violently eject that which does not belong. The principle of 'dudula' resembles what Mbembe calls nanoracism, a type of racism which 'consists in placing the greatest number of those whom we regard as undesirable in intolerable conditions, to enclose and marginalise them daily, to continually inflict on them an endless series of racist jabs and wounds, to rob them of all their acquired rights, *to smoke them out of their hives* and dishonour them to the point where *they have no choice but to self-deport*' (Mbembe, 2016, p. 31, italics not in original). In the film, *Fear and Loathing*, one member of Operation Dudula called Dimakatso says foreigners will not only leave South Africa, but they will also run away because the purpose of dudula is 'to smoke them out of their hives' so that they can 'self-deport'.

Writing about the experiences of outsiders in Europe, Mbembe (2016, p. 31) argues that outsiders are always confronted by someone:

> an institution, a voice, a public or private authority – asking them to justify who they are, why they are here, where they come from, where they are going, why they don't go back to where they came from; in other words, a voice or authority which deliberately seeks to cause them a large or small shock, to irritate them, to hurt them, injure them, to get them to lose their cool and self-composure as a pretext to violate them, to slander and debase without restraint that which is most private, most intimate, and vulnerable, in them.

This is an apt summary of the South African migrant experience. As a migrant in South Africa, one must always, and often without warning, engage in endless rituals of self-verification. As a migrant, you are guilty until you prove yourself innocent. How did you get this job when you are not South African? How did you acquire this document? Is it legit or fraudulent? Why do you live in a Mandela house? Are you South African? Where is the original owner of the house? Often, these questions do not seek to solicit a response, but to criminalise, and if possible, eliminate through violence.

Migrants around the world are hurt, injured, violated, slandered, and debased both physically and psychologically. The Zimbabwean migrant, Sabelo Ncube, whose story we discussed above, is a case in point. Sabelo is considered a foreigner although his mother is South African, and he has lived all his life in South Africa. Like the Nigerian migrant whose story we also discussed above, Sabelo has documents to prove that he is a South African by birth, but the vigilante group does not care. He must go back to his country, but which country must he go back to? He has no home or family in Zimbabwe, given that his father came to South Africa during the colonial era. After Operation Dudula evicted him from his home, Sabelo told Ayanda Charlie, the reporter, that he felt as if he was naked. Nakedness is the ultimate form of dehumanisation. The migrant must be humiliated and dishonoured until he/she self-deports. The eviction leaves Sabelo feeling powerless and useless because he cannot defend himself and his children. In most African cultures, fathers have a responsibility to protect their children

Further Thoughts: The Figure of the Migrant in Contemporary Discourse **149**

from danger. Sabelo could not protect his children because the vigilante group is well armed and dangerous.

To evict a man from his house is not only to deprive him of shelter but also to challenge his masculinity. In theorising the border and the migrant in the contemporary neoliberal order, Achille Mbembe (2019) argues that the 21st century is obsessed with

> 'borderization', that is, the process by which certain spaces are transformed into uncrossable places for certain classes of populations, who thereby undergo a process of racialization; places where speed must be disabled and the lives of a multitude of people judged to be undesirable are meant to be im-mobilized if not shattered. (p. 9)

Sabelo's life is shattered when he is evicted from his home. In this world, human beings are classified into those who belong and those who do not belong, those who have value and those who do not have value. Those without value deserve to die, and if they die, their death will not be accounted for. Sabelo and the nameless Nigerian migrant represent these kinds of people whose stories do not matter, whose lives do not matter. The vigilante group tells Sabelo that he must leave because his story is over/*indaba yakho aiseko*.

We reflect on these stories because they resonate with our own experiences of living and working in South Africa, as migrants. South Africa has, in recent years, become an increasingly hostile space for African migrants. While the situation is probably worse for illegal migrants who are often treated as the ultimate outsiders, African migrants often have similar experiences regardless of their legal status. One of the contributors to this book, Rodwell, is a Zimbabwean migrant who came to South Africa at the height of the Zimbabwean crisis in 2007. He lived in Mpumalanga Province where he witnessed firsthand the exploitation of migrant labourers from Zimbabwe and Mozambique on South African farms. When he first arrived in South Africa, he briefly worked on an orange farm. Oranges are usually harvested in a period of three months and most farmers in South Africa rely on seasonal labourers. Seasonal farm labourers do not have a fixed salary. In 2007, those who harvested oranges were paid 38 cents per bag of oranges, and to make 38 rands, one would have to fill up 100 bags of oranges. Harvesting oranges is a pain-staking exercise. Farm workers use heavy metal ladders which they often carry from one orange tree to another and a 10–15 kg bag of oranges around one's neck. It is a bloody job because orange trees have sharp thorns that often mercilessly piece the skin as one rushes to fill up as many bags as possible. Sometimes, the harvesting is interrupted by police who often raid farms looking for illegal immigrants. When the police come to raid farms, illegal immigrants runway into the bushes, leaving everything behind. In some instances, farm owners connive with the police to arrest illegal immigrants a few days before payday to avoid paying salaries.

In her debut novel, *We Need New Names*, Zimbabwean writer, NoViolet Bulawayo (2013) narrates the experiences of African migrants in the United

States which in many ways resemble the experiences of undocumented migrants in South Africa:

> The jobs we worked. Jesus-Jesu-Jesus, the jobs we worked. Low-paying jobs. Jobs that gnawed at the bones of our dignity, devoured the meat, tongued the marrow. (p. 247)

The figure of the migrant in the contemporary world resembles that of Agamben's homo-sacer, who must do the dirty work that the locals do not want to do for very little pay, without being acknowledged.

In 2007, Rodwell stayed with his elder brother in a small village called Matlala in Mpumalanga. His brother (let's call him Matukeni) was a carpenter who made different kinds of furniture for people in the community. Although he had left a wife back home, Matukeni stayed with a South African woman. Rumour had it that the woman was a retired prostitute who used to ply her trade in Pretoria and had returned to the village because she was tired of the demands of city life. The woman was a drunkard and a chain smoker although she was jobless. Matukeni would often give her money to buy beer and cigarettes, something that Rodwell thought was unreasonable given that Matukeni had a family in Zimbabwe. Sometimes, the woman, Tebego, would brew traditional beer in the house and call her relatives to come and have a drink. Tebego had a very short temper especially when she was drunk, and she often demanded money from Matukeni whenever she wanted to go and drink with her friends. Often, when she returned from the bottle store, she would shout at everyone, demanding things, including cigarettes. Rodwell often wondered what the woman had given his brother. Was it a love portion or his own foolishness?

Later, Rodwell learnt that his brother was in fact in some kind of hostage situation. The woman was in her village, where she had friends and relatives. Matukeni was an outsider, a Zimbabwean migrant. If he had divorced her, she would have easily organised people to either steal from him or shoot him. Rodwell remembered that in the village, locals often behaved as if they were entitled to foreigners' money. They would often demand 2 rand 'for smoke' and failure to pay one's dues could be fatal. Matukeni's business was doing well but the money was never enough because he was technically running two homes, one in South Africa and another in Zimbabwe. His wife did not know that he was living with another woman in South Africa. His life remained in limbo because he was being extorted, not only by his 'chain-smoking' girlfriend but also by her numerous relatives, who often demanded money for a drink, a beer, or a packet of cigarettes, depending on what they fancied.

In that community, migrants were often called by derogatory names such as *makwerekwere* (if they were African) or *my friend* (if they were Asian). The term makwerekwere referred to people who spoke languages that were unintelligible to the locals. *Makwerekwere* were not only different in the eyes of the locals but also strange. In the same yard where Rodwell and Matukeni stayed, there was a grocery shop owned by a Bangladesh national named Jangri. It was at this grocery shop that Rodwell witnessed his first armed robbery incident in South Africa.

Jangri, the shop owner, had a South African security guard called Clipper who literally lived off the shop. It was not clear whether he had a salary for his security services or he was paid in kind. However, he would often come to the shop in the middle of the night to demand bread claiming he was hungry.

Rodwell often wondered what kind of security guard Clipper was because he rarely stayed at the shop. On one occasion, two criminals came to the shop, ordered everyone to lie on the floor and demanded money from the shopkeeper. Each time the latter said he did not have money; the criminals slashed a part of his body with a knife. This happened in broad daylight. When the criminals were done, they walked away with plastic bags full of groceries, as if they were coming from a normal shopping spree. Later, rumour emerged that Clipper was behind all the robberies that happened at the shop almost every month.

While these stories are not representative of all migrants and/or migrant experiences, they shed light on contemporary migrant experiences not only in South Africa but also around the world. The migrant is often perceived as a problem, one who is not like *us* and one with whom *we* share nothing in common. He/she is a vector of all kinds of socio-economic problems, from crime, unemployment, and poverty to poor service delivery. One would obviously have to be careful not to generalise and create an impression that South Africa is a hostile destination for all migrants. South Africa is indeed home to many people from different parts of the world, but it has, in recent years, embraced what Mbembe (2016) calls 'the principle of apartheid' which is obsessed with the segregation of human beings into two irreconcilable worlds:

> On one side, therefore, is me – the basic nexus and source of orientation in the world – while, on the other, are the others with whom, however, I can never completely fuse – others with whom I may relate, yet never genuinely engage in relations of reciprocity or mutual implication. (Mbembe, 2016, p. 25)

The others, in the context of South Africa, are the migrants, especially those from African countries. These are the permanent outsiders who can never be redeemed. It did not matter whether they acquired papers to legalise their stay or not, they remained foreigners who must go back to their countries. We must, however, emphasise that this is not a unique South African experience. In her novel, *We Need New Names*, No-Violet Bulawayo tells the story of Uncle Kojo, a Ghanaian migrant who has lived in the United States for 30 years, but he still does not have papers. What does it take for a migrant to be seen as a fellow human being who feels pain just as *we* do? The figure of the migrant, at least in South Africa, is an enigmatic one. He/she is an embodiment of contradictions. On one hand, the migrant must do low-paying, back-breaking jobs for little pay. He must do the dirty work that *we* do not want to do, yet on the other hand, it is also the migrant who must shoulder the responsibility for the rising unemployment. Official regulations insist that migrants must register their shops and contribute to the fiscus, yet we are also told the migrants have taken everything from *us*, 'we cannot recognise our own country'.

This book has shown that in everyday social discourse, migration is imagined mainly in two ways: as positive and negative, as empowering and disempowering. Migrants provide cheap labour that business needs, but they also exacerbate problems such as unemployment, crime and service delivery. To migrate is to secure economic freedom but it is also to embrace new unknown challenges with which one must wrestle and win or lose.

The foregoing discussion raises a few questions. How does the proliferation of digital technologies enable people from different parts of the world to share experiences and opportunities? How do experiences of migration shared on digital platforms help our understanding of the contemporary world? Can discourses of migration help us understand migration patterns and popular attitudes towards migrating to certain destinations? In the past, those who migrated to faraway places barely had an opportunity (or the means) to communicate their experiences to friends and relatives back home in real-time. There was no way of telling whether the migrant had travelled well or successfully settled in the host destination. Many Zimbabweans who migrated to South Africa in the late 1880s in search of employment opportunities on the Rand perished on the way, others died in the mines while some went back home after so many years that their relatives could hardly recognise them. Most of the migrants made the long journey from Zimbabwe to Johannesburg on foot and the only available means of communication was word of mouth.

This book has shown that the advent of digital technologies has significantly transformed migration and the ways in which migrants communicate to each other about their destination countries and their experiences there. While social media platforms have revolutionised communication by enabling the creation of digital diasporas and transnational public spheres where migrants share ideas and experiences, the same social media have also created challenges because it is difficult to verify information shared on these platforms. We have already mentioned that migrants often tend to exaggerate their gains in the destination country to maintain a false image of success and impress relatives and friends back home. However, notwithstanding these challenges, social media platforms have become platforms of choice for both migrants and potential migrants to, not only discuss problems in their home countries but also share opportunities available in host destinations.

References

BBC. (n.d.). *Fear and Loathing in South Africa – BBC Africa Eye documentary*. https://www.youtube.com/watch?v=rogZ8BYg-kM

Bulawayo, N. (2013). *We need new names*. Chatto and Windus.

Fraser, N. (2007). Transnationalizing the Public Sphere On the Legitimacy and Efficacy of Public Opinion in a Post-Westphalian World. *Theory, Culture & Society, 24*(4), 7–30.

Mbembe, A. (2016). The society of enmity. *Radical Philosophy, 200*, 23–25.

Mbembe, A. (2017). *A critique of black reason* [Translated by Laurent DuBois]. Duke University Press.

Mbembe, A. (2019). Bodies as borders. *From the European South, 4*, 5–18.